P9-DGU-700

BRAVE
NEW
SCHOOLS

BERIT KJOS

HARVEST HOUSE PUBLISHERS
Eugene, Oregon 97402

Cover by Garborg Design Works, Minneapolis, Minnesota

BRAVE NEW SCHOOLS

Copyright © 1995 by Harvest House Publishers
Eugene, Oregon 97402

Kjos, Berit.
    Brave new schools / Berit Kjos.
        p. cm.
    Includes bibliographical references.
    ISBN 1-56507-388-6 (alk. paper)
    1. Education—United States—Aims and objectives. 2. Education—United States—Forecasting. 3. International education.
    I. Title.
    LA210.K523 1996
    370'.973—dc20   95-34984
                                           CIP

Printed in the United States of America.

98   99   00   01   /   BC   /   9   8   7   6   5   4

Acknowledgments

I want to thank the faithful nationwide team that has worked together to produce this book. Concerned parents and dedicated researchers from across the country have provided invaluable information, documentation, insights, and firsthand classroom reports. Loyal friends helped critique and correct, making sure the manuscript was reader-friendly and easy to understand. Many promised to pray each day. My supportive husband and high-tech sons helped me master my computer, searched library archives for missing footnotes, encouraged, shopped, and gave me time to work. Without their help, encouragement, and prayers I couldn't have written this book.

The list of all who helped would fill a chapter. Most of us have only met by phone and fax, but we are linked together in a common purpose: to share the truth about our changing schools and culture.

Most of all, I thank God, who answered all our prayers. His daily strength, wisdom, and guidance enabled us to finish the task without discouragement. Considering the immensity of today's cultural transformation, we could easily have given up. After all, we are only a small minority. But God has shown us that in Him we serve on the winning team. We may not stop the shift from Judeo/Christian values to New Age globalism, but we can inform communities and warn parents so that they can prepare their children to face a new world. Since our Shepherd goes before us and lives His life in us, we look ahead with hope, not fear.

"Thanks be to God, who always leads us in His triumph!"

Contents

We are . . . in the process of creating a new civilization.

—Newt Gingrich in Foreword to
Creating a New Civilization

*A new civilization is emerging in our lives, and blind men every-
where are trying to suppress it. This new civilization brings with
it new family styles, changed ways of working, loving, and living,
a new economy, new political conflicts, and beyond all this an
altered consciousness as well.*

—Alvin and Heidi Toffler in
Creating a New Civilization

*We've got to revolutionize education. The old answers are not
good enough anymore.*

—Former President George Bush
promoting America 2000,
the Republican version of Goals 2000

Before
You Begin . . .

Remember the frog that landed in a pan of water and stayed until it boiled? Had the pan been hot, the frog would have noticed and hopped out. But the water felt cool at first, and the frog sensed no danger. It simply relaxed and conformed to the gradual change. Subdued by the rising heat, it grew too sluggish to act. By the time the water actually boiled, the frog was dead.

I know that carefree feeling. When my oldest son entered the public school system over two decades ago, our local elementary school seemed safe and friendly. A fatherly principal welcomed him, and friendly teachers used the same teaching techniques that had taught me to read and multiply long ago: phonics, drills, memorization. . . . How could I suspect that these proven teaching methods were about to be replaced by classroom experiments using children as guinea pigs for social engineering? I had no way of knowing that truth, facts, logic, and history would soon be replaced by an unrelenting emphasis on myths, feelings, imagination, and politically correct stories. I saw no reason to believe that our values would soon be ridiculed, redefined, and subjected to unthinkable tests.

If someone had told me that globalist educators were determined to mold our children into a compliant workforce for a new global society by year 2000, I wouldn't have believed them. If a friend had warned me that political leaders would use our schools to transform the world into a "global village" held together with the cords of pantheistic oneness and a computerized surveillance system, I might have laughed. How could our elected representatives agree to something so outlandish? That could never happen in America. This was the land of the free! After all, we have our Constitution. No one can take our rights—or our children—from us!

Ten years later my third son started school. By that time I had read enough textbooks and talked with enough teachers and parents to know that our schools were changing. The more I researched, the more alarmed I became. The foundational goals of education had been turned upside-down, not only in my own community but across the country and around the world. Socialization—the "right" attitudes, beliefs, and behavior—had replaced academics as the main outcome of education. In spite of the nice-sounding promises, individualism was *out,* and group thinking and universal values were *in.* The minds of children were being molded through the latest techniques in behavioral psychology.

If this monstrous system is put in place by A.D. 2001 as planned, all children will be monitored through a national computerized data transmission system designed to build a permanent, personal file on every child. No one will be safe from the watchful eyes and controlling arms of the new system—not children taught at home or in private schools, not their parents, not anyone.

This transformation transcends political as well as national lines. The main body of President Clinton's massive education law, Goals 2000, was first drafted by Education Secretary Lamar Alexander during the Bush Administration and introduced to the public in 1991 as America 2000. The two, Goals 2000 and America 2000, are essentially the same "outcome-based" system. Today, many of its functions and proposals have been transferred into private, nongovernmental groups or merged with the Department of Labor and the Department of Health and Human Services. This makes sense, since the strategies for molding the global workforce stress mental and emotional "health," not factual learning.

It is impossible to summarize the worldwide educational agenda in a few pages. You might find it too strange to believe. That is why I wrote this book. But before you start reading it, let me give you some helpful suggestions:

First, preview the Chronology of Events on page 223. It will clarify the globalist agenda and show the steps that brought us to the dawning of an international education system.

Second, scan the Glossary (p. 249). It defines and explains new words and concepts that are part of educational restructuring. These words will be highlighted when you first meet them in the chapters of the book. Their true meanings may surprise you.

Third, look for answers to the questions below. Those answers will help you respond wisely to people who, like the proverbial frog, have become so accustomed to the changes that they fail to see the danger signs. These people may ask you—

- What can be wrong with global oneness?

- Don't we need international education?

- Won't multicultural education build understanding and tolerance?

- Why do **Higher Order Thinking Skills** do the opposite of what they promise?

- Teaching environmental consciousness and political activism is essential to creating a better world, isn't it?

- Why shouldn't the whole community be partners with parents in raising children for the twenty-first century?

Fourth, don't blame the local teachers. They are caught up in a movement they can't stop. Because their intentions are usually good, they often feel confused or angry when confronted by parents who question their efforts. They simply don't understand how lessons that seem so good to them could seem so bad to others. As you read, look for practical tools to help them see the difference.

If you are a Christian teacher being pressured to cooperate with the new system, the facts in this book may discourage as well as encourage you. Know that when God puts His people in the heat of the battle, He also promises to meet all their needs.[1] Armed with truth, faith, and the essential facts, you will be ready for your local battle.

Fifth, be alert to the difference between well-meaning local educators and the educational establishment (national and international) who have planned the transformation. The latter call themselves "change agents" and are training an army of like-minded revolutionaries for our local schools.

"We need change agents in charge of those schools, not preservers of entrenched interests and encrusted practices,"[2] writes Chester Finn, director of the Educational Excellence Network, who helped former President Bush and Lamar Alexander promote America 2000.

These change agents are trained to twist the rules to win public support. As North Carolina school superintendent Dr. Jim Causby said in his 1994 speech at the *Second Annual Model Schools Conference*[3] in Atlanta:

> We have actually been given a course in how not to tell the truth. How many of you are administrators? You've had that course in public relations where you learn to put the best spin on things.[4]

To stay ahead of critics, leading educators keep changing the labels. Thus, what many know as Outcome-Based Education, or OBE, is also called Quality Learning, Total

	TRADITIONAL OR ASSUMED MEANING	MISLEADING OR STATED MEANING	REAL MEANING behind the misleading promises
WORLD-CLASS STANDARDS	New standards needed for global challenges.	"High standards" needed for the 21st century global economy.	Low standards for literacy, comprehension, and factual knowledge. "High standards" for the beliefs, attitudes, and group thinking needed to prepare **human capital** for the 21st century.
MASTERY LEARNING (ML)	Students must master key subjects, i.e., learn the content.	Given enough time, all students can learn—and achieve the "same high level."	Psychological strategies for conditioning students to new beliefs, values, and ways of thinking. Failure to meet attitudinal, not factual, standards means drilling until students demonstrate the "right" responses.
OUTCOME-BASED EDUCATION (OBE)	Educating students according to planned results.	A systemic plan to prepare *all* students to meet high standards.	The national delivery system for **Mastery Learning.** A multilevel process for setting educational standards at the national level and making sure local schools prepare students individually to meet **affective** standards.
MULTI-CULTURAL EDUCATION	Learning about other cultures.	Learning to respect and understand all cultures and lifestyles.	"Becoming" a multicultural person, open to the pluralistic beliefs and lifestyles of *all* except those who cling to Judeo-Christian values.
LOCAL CONTROL	Elected school board represents local parents.	Local schools choose and mange their own learning programs.	The lowest level of a new centralized bureaucracy. A selected panel of supportive citizens will make sure students learn what national standards and tests require.

Quality School Restructuring, Performance- or Achievement-based Education. . . . Whatever the label, it refers primarily to the national/international system that demands
specific "outcomes" from students and uses the psychological strategies of Mastery Learning to achieve the planned
result. John R. Champlin, a leading change agent, summarized the deceptive plan in the *Journal of Quality
Education:*

> While OBE has become a "tainted" term . . .
> many of the significant practices and concepts will
> continue under another label, one that will not take
> away even a particle of what a well-conceived, well-
> managed OBE program offers. . . . We need to learn
> our lessons well—for keeps this time.[5]

To sell OBE to the public, change agents promote it as
"local control" and "decentralization." They are not telling
you the truth. As you will see in Chapter 7, what students
must learn at the local level will be determined at the
national level.

The chart on the previous page shows how educators
"put the best spin" on their deceptive plans. Ponder the
three sets of meanings. They expose the heart of the transformation.

Finally, don't forget that OUR GOD STILL REIGNS.
He has the world in His hands, and nothing can hinder His
eternal purpose or timetable. When you trust and follow
Him, you can be confident that "your Lord who goes before
you will Himself fight on your behalf."[6]

1

New Beliefs
for a Global Village[1]

The purpose of education and the schools is to change the thoughts, feelings and actions of students.[2]

—Professor Benjamin Bloom
called "Father of Outcome-Based Education"

Nations that stick to stale old notions and ideologies will falter and fail. So I'm here today to say, America will move forward. . . . New schools for a new world. . . . Reinvent—literally start from scratch and reinvent the America school . . . . Our challenge amounts to nothing less than a revolution in American education.[3]

—President George Bush
announcing America 2000

You can only have a new society. . . if you change the education of the younger generation. . . .[4]

—Marilyn Ferguson
The Aquarian Conspiracy

*C*ome to the medicine wheel!" The teacher's cheery voice beckoned the Iowa fourth graders to a fun Native American ritual. "And wear your medicine bags."

Jonathan grabbed his little brown pouch and hurried to his place. His favorite teacher made school so exciting! She brought Indian beliefs about nature into all the subjects— science, history, art, reading. She even helped the class start The Medicine Wheel Publishing Company to make writing more fun.

She taught Jonathan to make his own **medicine** bag— a deerskin pouch filled with special things, such as a red stone that symbolized his place on the medicine wheel astrology chart. This magic pouch would empower him in times of need, such as when taking tests. Jonathan wanted to show it to his parents, but his teacher said no. He didn't know why.

Sitting cross-legged in the circle, the class chanted a song to honor the earth: "The Earth is our Mother, We're taking care of her. . . . Hey younga, ho." Then the teacher read an Indian myth from the popular classroom book *Keepers of the Earth.* It told about a beautiful spirit woman who came to save a starving tribe of Sioux Indians. This mystical savior brought sage to purify the people, and she showed them how to use the sacred pipe—a symbol of

15

"the unity of all things"—for guidance and prayer to the Great Spirit.

Few students could miss the point of the story: All is one—the earth, people, and animals—around the world. As long as the tribe remembered "that all things were connected as the parts of the Pipe, they lived happily and well."[5] Spiritual oneness, not Western individualism, would bring happiness. In the teacher's guide, the authors Michael Caduto and Joseph Bruchac explain that this blend of myth and ecology meets today's need for "spiritual and religious values," including "deeper spiritual ties with the Earth."[6]

From coast to coast, the same kind of multicultural *experiences* inspire students to stretch their view of God—an essential part of today's social transformation. Connecticut fourth-graders use **guided imagery** to "experience" Indian tribal life and meet "wise" spirit helpers.[7] Colorado sixth-graders enjoy "spirit dances" wearing their class-made masks.[8] Oregon students celebrate Winter Solstice by acting the roles of the Sun God, Moon Goddess, drummers, and animal spirits.[9] California students wear masks that help them identify with their favorite Greek gods and goddesses.[10] **Earth-centered** religions are *in*.

During a public school dedication of a small parcel of Colorado land, an officiating pastor said, "Now we are going to stomp our feet like tom-toms and pray to the Great Spirit." After the ceremony a mother explained to her confused son, "No, the Great Spirit is *not* the same as God."[11]

Having rejected biblical Christianity, educational "change agents"[12] have realized that some kind of **global spirituality** is needed to fuel a collective pursuit of global unity. Although Native American spirituality provides the perfect model—and brings the least resistance from concerned parents—any of the world's New Age or neopagan religions will do. Offering a common alternative to the biblical God, they all blend one or more of the following:

- **Pantheism:** All is God and God is all, since a universal force infuses all things with spiritual life. Today's popularized versions encourages everyone to "look within" for the strength, wisdom, and guidance needed to empower oneself for success.

- **Monism:** All is one, joined together through the pantheistic spirituality.

- **Polytheism:** Many gods. Since the pantheistic deity makes everything sacred, people can worship anything or anyone they choose. Children learn that in the end, all the world's gods lead to the same happy spirit world.

Few classroom texts dare mention the terrors and tortures that have always oppressed pagan cultures—those that sought power and wisdom from occult forces. Instead, ancient paganism has donned a new mask. Sometimes called neopaganism, it is simply an idealized blend of any of the world's pagan religions. Disguised as personal empowerment and harmony with nature, this global or earth-centered spirituality seduces both young and old who ignore the tragic lessons of history.[13]

Oneness is the heartbeat of global spirituality. Taught to believe in the basic oneness of all life, students are trained to demonstrate this unity through a planned set of values, attitudes, and behaviors. The "right" kinds of assignments bypass reason and establish the new ideals in their minds. So when sixth-graders in North Carolina had to design a global postage stamp that would show "what the world would need to make it a better place," they used their imagination, not facts, to form new goals. When ninth-graders wrote a "constitution for a perfect society,"[14] they practiced building their dreams on mythical idealism, not the truth about human nature. Chapter 3 will show you how easily these fragile foundations can be manipulated for political purposes.

"The teaching profession prepares the leaders of the future," wrote NEA (National Education Association) leader William Carr, secretary of the Educational Policies Commission. "The statesmen, the industrialists, the lawyers, the newspapermen. . . . all the leaders of tomorrow are in schools today."[15] Half a century ago he called for the global beliefs and values that now infuse education:

> The psychological foundations for wider loyalties must be laid. . . . Teach those attitudes which will result ultimately in the creation of a world citizenship and world government . . . we can and should teach those skills and attitudes which will help to create a society in which world citizenship is possible.[16]

Today students across the country are asked to demonstrate those "skills" and "attitudes" on standardized tests. Traditional knowledge and reason have been replaced by a radical new emphasis on politically correct attitudes that supposedly demonstrate the mental health needed for world citizenship. These attitudes are included in the "competencies" and work "skills" defined by the Department of Labor.[17]

The process for change is already in place. Initiated by former President Bush, the new education system cuts across partisan lines. Focused on socialization rather than traditional education, it fits as easily into the U.S. Department of Health and Human Services or the Department of Labor as into an Education Department. Many of the new functions—such as national testing and the school-to-work linkage—now operate through "private" organizations which receive government funds but are not accountable to concerned parents.

Students who resist the change face growing intolerance and pressures to conform. Unless the process is reversed, they will fail to earn their entrance pass to work or higher education.[18] The following story about Matt

Piecora gives a small glimpse of the confusion faced by children who cling to traditional beliefs.

No Room for Traditional Beliefs

Matt Piecora was only following instructions. The fifth grader at Mark Twain Elementary School near Seattle didn't know that his answers had to fit the new cultural standard. So when his teacher told him to complete the sentence "If I could wish for three things, I would wish for. . ." Matt wrote "infinitely more wishes, to meet God, and for all my friends to be Christians."

Since each student's personal expressions would be posted on a wall for open house, they had to be just right. Matt's didn't pass. The teacher told him that his last wish could hurt people who didn't share his beliefs. To avoid offense, he agreed to add "if they want to be."

Another sentence to be completed began, "If I could meet anyone, I would like to meet . . . " Matt wrote: "God, because he is the One who made us!" The teacher urged him to add "in my opinion."

When Debbie Piecora, Matt's mother, bent down to read her son's paper posted on the bottom of the wall, she immediately noticed the phrases that followed Matt's original sentences. "How come you wrote this?" she asked him.

"The teacher didn't want me to hurt other people's feelings like Mormons and people like that," he answered.

"But these are just your wishes."

"I thought so, Mom." Matt looked puzzled.

Defending her actions, the teacher later explained that she wanted diversity in her multigrade classroom and was just looking out for her other students. But if the public display was supposed to "express the students' diverse views," why did she censor only Matt's views? Troubled, Dan and Debbie Piecora pondered the paradox. Didn't their son's expression fit the needed "diversity"?

Apparently not. Like other parents across the country, the Piecoras are realizing that Judeo-Christian absolutes have become intolerable to educators who seek more **universal values**. To match international as well as national goals, schools must train students to open their minds to new possibilities and to discard the old truths that block "progress" toward global oneness. In the name of tolerance, diversity, and understanding, traditional beliefs are being squelched and more "inclusive" earth-centered beliefs are filling the vacuum.

The chart opposite, which compares the new meaning of "Good Thinking" with the new meaning of "Poor Thinking," illustrates these ambiguous values and deceptive labels. Part of a proposed core curriculum for Los Altos, California, it presents local guidelines designed to match national standards. Notice the bizarre logic in the introduction. Ponder the two-pronged guidelines that disqualify belief in biblical absolutes and encourage students to try new paths. Consider these questions: Would Matt be considered a good or a poor thinker? Would your child?

This formula for "good" thinking may help students solve rational problems, but it forces students like Matt to rethink their home-taught beliefs and values. Contemporary **change agents** know this well, and so they use the formula to turn students of all ages from time-tested truths and factual knowledge to the shifting sands of myth, speculation, and planned ambiguity. The Kansas Board of Education called it "new thinking, new strategies, new behavior and new beliefs."[19]

At the core of psychological strategies such as **critical thinking** and **values clarification**, this formula undermines rational resistance to the new social philosophy. Raymond English, Vice President of the Ethics and Public Policy Center, summarized the scheme well. In 1987, he told the National Advisory Council on Educational Research and Improvement that—

Good Thinking Versus Poor Thinking[20]

This model helps us make some valid and useful distinctions between good and poor thinking. Here we wish to distance ourselves from those who equate good thinking with a long list of discrete mental operations and those who describe poor thinking in terms of several logical errors.

Good thinkers are willing to think and may even find thinking enjoyable. They can carry out searches when necessary and suspend judgment. They value rationality, believing that thinking is useful for solving problems, reaching decisions, and making judgments. Poor thinkers, in contrast, need certainty, avoid thinking, must reach closure quickly, are impulsive, and rely too heavily on intuition.

THE GOOD THINKER:	THE POOR THINKER:
Welcomes problematic situations and is tolerant of ambiguity.	Searches for certainty and is intolerant of ambiguity.
Looks for alternative possibilities ...	... is satisfied with first attempts.
Is reflective ... searches extensively when appropriate.	... is overconfident of the correctness of initial ideas.
Revises goals when necessary.	Does not revise goals.
Is open to multiple possibilities.	Does not seek alternatives to initial possibilities.

[C]ritical thinking means not only learning how to think for oneself, but it also means learning how to subvert the traditional values in your society. You're not thinking "critically" if you're accepting the values that mommy and daddy taught you. That's not "critical."[21]

No wonder parents are concerned! "I try to instill God's truths in my son, but it seems like the school wants to remove them," said Dan Piecora.

He is right. The *old* Judeo-Christian beliefs must be crushed before the *new* beliefs and values can be established. A student's right to free expression means little to those who put social change above Constitutional freedom. While educational change agents used "separation between church and state" to ban biblical truth from public schools, many of the same leaders now wholeheartedly endorse pagan indoctrination. A public school in St. Paul, Minnesota, which openly practices Native American spiritism, illustrates today's strange partiality toward the "right" spiritual foundation for world-class education.

Indian Ritual, Global Model

When Rachel Holm,[22] a Minnesota mother, visited Mounds Park All-Nations School, she found magic dream-catchers in every classroom, mystical drawings of a spiritualized earth, and a ring of stones in the schoolyard for medicine wheel ceremonies. She heard politically correct assumptions about the evils of Western culture and the goodness of pagan spirituality. *How can public schools promote Native American rituals but censure Christianity?* she wondered.

Her tour of the school began in the All-Nations room, where the student body had gathered for Monday morning "circle time"—a time of "peer teaching" and "cooperative learning." She listened as eighth-graders, one by one, imparted their wisdom to the younger students, much like tribal elders would impart advice to younger braves.

A celebration of ritual drumming and dancing followed. "During the drumming, if you have a good feeling, you look at the drum," explained Laura, a student assigned to guide Mrs. Holm for the day. "Suddenly the top of the drum becomes black and smoky and you see a face on the drum. It's a human face that is neither happy nor sad."

One of the boys mentioned that women must never touch the drum, because "the spirit of a woman" inside the drum could be offended if another female touched it.

The circular walls of the All-Nations room were covered with large medicine shields made by sixth-graders. "They're made from things that symbolize each person's dreams and feelings," explained Laura. "They protect us from all kinds of dangers such as kidnappers and bad spirits."

A glass case in the main foyer displayed drawings of an Ojibwe Indian creation myth. "Is this story true?" asked Mrs. Holm. "Oh, yes," answered Laura.

"How do you know?"

"Well, I've heard it two or three times." Laura's revealing answer illustrates an important shift in classroom emphasis: Children are learning to base their conclusions—even their understanding of God and His creation—on myth and imagination instead of truth and reason.

Every classroom displayed at least one *dreamcatcher*— a magical spider web inside a sacred circle. The students explained that dreamcatchers protect them from evil spirits and nightmares by catching the bad dreams but permitting good dreams to pass though the center. According to fourth-grade teacher Ms. Preston, the amber crystal in the center of her dreamcatcher meant proper spiritual alignment with the energy of the universe.

This cosmic energy was defined in an article by the principal, Dr. Cornel Pewewardy, which Mrs. Holm had read before her tour:

> In Native American philosophy and thought, "medicine" is a vital energy source that we draw upon and use for direction and for wholeness. **Holistic education** equates to responsibility for the whole universe: We are all related.[23]

In the same article Dr. Pewewardy explained that "the school attracts students, staff and volunteers who do more than emphasize a Native American philosophy, we espouse and live it. We do so for the betterment of our children, ourselves and our world—one world."

What happened to the separation between church and state? Apparently today's purveyors of earth-centered religions have sidestepped this question by changing the labels. Native American spirituality is not "church" in today's politically correct circles. "We don't call it religion—we call it spirituality," explained Mounds Park eighth-grade teacher Jackie Lannon. "For the Native American, their spirituality is their culture and their culture is their spirituality . . . you can't really separate the two."[24]

The same can be said for Christianity, but today's change agents don't seem to listen. They have changed the rules and revised our history. Good and evil have been turned upside down—and our children are learning to love the latter.

History from a Pagan Perspective

Students in a public elementary school in Texas were enjoying a classroom assignment called "The Witches' Brew." They had to match all kinds of exciting people— witches, warlocks, astrologers, and shamans—to the corresponding "occupation." Then they linked a list of magic practices to the right definition. It was easy! Television, books, and cartoons had already taught them a lot about how those occult practices could give them spiritual power.

The occult words and meanings made sense to the students. Why shouldn't they empower themselves with the spiritual forces in nature? Captain Planet and other superheroes do it all the time! What could possibly be wrong with the old rituals that used to connect people to Mother Earth? Those nice tribal people had real power. Besides, the introduction to the lesson showed how it all fit into history:

> Once upon a time witches could be seen gathering on Walpurgis Night (the eve of May Day) in the Harz Mountains in Germany for the witches' Sabbath. Once upon a time wizards were consulted by leaders of government, and astrologers influenced world events. If these things seem bizarre (outlandish, peculiar) today,

they shouldn't. For the second half of the twentieth century has seen a rekindling of interest in the occult arts.

On more than one college campus warlocks conjure,
and in the cities witches brew magic potions and cast
spells. In such circumstances it is wise to know some
of the terminology associated with witchcraft.[25]

Ask yourself, *Is this story true?* Is it good? Why might
your answer differ from that of a contemporary change
agent?

On the surface, lessons like "The Witches' Brew" seem
designed to bolster a student's vocabulary. But that's not
all. Fulfilling a far more significant purpose, they are part
of the plan to restructure not only what schools teach but
also what children think and believe. This assignment
illustrates a four-pronged assault on traditional values.
Notice how it—

- Validates witchcraft, one of the many masks for the
  all-inclusive global spirituality;

- Invalidates objections based on Christian convictions;

- Prepares students to accept occult terms and
  explore pagan concepts;

- Encourages students to welcome today's revival of
  pagan spirituality.

No part of the assignment mentions the dangers of
occult connections. The old adage "Tell the truth, the whole
truth, and nothing but the truth" doesn't fit anymore.
Contemporary lessons in multiculturalism are designed to
sell earth-centered beliefs and values, not simply to build
objective understanding of the world's diverse cultures.
Facts that disprove the intended conclusions are simply

censored. After all, if students were allowed an unbiased view of paganism—one that showed all the relevant facts and presented all the fears, oppressions, and terrors that accompany polytheism—rational children would shun it.

Global-minded educators and environmentalists can't allow that to happen. They know that the new beliefs and values must be couched in some kind of religious faith and experience.

"Every transformation," writes Lewis Mumford in Robert Muller's *World Core Curriculum Journal,* ". . . has rested on a new metaphysical and ideological base . . . a new picture of the cosmos and the nature of man."[26]

It doesn't matter if the "new ideological base" is actually old and tried, as long as it takes civilization beyond the Western or Christian culture. The change agents who planned the next-century "global village" have recognized the importance of a global spirituality that emphasizes universal oneness rather than national or religious loyalties.

Of course, the biblical basis for oneness was unacceptable. It was an obstacle. So in the early sixties, humanist activism closed the door to biblical truth in public schools. Three decades later, many of the same humanist leaders were calling for a return to the sacred. They had experienced the powerlessness of atheism and were seeking answers in the world's timeless alternatives to God.

Notice in the following three-view chart that humanism is merely a downward step on the slide toward global spirituality.

To block resistance to this spiritual transformation, national and international change agents have implemented a plan to build into the minds of students a mental framework, a new worldview or paradigm, that will accommodate global spirituality but exclude Christianity. Some years ago, most of us didn't talk about worldviews or **paradigms**. We assumed that most people shared a Judeo-Christian worldview. That's no longer true. While the people we meet in our communities may represent any of the three paradigms

CHRISTIANITY (BIBLICAL ABSOLUTES) Old Religion	HUMANISM (RELATIVE VALUES) No Religion	GLOBALISM (GLOBAL ABSOLUTES) New Religion
The Bible reveals reality	Science explains reality	Feelings and experience define reality
God is transcendent and personal	God is a nonexistent crutch	A pantheistic god(dess) or force is present in all
God created the earth	The earth evolved by random chance	The earth evolves by its own (or cosmic) power
Trusting God is key to success	Trusting self is key to success	Trusting one's inner god-self is key to success
Good and evil are incompatible	Good and evil are relative	Joining good and evil brings wholeness

© 1994 Berit Kjos

shown on the above chart, most are steadily drifting with the rest of our culture into the globalist paradigm.

Humanist educator John Dewey laid the foundation for this paradigm shift at the start of this century. Half a century later, long after his radical ideas had transformed our universities and teacher's colleges, the counterculture of the sixties swept a new breed of religious revolutionaries into mainstream America. One of the more famous idealists was Aldous Huxley, author of *Brave New World* and a Fabian socialist who pushed Zen meditation and psychedelic drugs—a trance-forming blend almost certain to invoke spiritual "enlightenment" from demonic sources.[27] Many of his questionable insights dealt with education and transformation.

According to Huxley, education must provide a mental "framework...within which any piece of information acquired in later life may find its proper and significant place."[28] In the old days, that mental framework was the biblical worldview. Huxley, like most of today's change agents, called for a New Age/global framework. Like a filter, it blocks facts and ideas that don't fit, but it welcomes information that strengthens the framework.

A familiar tale told to first-graders in Pennsylvania shows what happens when old stories are squeezed into the mold of the new paradigm. We all know the story of the Little Red Hen who wanted some bread to eat. She asked some of her barnyard friends to help make it. But the cat, the dog, and the goat all said no. Finally she did all the work herself. However, when the bread was done, her unwilling friends came to help her eat it.

"Won't you share with us?" they begged.

"No," she answered. "Since you didn't help, you don't get anything."

In the context of the old paradigm, the moral of the story is: You get what you work for. But the new paradigm point is different. Listen to the kinds of questions the first grade teacher asked her class: "Why was the Little Red Hen so stingy? Isn't it only right that everyone gets to eat? Why wouldn't she share what she had with some who had none?"[29]

Later, the concerned mother who heard and reported this story, asked, "What kinds of values were the children taught?" The new story emphasizes love and sharing, but what is missing? How might it confuse a child's values?

A new mental framework is essential to the paradigm shift. But to establish the new, the old patterns must be blurred and broken. Educators know that children who are fed a daily diet of biblical truth will resist their plans for change. They also know that students bombarded with dubious suggestions as well as outright paganism will probably reject Christianity. If schools can build the new kind of framework or filter in the minds of children early enough, the new global beliefs will fit right in. In other words, the battle for the hearts of America's children will be won by the side that first trains children to see reality from its point of view.

While many Christian parents are ignoring the battle, educational change agents have never fought harder. They use an upgraded version of the strategy that Aldous Huxley outlined in *Brave New World*. Like Huxley's futuristic fantasy, the rest of this book will show some of the calculated steps toward total social transformation:

- Rewrite history to discredit nationalism and promote globalism.

- Teach thinking "skills" based on feelings and experience, not facts and reason.

- Encourage loyalty to peers and teachers, not family and churches.

- Immerse students in global beliefs and values.

- Condition students to serve a "greater whole."

- Block opposition to the new global paradigm.

In the final chapter, you will find some of the tools needed to resist this incredible transformation. But it won't be easy, for the wheels set in motion decades ago have progressed and accelerated far beyond any human grasp or measure. None of our children—even homeschoolers and those who attend Christian schools—will be free from the tentacles of national and international controls if the global plan is fully implemented.

Since this ominous transformation extends far beyond American borders to an imagined global union, let us begin with a behind-the-scenes look at the international agenda.

2

The International Agenda

*[A] major goal . . . should be . . . to organize a worldwide educa-
tion program. . . . In the process, we should actively search for ways to
promote a new way of thinking about the current relationship between
human civilization and the earth.*[1]
> —Al Gore, *The Earth in the Balance:*
> *Ecology and the Human Spirit*

The basic goal of education is change—human change. . . .[2]
> —Harold Drummon
> former President of the Associationfor Supervision
> and Curriculum Development (ASCD)

*Enlightened social engineering is required to face situations that
demand global action now. . . . Parents and the general public must
be reached also, otherwise, children and youth enrolled in globally
oriented programs may find themselves in conflict with values
assumed in the home. And then the educational institution frequently
comes under scrutiny and must pull back.*[3]
> —John Goodlad
> Foreword in *Schooling for a Global Age*

*W*e can't teach that only America is good," said Seema Desai, a tenth-grader who moved from India to Florida in 1993. "That would hurt my feelings."[4]

Seema had joined an impassioned war, led by the local teachers' union, against three Lake County school board members who wanted Florida schools to emphasize America's unique merits. Seeking to overturn a requirement that would "indoctrinate" students with the intolerable old-paradigm notion that America is best, the union had sued the school board. Such ethnocentric teaching, it argued, emphasizes one culture over another. Therefore it breaks a state law that requires multicultural education.

Did you know that multiculturalism ruled out loyalty to our country? I didn't. Like most parents, I believed that multicultural education simply helps students understand other cultures and people. In reality, it trains students to view the world and its people from a global and pantheistic perspective rather than from a national and Judeo-Christian perspective. In other words, it is designed to speed the paradigm shift—the current transformation toward a radical new way of thinking, believing, and relating to "our global family."

This paradigm shift is supposed to prepare students for life in the next-century "global village," the envisioned worldwide community of people joined together through high-tech superhighways and a common set of values. To mold world-class students, social engineers are testing the latest techniques in behavior modification on our children. As you will see in coming chapters, children must either reject their old home-taught faith or stretch it far beyond biblical boundaries to include the world's pantheistic, polytheistic belief systems.

"Multicultural education . . . strives to integrate multiethnic and global perspectives," wrote Christine Bennet in *Comprehensive Multicultural Education,* a popular textbook for student teachers. Its goal is not to teach factual history, but to "challenge [the student's] cultural assumptions" and mold global citizens with an "emotional commitment to the fundamental unity of all humans. . . ."[5]

In other words, a new commitment to universal oneness must supersede commitments to God and country. While grandiose dreams of global unity reach back to the beginning of history, it was more recently documented in 1973 by the authors of the Humanist Manifesto II. They wrote, "We deplore the division of humankind on nationalistic grounds. We have reached a turning point in human history where the best option is to transcend the limits of national sovereignty and to move toward the building of a world community. . . ."[6]

Professor Philip Vander Velde, who taught "Foundations of Education" at Western Washington University, authored the book *Global Mandate: Pedagogy for Peace.* Reflecting the views of countless other change agents, he wrote:

> . . . unless a new faith . . . overcomes the old ideologies and creates planetary synthesis, world government is doomed. . . . Nation-states have outlived their usefulness, and a new world order is necessary if we are to live in harmony with each other. . . . The task of reordering our traditional values and institutions should be one of the major educational objectives of our schools.[7]

These revolutionary beliefs didn't originate with Vander Velde. When he penned these chilling words in 1985, his book merely articulated a transformation that was already well under way. Since then this philosophy has permeated curriculum and teaching strategies from coast to coast.

Today's history lessons are designed to reflect and fuel the paradigm shift. Alarmed parents in every state report that they do.[8] "My son told me that he had seen some videos in his high school history class," said Pam Hoffecker, a Pennsylvania mother and coauthor of *Outcome-Based Education*. "One of the videos, *The Columbus Controversy*, gave a politically correct view of Christopher Columbus. The other, *The Puritan Experience,* was about a girl who disobeys her parents, skips church, and helps the Indians. It showed that a formal religion like Christianity is bad, but disrespect toward traditional authority is good."

My friend Pam borrowed the whole series from the school. Later she summarized in a telephone conversation what she had seen:

> When I looked at the video about Columbus, I was very upset. It began with a teacher grabbing a purse from a student's desk and saying, "This is my purse. I didn't steal Samantha's purse. I discovered this purse." Columbus was presented as an antihero who sought gold and slaves, brought genocide to the indigenous, and should be ridiculed. It never mentioned that the supposedly peace-loving Carob Indians owned slaves and would fatten, castrate, and eat male babies in cannibalistic rituals. True, the European immigrants did exploit Indians, but there are two sides to the story. . . .[9]

As Pam told her story, I shared her sadness at the growing hatred for a culture that has offered security, freedom, and peace to millions of people from around the world. Her son, Timothy, had heard the missing facts from his parents, but most children who learn history from the new-para-digm perspective will never know why America was called the land of the free.

One thing is certain: The 1994 National Standards for American History would not provide the needed balance. That the newly elected conservative U.S. Senate refused to approve them made little difference. Long before those standards were discussed in public, they had become the unofficial standards in our tax-funded **regional education laboratories,** curriculum guidelines, and in our public schools. In fact, Gary Nash, who authored our nation's most popular social studies text in the early nineties,[10] led the panel that wrote the official History Standards.

Rewriting History

"Imagine an outline for the teaching of American history in which George Washington makes only a fleeting appearance and is never described as our first president," suggested Lynne Cheney, former Chair of the National Endowment for the Humanities, "or in which the foundings of the Sierra Club and the National Organization for Women are considered noteworthy events, but the first gathering of the U.S. Congress is not. . . . This is, in fact, the version of history set forth in the soon-to-be released National Standards for United States History." She continued:

> . . . not a single one of the 31 standards mentions the Constitution. True, it does come up in the 250 pages of supporting materials. It is even described as "the culmination of the most creative era of constitutionalism in American history"—but only in the dependent clause of a sentence that has as its main point that students should "ponder the paradox that the Constitution sidetracked the movement to abolish slavery. . . ."

African and Native American societies, like all societies, had their failings, but one would hardly know it from the National Standards. Students are encouraged to consider Aztec "architecture, skills, labor systems and agriculture." But not the practice of human sacrifice. . . .

What went wrong? . . . According to [an unnamed member of the panel], those who were "pursuing the revisionist agenda" no longer bothered to conceal their "great hatred for traditional history."[11]

Gary Nash represents the academic bureaucracy charged with training America's youth. His debate with Lynne Cheney on the MacNeil/Lehrer News Hour on October 26, 1994, highlights the two opposing paradigms in American culture.

Cheney: There is very little sense here of our nation's greatness, of our progress. . . . It is a very grim and gloomy picture of the American past. . . . You don't find Robert E. Lee . . . Thomas Edison, and many other people who have the misfortune to have been born white males.

Nash: The hundreds of teachers, and the hundreds of historians from every part of the country who were collaborators and coauthors of this document would truly disagree that this is a gloomy, dark picture. . . . We do not top up lists of names for students to absorb, in fact to memorize and attach to dates. . . .

Cheney: We are asked to look at King Mansa Musa, an African king, and to admire his wealth. The point is that we don't hold everyone to the same standard. When we look at a phenomenon in another country we say, "Oh, that was wonderful. . . ." When we look at it in this country, it becomes an object of derision. . . .

Nash: There are hundreds and thousands of people who have reviewed this book who have never raised that objection. We have sent out over 6000 copies of five drafts of this book for review to every corner of this country. And this is the first criticism of this sort. . . .

Cheney: The fact that Mr. Nash didn't receive a lot criticism perhaps speaks for the state of history. . . .

She is right. America's perception of the past *has* changed. Not only do recent social studies texts bring shame and anger to our country but they drive a wedge between parents and children. Poll after poll shows that the majority of adult Americans still believe in God and appreciate the nation He established. But their children are taught that the Judeo-Christian values have failed us, and that now it is time to discard the old stories and find new models in the world's earth-centered cultures.

Contrary to revisionist rhetoric, the facts of history prove America's uniqueness. For over two centuries our nation offered shelter and freedom to the world's oppressed people. It built schools and hospitals in needy nations that showed no concern for their own poor. It demonstrated a compassion toward faraway tribes that was unthinkable in earth-centered cultures. Yet the very cultures that abandoned their poor to karmic[12] laws and their enemies to cruel tortures have now become classroom models for unity and tolerance. It makes no sense.

The next chapter will explain why: the new paradigm abandons facts and reason as the basis for action. It also undermines nationalism, discredits the "obsolete" traditions of capitalism and national sovereignty, and transfers children's loyalties from America to a Utopian global welfare state.

March to Global Oneness

While Gary Nash and his panel of historians were rewriting American history, other revisionists were gathering worldwide support for an international education system. Around the world, students would learn the same basic beliefs and values using the same psychological strategies. If the revisionists could inspire the children with a common vision of a planet without national boundaries, the battle for global governance would be won.

They have come a long way. As if pulled by invisible strings, teachers around the world were introducing the same kind of psychosocial curriculum designed to reprogram children's minds until their beliefs and attitudes conform to global ideals. A report in the *American Sociological Review* summarized their global progress. It found that—

> primary-school curricula have become remarkably similar around the world, reflecting the increasing global dominance of a single concept of modern society.[13]

How did this happen? The Chronology of Events (see page 223) traces the steps back to 1905, but in this section we will begin in November 1985. Leading educators from 12 nations had gathered in the Netherlands for an international-curriculum symposium. One of the sponsors was the ASCD (Association for Supervision and Curriculum Development), the influential curriculum arm of the powerful NEA (National Education Association). Its executive director, Dr. Gordon Cawelti, was one of the main speakers.

According to *Education Week*, Dr. Cawelti "urged representatives of other Western nations and Japan to press for the development of a 'world-core curriculum' based on knowledge that will ensure 'peaceful and cooperative existence among the human species on this planet.'"[14]

Knowledge that would ensure peace and cooperation? What kind of knowledge would that be?

Education Week explained: "Cawelti's world-core curriculum would be based ... on proposals put forth by Robert Muller, assistant secretary-general of the United Nations, in his recent book *New Genesis: Shaping a Global Spirituality.*" Do you wonder what kind of "global spirituality" that might be? Here is one description:

Once again, but this time on a universal scale, humankind is seeking no less than its reunion with the "divine," its transcendence into ever higher forms of life. Hindus call our earth Brahma, or God, for they rightly see no difference between our earth and the divine. This ancient simple truth is slowly dawning again upon humanity. Its full flowering will be the real, great new story of humanity as we are about to enter our cosmic age. . . .[15]

After the symposium, Cawelti expressed his appreciation for the positive response to his suggestion. Despite "the pride all countries have in their own core curriculum," he said, all shared a common response "to the urgency of defining what global interdependency means for the schools."[16]

Since the ASCD so heartily endorsed Muller's World Core Curriculum, how have Muller's ideas influenced our schools? The answer will help us understand the seductive pull of holistic education, which has suddenly won mainstream support. It provides globalists with the spiritual link needed for a plausible vision of a united world, of connectedness with nature, and of the oneness of the human family around the world.

This is no trivial fringe vision. The much-acclaimed Czech President Vaclav Havel, who joined Mikhail Gorbachev and other world leaders in San Francisco for the 1995 anniversary celebration of the U.N. Charter, shared the same dream in a speech in Philadelphia on July 4, 1994, when he was awarded the Philadelphia Liberty Medal. Compare his words with those of Robert Muller:

The central political task of the final years of this century, then, is the creation of a new model of coexistence within a single interconnected civilization. . . . The only real hope for people today is probably a renewal of our certainty that we are rooted in the Earth, and at the same time in the cosmos. This awareness endows us with the capacity for self-transcendence. . . . Transcendence is the only real alternative to extinction.[17]

The Robert Muller World Core Curriculum

During a visit to Arlington, Texas, some years ago, a friend took me to see the original Robert Muller school. While she waited in the car, I walked past a little Buddha, climbed the steps to the front door, and rang the bell. Gloria Crook, the director opened the door and asked why I had come. I listed my credentials: I was interested in global education, I was concerned about the environment, and I was an immigrant from Norway—a country well-known for its global concerns and admiration for the United Nations.[18] I must have passed the test, because she invited me in and led me into a massive hallway. Looking to the left, I saw a room full of young mothers and pregnant women in Yoga position. On a table next to the doorway I noticed a stack of papers. The title startled me: "Occult Meditation."

To those who don't know God, the occult seems good, not bad, I thought to myself.

"Are you familiar with Alice Bailey?" she asked me as we entered a large cluttered office.

"Yes," I nodded, well aware of the occult messages she channeled from her favorite spirit guide. "Didn't she write books full of messages she received from the Tibetan Master, Djwhal Khul?"

"Yes," answered Ms. Crook. "Here, sit down and look at some of them." She pulled down several of Bailey's books from a shelf and put them in my lap. I prayed silently as I flipped through the pages of the first one, *Education in the New Age.*

Then she handed me the *Robert Muller World Core Curriculum Manual.* I turned a few pages and read:

The underlying philosophy upon which the Robert Muller School is based will be found in the teaching set forth in the books of Alice A. Bailey by the Tibetan teacher, Djwhal Khul. . . . [19]

The back of the manual contained two certificates. The first announced that The Robert Muller School "is a participating institution in the UNESCO Associated Schools Project in Education for International Cooperation and Peace." The other confirmed its accreditation by the Southern Association of Colleges and Schools. On behalf of the Southern Association's review team, Dr. Eileen Lynch wrote:

> The visiting team was so impressed with the Robert Muller School that they thought the educational process and the general curriculum would be most valuable as a model for teacher education. . . . Throughout this report the committee has recommended that information of the school's educational processes be shared with educators everywhere as much as possible.[20]

Finally Ms. Crook pulled two large golden frames from the wall and showed them to me. The first pictured a beautiful calligraphic rendition of "The Great Invocation," an occult prayer used around the world to invoke a global outpouring of spiritual light and power.

The other frame displayed a letter from the White House. President Bush had sent his greetings and appreciation for the contributions made by the school. *Did the former president know whom he had endorsed?*

Whether Bush knew Muller or not, the former U.N. leader is no stranger to the educational establishment. You saw that Muller's outline for a World Core Curriculum was endorsed by the powerful ASCD and recommended to enthusiastic educators at an international curriculum symposium. Two years later it was promoted by Andy LePage in his well-endorsed book on holistic learning, *Transforming Education*. In the nineties it is spreading into local school districts.

For example, Eugene, Oregon, School District 4J developed and published its "Integrated Curriculum K-5" in 1989. Page 11 in this public school curriculum acknowledges that "the three curriculum strands are adapted from the World Core Curriculum by Robert Muller. . . ." The three curriculum strands match those in Muller's book: "Oneness with the planet," "Unity with people," and "Harmony with self." Muller's fourth strand, which deals with evolution through time, is incorporated into the other three strands. In *New Genesis*: Muller pulls the strands together into one Utopian vision:

> The ecumenical teachings of the Christ [not the biblical Jesus]—peace, justice, love, compassion, kindness, human brotherhood . . . must also find their way in worldwide global education. We must give the newcomers into the ceaseless renewed stream of human life the right education about their planetary home, about their human family, about their past, present and future, about their place in the universe and in time, so that they can flower to their utmost beauty—physically, mentally and spiritually—and become joyful and grateful members of the universe or kingdom of God.[21]

Muller's vision can be seen at a glance in two diagrams for "Defining World Class Education" designed by the Iowa Department of Education. The first diagram, called "The Old Story: Conventional Wisdom," shows an oval picture of the earth with its land and oceans. The globe is surrounded by arrows pointing toward the center and bombarding the planet with terrors like "Domination," "Biocide," "Ecocide," "Earth Is Man's to Exploit," "WAR," "Intercultural Conflicts," and "Boundaries."[22]

The second diagram shows students "the right education about their planetary home." It pictures a rounder, more mystical planet. Titled "The New Story: Transformation," it shows arrows radiating out from the earth. Here the descriptions reflect the vision of a healthy, harmonious planet: "Beyond War," "Humanity Evolving," "Reverence for all Life," "Interconnectedness: We are All One," and "**Gaia**" (a spiritualized Earth renamed after an ancient Greek goddess).

This mystical teaching tool was fabricated by *tax-funded educators,* not fringe fanaticals. The paradigm shift it promotes has gained enough acceptance to be established in local classrooms as well as global symposiums. Listen to the message in "The Peacemakers Planetary Anthem," sung to the melody of the Star Spangled Banner, during an assembly at an elementary school in Sunnyvale, California. Encouraging children to imagine a peaceful planet with pristine forests and crystal-clear rivers, it begins with this millennial view:

> O say can you see
>   by the one light in all,
> A New Age to embrace
>   at the call of the nations. . . .[23]

Now compare the material in the previous paragraphs with Muller's vision of a world united through global education and evolving spiritually toward ultimate perfection:

> We need a new world education. Global education, namely the education of the children into our global home and into the human family, is making good progress. But we have to go beyond. We need the cosmic education foreseen by the religions and by people like Maria Montessori. We need a holistic education, teaching the holism of the universe and of the planet. . . [24]

Muller didn't mention Waldorf Schools, but they fit right in. Their founder, Rudolf Steiner (1861–1925), shared Alice Bailey's occult roots in Theosophy, but broke away to start his own cult, Anthroposophy, which he described as "knowledge produced by the higher self in man."[25] Like the Robert Muller schools, Waldorf schools offer holistic education and have long used the strategies now implemented in all states through mastery learning: whole language instead of phonics, stories and "literature" instead of factual history, and a strong emphasis on myth, imagination, guided imagery, art, creativity, movement (eurythmy), and spiritual oneness with nature.[26]

Global Education is still Muller's driving ambition. His main headquarters are now in Costa Rica, where he serves as Chancellor of the University of Peace, which is sponsored by the United Nations as a model for education in the next century.

In 1989, UNESCO (United Nations Educational, Scientific, and Cultural Organization) awarded Muller its Peace Education Prize. In his acceptance speech, Muller shared his vision of the new world education program. Part of his dream was—

- that all schools and universities of this Earth will teach peace and nonviolence and become schools and universities for peace;

- that UNESCO will study and recommend by the year 2000 a world-core curriculum for adoption by all nations;

- that all human beings of this earth become instruments of peace, thus fulfilling the cosmic function deeply engraved in each of us. . . . [27]

By the time Muller shared this vision, the world had already made a giant leap toward fulfilling it.

The World Conference
on Education for All (WCEFA)

When delegates from 155 countries met in Jomtien, Thailand, in 1990 to plan the international agenda for education, Muller's heart must have been singing. His vision for world education was nearing reality. Within five days in early March, the world's leaders reached consensus on six international goals. Like the six U.S. goals prepared by the Bush administration (America 2000) and later adopted by the Clinton administration (Goals 2000 added two goals), the international goals call for implementation by the year 2000. Notice the similarities between the two sets of goals from the chart opposite.

These goals were designed to inspire a common vision and draw a groundswell of support. They must appeal to the public while hiding their true purpose. For example, the first international goal, "expansion of early childhood care . . . including family and community intervention," sounds good to tired, frustrated parents who would welcome community support. But few parents realize that this goal set the stage for "parent educators" or other school-based authorities to intervene when parents don't follow their new-paradigm guidelines. If this sounds hard to believe, the rest of this book will convince you.

To bridge the gap between domestic and international education, educators and politicians formed a U.S. branch of the WCEFA. Called the United States Coalition for Education for All (USCEFA), it first met in Virginia in 1991 with Barbara Bush as its Honorary Chairwoman. For three days, nearly 300 leaders from over 28 countries "worked together to find ways to build stronger partnerships. . . ."[30]

The USCEFA partnerships include educational organizations, universities, international business and media groups, and local teachers and principals. Some of the links are familiar: the National Education Association, the National Center for Education Statistics, Apple Computer, Encyclopaedia Britannica Education Corporation, and

	THE NATIONAL GOALS America 2000 and Goals 2000[28]	THE INTERNATIONAL GOALS World Conference Education for All
1. Readiness for school	"By the year 2000, all children in America will start school ready to learn."	"Expansion of early childhood care and developmental activities, including family and community interventions...."
2. Certificate of Initial Mastery	"By the year 2000, the high school graduation rate will increase to at least 90%.	"Universal access to, and completion of, primary education (or whatever higher level ...each country considers as 'basic')...."
3. Achievement, citizenship	"By the year 2000, American students will leave grades four, eight, and twelve having demonstrated competency...."	"Improvement in learning achievement at all grade levels ...an agreed percentage attains or surpassed a defined level...."
4. Science, Math, Reading	"By the year 2000, U.S. students will be first in the world in science and mathematics."	"Reduction of the adult literacy rate to at least one-half its 1990 level by the year 2000, with sufficient emphasis on female literacy...."
5. Adult literacy and lifelong learning	"By the year 2000, every adult American will be literate and will possess the knowledge and skills necessary to compete in a global economy...."	"... basic education and training in other essential skills .... program effectiveness assessed in terms of behavioral changes and impacts on health, employment, and productivity."
6. Behavior modification for safe, drug-free schools	"By the year 2000, every school in America will be free of drugs and violence and will offer a discipline environment conductive to learning."	"... the knowledge, skills, and values required for better living and sound and sustainable development ...through all education channels including the mass media ...and social action, with effectiveness assessed in terms of behavioral change."[29]

[Ted] Turner Educational Services. The religious partners include World Vision and The Baha'i Foundation.

These partnerships between governmental and non-governmental groups are essential to the network of support on every level: local, state, national, and global. Chapter 7 will explain more about this deceptive strategy, and show how mainstream churches have been lured into partnerships designed to weaken the very families they serve.

The USCEFA met again in December 1994. To set the stage, it prepared a report with some familiar guidelines. They turned out to be the same ones that are being promoted in local communities across America: **lifelong learning**, **partnerships**, communication technologies.

These "innovations can be used creatively to bring about change from the local to the international levels,"[31] the report explained. They must be implemented in one package, not piecemeal. After all, education is "the key mechanism for attaining a global society that is peaceful and just, and provides a decent living for all its present and future citizens."[32]

Few people would disagree with such noble goals. The problem is the plan for their attainment. Later you will see that the new path to peace mapped out by leading educators looks more like the mystical steps to occult oneness described in *Celestine Prophecy,* James Redfield's top-selling book on spiritual evolution toward New Age perfection, than anything the Western world has ever seen.

The following USCEFA standard sounds strangely similar to the 1995 *state* standards written to conform to *national* standards:

> Schools will need to reach learners as never before, developing responsibility for learning, encouraging self-esteem and motivation, stimulating curiosity and emotions, concentrating on higher order [thinking] skills and instructing people how to work together.[33]

These goals sound good, don't they? But the next chapter will show you what these new-paradigm euphemisms actually mean:

- trading facts for imagination so that children cannot think or reason independently;

- teaching occult formulas for empowerment to help students feel good about themselves and school—at least for a while;

- providing daily lessons in group conformity to quench individual choices;

- using **cooperative learning** so that all students will progress to the same mediocre level.

This kind of "education for all" leads to global socialism, not responsible democracy. It breeds intolerance and religious persecution, not respect and religious freedom. It produces a pliable workforce that can easily be manipulated, not individuals who stay true to their conscience. It follows the blueprint of Soviet indoctrination, which should come as no surprise considering the secretive Soviet-American educational exchange agreements led by the Carnegie Foundation during the eighties.[34] It aims to destroy everything that Americans once called good.

Listen to this warning from Thomas Sowell, respected economist and Senior Fellow at Stanford University's Hoover Institution. In his review of Friedrich Hayek's exposé of socialism, *Road to Serfdom,* he writes:

> At the heart of the socialist vision is the notion that a compassionate society can create more humane living conditions for all through government "planning" and control of the economy. . . .
> The rule of law, on which freedom itself ultimately depends, is inherently incompatible with socialism. People who are free to do as they wish will not do as the economic planners wish. Differences in values and priorities are enough to ensure that. These differences

must be ironed out by propaganda or power, if socialism is to be socialism. Indoctrination must be part of
the program, not because socialists want to be brain-
washers, but because socialism requires brainwashing.

[I]dealist socialists create systems in which idealists are almost certain to lose and be superseded by
those whose drive for power, and ruthlessness in
achieving it, make them the "fittest" to survive under
a system where government power is the ultimate
prize. . . . The issue is not what anyone intends but
what consequences are in fact likely to follow.[35]

In the same article, aptly titled "A Road to Hell Paved
with Good Intentions," Sowell points out that "Marxism as
an ideal continues to flourish on American college campuses,
as perhaps nowhere else in the world." Collectivist visions
appeal to academic idealists and others who ignore the
lessons of history.

Others know well what Communism proved: that central controls lead to tyranny and poverty, not peace and
equality. Yet our lawmakers continue to pave the path to
lifelong management of our children while raising the
promise of "local control" as a smokescreen to pacify concerned parents.[36] Chapter 7 explains how the planned "community" will heed state, national, and global directives, not
local parents.

The goal of education is no longer to teach the kind of
literacy, wisdom, and knowledge we once considered essen-
tials of responsible citizenship; it is to train world citizens—a compliant international workforce, willing to flow
with the storms of change and uncertainty. These citizens
must be ready to believe and do whatever will serve a predetermined "common good" or "greater whole." Educators
may promise to "teach students to think for themselves,"
but if they finish what they have started, tomorrow's students will have neither the facts nor the freedom needed for
independent thinking. Like Nazi youth, they will be taught
to react, not to think, when told to do the unthinkable.

In another excellent article titled "Indoctrinating the Children," Thomas Sowell summarized the process:

> The techniques of brainwashing developed in totalitarian countries are routinely used in psychological conditioning programs imposed on American schoolchildren. These include emotional shock and desensitization, psychological isolation from sources of support, stripping away defenses, manipulative cross-examination of the individual's underlying moral values, and inducing acceptance of alternative values by psychological rather than rational means.[37]

The next two chapters will show how this is happening—even in your own community.

Meanwhile, don't despair; you just made it through the heaviest part of the book. If you feel overwhelmed by the globalist agenda, know that hopeful answers are coming. Remember, when we know the truth, stand together, trust God, and do what He says, we join the winning team. "Thanks be to God, who always leads us in triumph."[38]

3

A New Way
of Thinking

*What's happening in America today . . . is a total transformation of
our society. We have moved into a new era . . . I'm not sure we have
really begun to comprehend . . . the incredible amount of organizational restructuring and human resource development. . . . [W]hat we
have to do is build a future. . . . The revolution . . . in curriculum is
that we no longer are teaching facts to children."*[1]

—Dr. Shirley McCune
addressing the 1989 Governors' Conference on Education

*We are now between two ages, on the threshold of a new epoch in
human history. . . . Nothing less than a universal liberal education
will suffice.*[2]

—Donald A. Cowan
President Emeritus of the University of Dallas

*"Old men in the bad old days used to renounce, retire, take to reli-
gion, spend their time reading, thinking—thinking!"*
"Idiots, swine!" Bernard was saying to himself . . .
*"Now—such is progress . . . men have no time, no leisure from plea-
sure, not a moment to sit down and think . . . safe on the solid ground
of daily labor and distraction, scampering from feely to feely . . ."*[3]

—Aldous Huxley, *Brave New World*

*T*he classroom discussion came to a close, and Ashley began to pack up her books. Her English class had studied Oedipus, the mythical king haunted by an oracle's tragic prediction that he would kill his father and marry his mother. Moments before the bell rang, the California tenth-grader heard her teacher announce a writing assignment:

> You're going to consult an oracle. It will tell you that you're going to kill your best friend. This is destined to happen, and there is absolutely no way out. You will commit this murder. What will you do before this event occurs? Describe how you felt leading up to it. How did you actually kill your best friend?[4]

"Yeah!" cheered some of the students gleefully. Others seemed more sober. A few raised their hands and asked if they could commit suicide to avoid murdering their friends.

"No," they were told. The oracle makes no mistakes and permits no other options.

Ashley felt eerie. What a strange assignment! Why would her English teacher tell her to imagine something so horrible? I don't want to do this, she told herself. Long after she told her parents, the awful feelings continued to churn inside.

The next day Ashley's mother called the teacher and asked that her daughter be given an alternate assignment. "I can't encourage my daughter to write a story about murdering her best friend," she explained.

"Certainly Ashley knows the difference between fantasy and reality," said Ms. Sawyer with a touch of sarcasm.

"Of course she does. But when you ask someone to imagine how she would go about murdering a friend, you could stir up nightmarish feelings."

"I have been giving the same assignment for years," answered Ms. Sawyer. Then she added the standard argument that parents across the country have learned to expect: "No one has ever complained about this before."

"That's a shame," responded the mother. "It seems to me that parents should be appalled!"

"If I give Ashley a different assignment she will be made to feel foolish."

"Are you saying that she will either get an F or be made to feel foolish? Is this a no-win situation for her?"

The teacher didn't answer, but the next day she carried out her threat. Staring straight at Ashley, she spoke to the entire class: "Of course you know the difference between fantasy and reality. And certainly you are capable of writing an assignment without becoming emotionally involved."

Ashley *did* feel uncomfortable—but not foolish. She knew that she had chosen wisely. She had refused to use her imagination to create horrible mental pictures that might never go away. Nor had she yielded to the demand for conformity to group standards. In spite of the teacher's warning, she was confident that she had done the right thing.

Ashley's assignment is not unique. This kind of emotional shock therapy has become standard fare in public schools from coast to coast. While topics may range from homosexual or occult practices to euthanasia and suicide, they all attack the old moral and ethical boundaries.

The New Paradigm

Ashley didn't know that her assignment illustrates a common classroom strategy used to desensitize students to traditional values. This strategy uses myths, shocking or disturbing stories, or hypothetical situations that

- evoke strong feeling;

- challenge traditional values;

- produce **cognitive dissonance**, a form of mental and moral confusion;

- elicit a response that demonstrates a change in attitude, that can be measured, and that becomes part of a child's individual electronic data file.

Each element of the strategy is part of a planned process to teach students the "new thinking, new strategies, new behavior, and new beliefs"[5] needed for full participation in the next-century workforce. "[Our objective] will require a change in the prevailing culture—the attitudes, values, norms and accepted ways of doing things,"[6] says Marc Tucker, President of the National Center on Education and the Economy (NCEE), the mastermind behind the Certificate of Initial Mastery (CIM). He, like other leading change agents, is calling for a paradigm shift—a total transformation in the way people think, believe, and perceive reality.

To accomplish this paradigm shift, change agents have tried to keep their true goals and methods hidden from opposing forces. "Old paradigms do not retire gracefully," wrote Chester Finn, who helped President Bush and Lamar Alexander promote America 2000, "and the avatars of new ones are often scorned and savaged. . . ."[7]

"Paradigm shifts are complicated," he added, ". . . but shift we will."[8]

New Age author Marilyn Ferguson outlined the transformation in *The Aquarian Conspiracy*. It is sobering to see that the changes she sought in the seventies have become reality in the nineties. Look at her "Assumptions" chart. Notice how she differentiates between the old paradigm's "right" information and the new paradigm's "right" things. To shift from the left to the right side, teachers as well as children must be made open to new concepts.

ASSUMPTIONS OF THE . . .[9]	
OLD PARADIGM OF EDUCATION	**NEW PARADIGM OF EDUCATION**
Emphasis on content, acquiring a body of "right" information, once and for all.	Emphasis on learning how to learn . . . pay attention to the *right* things, be open to and evaluate new concepts, have access to information. . . . (Emphasis added.)
Hierarchical and authoritarian structure.	Egalitarian. Candor and dissent permitted.
. . . emphasis on the "appropriate ages for certain activities."	Flexibility and integration of age groupings.
Priority on performance.	Priority on self-image as the generator of performance.
Emphasis on external world. Inner experience often considered inappropriate in school setting.	Inner experience seen as context for learning. Use of imagery, storytelling, dream journals, "centering" exercises, and exploration of feelings encouraged.
Emphasis on analytical, linear . . . thinking.	Augments left-brain rationality with holistic, nonlinear, and intuitive strategies.

As you can see, each paradigm has its own set of right values—and wrong ones. Everything that was part of the old paradigm is being discarded, but Ms. Ferguson's "egalitarian," integrated, feeling-centered learning has become standard practice in our land. Since the two paradigms are totally incompatible, today's change agents cannot tolerate Christian guidelines, nor can Christians embrace the new earth-centered values.

Christian children who read and know the Bible are likely to resist the global paradigm, and therefore educators want to reach children before they learn old-paradigm truths. To fulfill the first national/international goal (the U.S. version: "by year 2000, all children in America will start school ready to learn") all new students must be open to new global ideals and freed from the old uncompromising beliefs that block progress. Robert Muller explains why this is important in *The Birth of a Global Civilization*:

> In the long run, only the right global education will be our salvation on this planet. Children are born with more or less the same senses into the world. But very soon they are "wired in" by a culture, a religion, an ideology, a nation. There is only one thing with which they are never really wired in: their membership in the entire human family. . . . The lack of proper world education [is] one of our most glaring and dangerous deficiencies.[10]

Which culture or religion has "wired in" your children? If biblical truth has shaped their worldview, they will recognize and resist occult ideals. On the other hand, if their beliefs have been molded by television, movies, and multicultural books, the schools will merely reinforce the new paradigm established in their minds. These children, who have no strong ties to church and traditional values, are considered *ready to learn*. The others are not; they must be retrained or *remediated*.

Professor John Goodlad used the word *resocialize*. One of the most influential change agents in the global as well as the national arena, he has served on the governing boards of UNESCO's Institute for Education[11] and Global Perspectives in Education. In 1970 he warned his fellow educators that "most youth still hold the same values as their parents. . . . If we do not alter this pattern, if we don't resocialize. . . . our society may decay."[12]

Mastery Learning

The strategy for resocializing our children is best known as Mastery Learning. On the surface its promise to parents sounds good: Given enough time, every child can learn. However, like most of the new educational labels, this doesn't mean what we think it says. It refers not to solid factual learning but to the psychological process of conditioning students to new-paradigm thinking. It is based on the behavior modification formulas of B. F. Skinner, who said, "Operant conditioning shapes behavior as a sculptor shapes a lump of clay,"[13] and "I could make a pigeon a high achiever by reinforcing it on a proper schedule."[14]

What do pigeons have in common with children? Behavioral psychologists might answer that both can be trained to respond to stimuli in predictable ways, given enough time and the *right* kind of stimulus. Of course there are obvious differences between the level of achievement that can be expected from a pigeon and from human children. There are also different levels of ability among children (although educators seem reluctant to admit that fact). Some students can memorize and retain huge amounts of abstract information (I'm not among them). Others can grasp mathematical concepts that mystify me.

The new education system promises "high standards" for all students. The second goal (of Goals 2000 and America 2000) states that "by the year 2000 the high school graduation rate will increase to at least 90 percent." Obviously, the "high standard" that 90 percent of students will attain can be no higher than their capacity and study habits will allow. In other words, the threshold must be set low enough for almost everyone to reach the same "egalitarian" level.

Remember, the word *high* is relative. The "high standards" will be high only to the neediest students—those who were failing both academically and socially. Those same "high standards" are tragically low to the students who aim for college and beyond. How would you have survived high school, college, or work if your teachers had followed this bit of advice from Professor Kenneth Goodman, a leading **Whole Language** theorist at the University of Arizona?

> What we say is, you learn to spell by reading and writing. In that context, there is some risk taking, and kids invent spelling. We don't want to discourage kids from using words just because they can't spell them.[15]

"Our state's educational leaders decided it was terribly insulting for kids to have to learn number tables or how to spell words," said Maureen DiMarco, the top education adviser to California's Governor Pete Wilson. "So we ended up with math books without arithmetic, and literature books without reading."[16]

Not only is the new teaching dumbed-down, it is entirely different. A broad knowledge base is no longer important; to the contrary, it is a detriment to the new training system. Students armed with facts and strong convictions resist manipulation. On the other hand, students with limited knowledge and few convictions can easily be conditioned and controlled. They may provide just the kind of manageable workforce for the global economy which many change agents envision.

In an article titled "Experts Say Too Much Is Read Into Illiteracy Crisis," Thomas Sticht, member of (Labor) Secretary's Commission on Achieving Necessary Skills, usually called **SCANS**,[17] explains:

> Many companies have moved operations to places with cheap, relatively poorly educated labor. What

may be crucial, they say, is the dependability of a labor force and how well it can be managed and trained—not its general educational level, although a small cadre of highly educated creative people are essential to innovation and growth. Ending discrimination and changing values are probably more important than reading in moving low income families into the middle class.[18]

The stimuli used to "change values" are the shocking stories, the values clarification exercises, and the questions and suggestions written into each student's **Individual Education Plan** (IEP). This IEP is continually adjusted to a student's progress and degree of resistance. The national or state assessments that measure progress match the SCANS competencies as well as national standards. Therefore Dr. Sticht's chilling statement cannot be dismissed as mere fringe sentiment.

Sophisticated, computerized assessment strategies have been developed to meet the need for continual learning, testing, remediation, and retesting. . . . In her excellent exposé of the globalization of our schools, former U.S. Department of Education official Charlotte Iserbyt quotes Dustin Heuston of Utah's World Institute for Computer-Assisted Teaching (WICAT). He says:

> We've been absolutely staggered by realizing that the computer has the capability to act as if it were ten of the top psychologists working with one student. You've seen the tip of the iceberg. Won't it be wonderful when the child in the smallest county in the most distant area or in the most confused urban setting can have the equivalent of the finest school in the world on that terminal and no one can get between that child and that computer?[19]

From the new-paradigm perspective, this indeed sounds wonderful." Each child will have his or her own personal high-tech program for learning. It will offer immediate rewards for "right" thinking and immediate corrections for old-paradigm thinking. As Mr. Heuston pointed out, "No one [especially parents] can get between that child and that computer." Parents may be allowed to monitor some selected computer programs, but not the ones that raise concern.

Teachers across the country already use hand-held computer scanners during class time and recess to record students' responses that indicate progress toward behavioral goals. They simply scan the students' bar-coded name and bar-coded response, then transfer the information into the computer at the end of the school day.

The scanners simplify record-keeping for teachers—but parents, beware! Jeannie Georges in her excellent report "Outcome-Based Education" asks a sobering question: "But what if Jennifer doesn't happen to fall directly into one of the categories expected by the computer? No time for extensive notes or explanations; just file her under 'authority-challenged.'"[20]

Challenging *parental* authority has been encouraged for years, but try resisting the new school authorities! Mastery Learning is full of rewards for compliance and punishment for resisters. While computerized "teaching machines" offer subtle corrections to correct unacceptable beliefs and group facilitators use ridicule and strategic arguments to shame students into compliance, the new system can simply remove students from homes that resist the new-paradigm values (see Chapter 7).

Both teachers and students are rewarded when students surrender their independence, "master" the new thinking "skill," and respond "correctly" to stimuli. Disturbing lessons like Ashley's on fantasizing murder speed the process. When hypothetical situations introduce new values and evoke strong feelings, students remember them better and question their own beliefs more readily.

At this point of cognitive dissonance, the curriculum may call for group discussion. This allows well-meaning teachers or trained facilitators to use the time of mental confusion to confirm new-paradigm suggestions through group consensus. Teachers trained to lead these group discussions use the same tools to manipulate students as do animal trainers: positive and negative reinforcement. If students conform, they will be accepted. If they fail to conform, they face rejection and exclusion. Since most students have neither the desire nor the discernment to resist this form of brainwashing, they will conform to the group and compromise their standards.

That is exactly what the change agents had in mind. In 1990 the National LEADership Network Study Group on Restructuring Schools released a study titled "Developing Leaders for Restructuring Schools: New Habits of Mind and Heart." It encourages teachers to "create dissonance" and "encourage risk taking."[21] Risk-taking involves testing the moral boundaries learned at home and moving beyond: Instead of trusting your parents, dare to "think for yourself," transcend old boundaries, create your own values, leap into the unknown.

Most students seem ready to take those risks—they no longer have the strong convictions needed to hold them back. The result is family and social disintegration. Jeannie Georges' report titled "Outcome-Based Education," gives this tragic glimpse of contemporary reality:

> Kids are being told there is no meaning to life. There is no right; no wrong. They are to make their own decisions based on feelings and whims, and—if the parent interferes or restrains the child or attempts to discipline the child—children are to turn the parent in to the state for mental or psychological abuse.
>
> Parents find it much more difficult to discipline and teach their children. After all, why should the child obey the parent and spell words correctly when the teacher gives them high marks for "creative" and/or inventive spelling? Why obey when the parent can be thrown in jail for disciplining his own child?

They teach there is no right way to spell a word; no right to way to pronounce it; no meaning in it; no absolutes. Life becomes meaningless. . . .

This process is being implemented for the disorganization of mind and behavior—or mental breakdown. What follows this despair is a total desolation with nothing left but mysticism. Those raised on mysticism and superstition are easy to lead—easy to program—easy to enslave.[22]

The change agents are, of course, well aware of this pain and confusion; they planned it. To them, *this* crisis, like so many others, is an essential step along the way. Each serious crisis creates a *felt need*. And each urgent need becomes an open door to a new solution—one that brings the paradigm shift closer to completion. *But the frog doesn't even notice that the water is starting to steam.*

Purging the Old Views

To minimize resistance to the paradigm shift, educators had to purge the old-paradigm views. NCEE President Marc Tucker proposes "breaking the current system, root and branch."[23] Coming from the mastermind behind the Certificate of Initial Mastery (CIM)—a reward for conformity and a likely entrance pass to work and college—this is no minor opinion.

That process began decades ago by censoring references to God, prayer, and traditional families from our history books. This secretive sabotage of America's heritage was documented by Professor Paul Vitz in his excellent book *Censorship—Evidence of Bias in Our Children's Textbooks.* Today the movement that spread silently underground for years has suddenly taken wings, but too few people have noticed.

"The revolution . . . in curriculum is that we no longer are teaching facts to children," said Dr. Shirley McCune,

Senior Director with the Mid-Continent Regional Educational Laboratory (McREL)[24] at the 1989 Governors' Conference on Education, where Governors Bill Clinton and Richard Riley worked with Lamar Alexander to formulate the six original goals for national and international education. "We no longer see the teaching of facts and information as the primary outcome of education. We have to understand that the only way anyone ever learns is from their own frame of reference. . . ."[25]

From the new-paradigm perspective, McCune is right. Today's restructured education is based on feelings and personal relevance rather than facts and objective reason. Much of the credit goes to a close associate of John Goodlad: educational psychologist Benjamin Bloom, called "the father of Outcome-Based Education." In his book *All Our Children Learning* he admits that—

> the purpose of education and the schools is to change the thoughts, feelings and actions of students.[26]

One of the quickest ways to change people's "thoughts, feelings and actions" is to hide or distort the basic *facts* and *assumptions* that have molded their culture. This tactic was used effectively to revolutionize the youth in Nazi Germany and Soviet Russia. Facts were censored. Only politically correct information was allowed. Literacy and general knowledge became less important than group conformity and obedience to the new leaders and their instructions.

This same strategy has been established in our schools through Professor Bloom's Taxonomy. At first glance his hierarchy of "thinking skills" makes sense: A sound body of factual knowledge should be the foundation of all thinking processes. But in reality this model instituted a different message. It reduced factual *knowledge* and *comprehension* to the rank of **lower-order thinking skills**, suggesting that traditional knowledge had become relatively insignificant, and could even be a hindrance. In contrast, the more subjective processes—application, analysis, **synthesis**, and evaluation—were elevated to higher-order thinking skills. (See chart on p. 68.)

"How in the world," you might ask, "can students apply, analyze, synthesize, and evaluate without facts? How can they reach a rational conclusion without comprehension?"

They can't. In the absence of foundational facts, those *higher-order thinking skills* can only lead to subjective, uncertain answers. Without a broad knowledge base, children are rudderless and headed for disaster. Deprived of the factual comprehension needed for moral, spiritual, and intellectual discernment, they cannot recognize deception. At the mercy of social revolutionaries, they are ready to embrace the New Age/neopagan view of "reality"—which has no basis in actual reality.

In other words, they can easily be manipulated. Well aware that knowledge is the foundation of all true thinking, Dr. Bloom had discovered a process that could control the *outcome* or end product of thinking, which was often an opinion or a value judgment. By censoring a student's knowledge base, the teacher could direct the student's thinking.

Bloom's process works. Through biased information, carefully designed hypothetical stories, and pointed Socratic questioning, students are persuaded that their home-taught beliefs and values are incompatible with the needs for the next century. This is exactly what Benjamin Bloom and his followers intended. In his *Taxonomy of Educational Objectives II,* Bloom wrote:

> . . . a large part of what we call "good teaching" is the teacher's ability to attain effective objectives through challenging the students' fixed beliefs and getting them to discuss issues.[27]

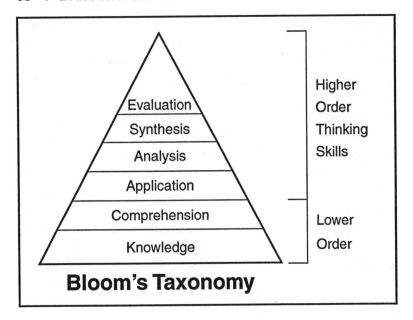

Bloom's Taxonomy

Change Beliefs Through Consensus

Why is it so important to "discuss issues"? Because group thinking is vital to **consensus building** and **conflict resolution**, two of the many nice-sounding buzzwords designed to sell the deception to the public. (See chart opposite.) Local school officials and well-meaning teachers are usually kept in the dark. Like most parents, they trust the system and are shocked when they learn the true intentions behind terms that sound so good. To help them and others understand today's transformation, we need to know—

- what most people expect these words to mean;

- what educators tell us they mean;

- what they really mean in the new-paradigm context.

THREE SETS OF MEANINGS FOR EDUCATIONAL BUZZWORDS

	EXPECTED MEANING	STATED MEANING	REAL MEANING
CONFLICT RESOLUTION	Resolving conflicts.	Learning to settle disputes peacefully.	Learning to synthesize beliefs: trading old absolutes for blended beliefs and compromised positions.
CONSENSUS BUILDING	Agreement through open discussion.	Seeking mutual understanding on any given topic.	Reaching a preplanned outcome by isolating, labeling, intimidating, censuring, or ignoring opposing voices.
COOPERATIVE LEARNING	Students working together.	Preparing to work in a global society with people whose values differ from yours.	A means of standardizing beliefs, values, attitudes, and behaviors, since all must express *respect* for each other's ways. Faster or more intuitive students help slower students reach same outcome.
CRITICAL THINKING	Rational, factual study and analysis.	Teaching students to think for themselves.	Criticizing traditional values and authorities, often through group discussion and forced decision-making.
HIGHER ORDER THINKING	Logical integration of facts.	Application, analysis, synthesis, evaluation.	Making conclusions based on a predetermined, politically correct set of opinions or judgments.
VALUES CLARIFICATION	Help students clarify and express the traditional values.	Discuss and clarify personal values.	Ridicule, reject, and replace old values with moral relativism and self-made choices—often determined through group consensus.

© 1996 Berit Kjos

There is nothing inherently wrong with a free-flowing exchange of facts and ideas. Organized discussions can be either good, neutral, or manipulative, depending on the purpose, direction, and control. But when teachers lead group discussions based on biased information toward a preplanned consensus or conclusion that conflicts with prior values, they are manipulating the students. Few children are equipped to resist this kind of pressure. Remember, Ashley was the only student in her English class who refused to yield to an immoral homework assignment.

A set of guidelines on group discussion was given to students at Homestead High School in Cupertino, California, along with a recent version of the infamous and much-used "Nuclear Shelter Assignment." (See p. 72.) Ponder these guidelines in the light of the assignment which follows.

GROUP DISCUSSION [28]

Group discussion is a way of thinking together. It is a method of pooling your ideas and information with that of others to come to some general conclusions. A leader generally guides the process of the group, but each person must have the responsibility of contributing his share.

THE PURPOSE OF GROUP DISCUSSION

- To gain information, facts, and ideas.

- To solve problems of interest.

- To learn to participate in discussion of social or public affairs.

- To learn principles of good leadership and social cooperation.

- To become open-minded and to respect the ideas of others.

- To make each feel he is taking an active part in the democratic way of life by expressing his own ideas.

It sounds good, doesn't it? However, "pooling your ideas" refers to the process of synthesis, which means the group must come to some kind of consensus. When a particular value conflicts with another value, students are forced to decide which option to take, which leads to situation ethics. For example, when a boy saw a friend steal a book, should he be honest and tell the truth, or should he be loyal to his friend and tell a lie? The students reached consensus together.

It doesn't matter how much the group's beliefs and values differ. Each group member must still agree to be open-minded, to respect and appreciate every other view, and to work toward a consensus. The method is based on an evolutionary decision-making process developed by Georg Friedrich Hegel. Each person brings his or her thoughts and ideas (his *thesis*) into the group. Then the group works together toward some kind of *common ground*, a "better" thesis, called a *synthesis,* since it blends or synthesizes all the ideas.

Thesis 1: I believe in God

Synthesis: We believe in many gods

Thesis 2 (antithesis): I believe in Buddha

Here is how the process might work: If one person believes in God (thesis 1), another in Buddha (thesis 2), and another in the Great Spirit (thesis 3), they may agree that "there are many gods" or that "every path leads to the same ultimate reality." This new thesis, of course, would not be considered *absolute* or *final* truth. It would merely be a higher step in the ongoing evolution toward ever greater understanding and perfection.

How does this *process* fit the old Judeo/Christian worldview?

How does the *conclusion* fit the old Judeo/Christian worldview?

How do both fit the new paradigm?

As you may expect, Christian children often feel anything but free to express their beliefs and ideas in this kind of group. But that's part of the plan.

Now take a look at one of the many versions of the nuclear shelter assignment.

> ...Suddenly the Third World War breaks out and bombs begin dropping everywhere. People are running to fallout shelters. You get a call from one of your fallout shelters asking for help.
>
> It seems that there are ten people, but there is only enough space, air, food, and water in the fallout shelter for six people for a period of three months. They want you to make the decision about who should go into the shelter....
>
> In making your decision, there are two important things to keep in mind. First, it's possible that the six people you choose might be the only six people left to start the human race over again. Therefore, the choice you make is very important. Second, if you don't make the choice in time, you will be leaving it to the ten to fight it out with the possibility that more than four might die.

The ten people you must assess include a bookkeeper and his wife, a black medical student, an historian, a singer, a scientist, a Rabbi, an athlete, a female college student, and a policeman with a gun. Whom would you choose? Who should die?

Notice that students are not given an option to share the shelter with the whole group. They *must* assign four people to death. Biblical answers and values don't fit the hypothetical context. The only permissible options concern the social significance of individuals—and here some choices will be more politically correct than others. In the end, the students must deny the inherent worth of some human lives and entertain the notion that it is good to sacrifice less important people on the altar of a "greater whole."

These disturbing views of human worth are taught through death education, sex education, and environmental, global, and multicultural education. Are students embracing them? They must. The mastery learning process prods them onward with its built-in rewards and corrections—often hidden in the student's computerized IEP program. If the students fail to comply, the new assessments (based on national requirements) will expose this failure and punish the school.

Since the new government tests match national standards, they show us what all students must learn to earn their graduation certificate. No one has exposed these connections more effectively than Anita Hoge. When researching Pennsylvania's EQA (Educational Quality Assessments) and its relationship to the National Assessment of Educational Progress (NAEP), she noticed an alarming emphasis on group conformity as a mark of good "citizenship." While emphasizing the new attitudes for citizenship, the NAEP, which developed the measuring scale, did not even consider *factual objectives* "such as (a) knowing structure of government and (b) understanding problems of international relations."[29] Apparently an understanding of the democratic process was considered unimportant—perhaps even a hindrance to the coming social order.

In the test assignment that follows, students were not given the option of saying no to vandalism. Instead, they had to role-play the part of vandals in the given hypothetical situation. The authors assumed that *all* students would participate given the right incentives.

There is a secret club at school called the Midnight Artists. They go out late at night and paint funny sayings and pictures on buildings. A student is asked to join the club. In this situation, I would join the club when I knew—

	YES	MAYBE	NO
1. my best friend asked me to join	☐	☐	☐
2. most of the popular students were in the club	☐	☐	☐
3. my parents would ground me if they found out I joined [30]	☐	☐	☐

Guess what the "right" answers were? Hint: The state seeks responses that demonstrate "willingness to honor self-made commitments to individuals or groups."[31] This response falls into the "citizenship" category which measures "personal responsibility and integrity." Knowing that today's global values give new meaning to words like "responsibility" and "integrity," one can begin to understand why the desired answers would be "yes" to 1 and 2.

The state also wants to know if students would respond to the threat of punishment. Therefore it gave students 1 point for a "no" to 3.

The key is control, says Anita Hoge. The establishment wants control over—

- knowledge (what students know and think);

- orientations (what they will be like, their attitudes and feelings);

- competence (what they can do).[32]

To control and change nations, leaders must know how to manage group behavior. A fascinating book by Gustave Le Bon called *The Crowd: A Study of the Popular Mind* shows why the group strategies used in international classrooms could produce a pliable population, one that can easily be manipulated for political and economic purposes. In it, Le Bon describes the moral weakness of the group mentality:

Little adapted to reasoning, crowds are quick to act. . . .
. . . how powerless they are to hold any opinions other than those which are imposed upon them. . . . [They are led] by seeking what produces an impression on them and what seduces them. . . .
Crowds possess a "collective mind which makes them feel, think and act in a manner quite different . . . . [The member of a crowd gains] a sentiment of invincible

power which allows [him] to yield to instincts which, had he been alone, he would . . . have kept under restraint.[33]

Could America be trading personal morality based on truth and reason for the moral relativism and irrational behavior of a crowd? "The great democratic danger," we read in *The Closing of the American Mind,* "is enslavement to public opinion."[34] If Americans yield to an impersonal group mentality, who will take charge? Who will control mass behavior?

Re-envision the World

Since traditional facts and reason are out, what is in? Dr. Donald A. Cowan has a ready answer:

> What will take the place of logic, fact and analysis in the coming age? The central way of thought for this new era will be imagination. Imagination will be the active, creative agent of culture, transforming brute materials to a higher, more knowable state. . . .[35]

This approach makes sense only when children are viewed through the deceptive filter of a holistic or panthe-istic paradigm. "Holism refers to what is holy," explains Jeffrey Kane, editor of *Holistic Education Review.* "The key here is to begin with respect for the sanctity, the spiritual integrity of the child as an autonomous human being. What is sacred must be treated with reverence."[36] He continues:

> To educate holistically is to create experiences and provide direction that will enable the child to unfold spirituality, to root himself or herself as a spiritual being in a physical world . . .[37]

To those who subscribe to this holistic paradigm, the child's inner voice transcends factual knowledge and all moral absolutes imposed by other people. Gone is the traditional understanding that children need instruction or wisdom from credible teachers, parents, pastors, or books. No longer do children need firm discipline to counter the selfish tendencies of human nature. Authority is transferred to self, and obedience is surrendered to personal feelings. But these feelings are being trained to respond to new-paradigm values—values that students "choose" under the manipulative guidance of the Mastery Learning process.

This process strips away the biblical foundations for a conscience, and with it the child's capacity for genuine remorse or repentance. After all, sin and guilt cannot coexist with the global beliefs and values supposedly needed to bring peace and unity to the world. Therefore children must be set free both from old authorities and from the limitations imposed by a Bible-trained conscience.

Today the various forms of values training or values clarification effectively erase those old moral values (right or wrong), social values (good or bad), and esthetic values (beautiful or ugly).[38] In their place stands the politically correct notion that children are naturally good and endowed with inner wisdom. Andy LePage, acclaimed author of *Transforming Education,* elaborates:

> Many, mostly traditionalists, still carry the cynical belief that we are, by nature, evil, irresponsible and untrustworthy. This belief is gradually being countered by a growing number who believe that, instead, and to the contrary, we are naturally inclined toward becoming life-affirming, cooperative, responsible and trustworthy. . . . Under [the] negative assumption, we logically act to repress and contain ourselves. Under the newer positive assumption, we logically act to liberate and express ourselves; even to fulfill ourselves . . . [It] is precisely . . . this limited view of ourselves as

human that has our world today in such disarray and despair. . . .

The way out is to be found in re-envisioning ourselves. . . .[39]

The arguments by global-minded educators for stressing "higher order thinking" might sound something like this: Don't bother teaching a lot of useless information. You don't know what facts will be relevant in the next century. Instead, teach children to ponder the universal truths in myths and symbols, to envision their own perfections, to imagine a better world, and to create their own stories of the future. This will help them connect with their inner wisdom, which in turn draws inspiration from the global mind. Then teach them persuasive communication skills and encourage them to share their self-expressions with parents and others in need of enlightenment.

THE NEW EMPHASIS IN EDUCATION	
OLD PARADIGM	**NEW PARADIGM**
Biblical truth	Earth-centered myths
Facts	Experience and feeling
Observation	Imagination
Logic	Speculation and feelings
Science	Politicized pseudoscience
Reality	Fantasy
Factual history	Fictional or multicultural stories
Objective thinking	Subjective feelings
Individual responsibility	Group thinking

© 1996 Berit Kjos

While parents are waking up to the unprecedented crisis, international educators are racing ahead with their agenda. Students around the world are learning to see the world through the framework of the new paradigm, and parents who question the classroom tactics are usually ignored, appeased, ridiculed, or reprimanded. Like Ashley's mother, they are made to feel that they alone imagine a problem, while the majority are sensible enough to appreciate the change.

But in fact the opposite is true. Listen to the prophetic words of Raymond Houghton, Professor of Secondary Education and Special Assistant to the President for Urban Affairs at Rhode Island College:

> . . . absolute behavior control is imminent. . . . The critical point of behavior control, in effect, is sneaking up on mankind without his self-conscious realization that a crisis is at hand. Man will . . . never self-consciously know that it has happened.[40]

As you can see, a war is raging for the minds of our children. But of course that is nothing new. Two thousand years ago God said, "See to it that no one takes you captive through hollow and deceptive philosophy, which depends on human tradition and the basic principles of this world rather than on Christ" (Colossians 2:8). Never has this warning been more relevant than today!

To keep our children from being caught up in deceptive philosophies, we need to train them to view reality through a biblical filter. If we don't, their schools, peers, and culture will teach them the new-paradigm perspective—and Christian beliefs and values will no longer make sense. The change agents will have won, and globalist leaders will determine their standards for their new universal values.

If you want to guard your child's mind, look again at the left column in the chart on the preceding page.

Then take time each day to train your children to—

- know biblical *truth*—the only source of genuine wisdom (Proverbs 2:6);

- learn the *facts* needed to defend what they know and believe;

- recognize the difference between *logic* and speculation;

- ground personal plans in *reality,* not fantasy;

- base their understanding of the world on *observation* rather than imagination;

- trust genuine *science* based on facts and logic, not social philosophy;

- learn the lessons found in a factual study of *history;*

- base actions in *objective thinking,* not subjective feelings;

- remember their *individual responsibility* before God and people.

When you train your children to look at daily and future events from God's perspective, you build into their minds a *mental framework* that will accept what is true and good but reject what is false and wrong. Remember:

> Be strong and courageous. Do not be afraid . . . for the Lord your God goes with you; he will never leave you nor forsake you (Deuteronomy 31:6).

4

Establishing a
Global Spirituality

What is needed is a shift in consciousness commensurate with the shift to a global society . . . [E]mphasize global interdependence. . . . Explore a major shift in belief systems with regard to our children and our future.[1]
— Phil Gang, Founding Director of The Institute
for Educational Studies (TIES) and Executive Director
of Global Alliance for Transforming Education (GATE)

As we look for answers [to saving the planet], more and more peoples are looking at the traditional peoples of the planet. . . . This is Indian history . . . our spiritualism, and we want to share it with the world.[2]
— Alan Ross, retired South Dakota school superintendent,
author of *Mitakuye Oyasin (We Are All Related)*

The group was now complete, the solidarity circle perfect. . . . Twelve of them ready to be made one, waiting to come together, to be fused, to lose their twelve separate identities in a larger being. . . . Tirelessly . . . the drums beat . . . "Come, Greater Being, Social Friend. . . ."[3]
— Aldous Huxley
Brave New World

*P*eter stared at his contribution to a large-scale mural of the earth. He had stopped for a moment to join a group of elementary students participating in a two-day art project called "Weaving the World Together." Like the others, Peter had chosen two distant parts of the world, then connected them with a piece of string. The message behind the project was obvious, since it had already been drilled into his mind through multicultural and environmental teaching in his school: All the people and nations of the world are interconnected; all are joined together into one big global family.

From Peter's neck dangled a new amulet, a symbolic object traditionally worn as protection against evil spirits. He had just made it in a workshop called "Tribal Neck Ornaments" which promised to teach students how to design their own "personal amulets." Standing nearby, Peter's mother was carefully balancing the products of two previous workshops: a bright, feathery Amazon Rain Forest bird and a grotesque tribal mask.

Earth Day had come and gone, but students from every elementary school in Sunnyvale, California, were still honoring Mother Earth and her indigenous people. At the annual Hands on the Arts Festival, which demonstrates the planned nationwide partnership between schools and communities, children could choose between 42 workshops teaching native art and rituals. Through tempting titles like "Indian Totem Poles," "Chinese Dragons," "South India Dances," and "African Drumming," the environmentally and politically correct expressions of the world's beliefs and practices beckoned: "Come, try, experience."

The students loved it. They wore their personalized Mexican spirit beads. They designed their own American Indian dreamcatchers, mystical spiderwebs inside sacred circles which supposedly would block bad dreams and welcome good dreams. They made medicine shields, Indian shields that identify and host their personal animal spirits. They created Panamanian "mythical figures and animals" and hugged their Southwest Indian "magical figures."

Oblivious to the occult dangers, they celebrated the return of the rhythms, rituals, and religions that once animated cultures from Norway to Africa and Alaska to Australia. Multicultural things are fun! Why shouldn't the world be one?

Unity in Diversity

Partnership, celebration, oneness. . . . These happy-sounding buzzwords that marked the Sunnyvale fair express the heart cry of today's cultural transformation. It seeks unity between nations, between cultures, between the school and the community, between people and nature. No wonder students pledge their loyalty to a spiritualized Earth, sing anthems to a coming New Age of peace, and celebrate a oneness that denies all religious barriers.

This oneness is central to the international education system. Chapter 2 showed that America's education goals match those of the World Conference on Education for All

(WCEFA). They also match the goals of the United States Coalition for Education for All (USCEFA), which helps link our national education system to the international system. While all three groups seek common values, the USCEFA emphasizes "the oneness of humankind." Hidden in these words is their joint understanding that the common values must be grounded in common beliefs and spirituality.

WCEFA	USCEFA	America 2000
Another and no less fundamental aim of educational development is the transmission and enrichment of *common cultural and moral values*. It is in these values that the individual and society find their identity and worth.[4]	Human survival and progress increasingly depend on the inculcation in the young of *values emphasizing the essential oneness of humankind*, the fragility of this planet ... and the ... rights of each individual.[5]	As we shape tomorrow's schools, we should rediscover the *timeless values* that are necessary for achievement.[6]

Everything must fit together. The old thoughts, ways, and beliefs that don't fit must be abolished. In a 1994 report on the Johnson City Central School District in New York, "a national model of instructional excellence," Dr. John Champlin calls for "a change agent" in every school, a "holistic system approach," and "revised beliefs, attitudes and relationships."[7] No minor figure in the educational arena, Dr. Champlin is the Director of Partners for Quality Learning, which was called the National Center for Outcome-Based Education until parents discovered the true nature of OBE. His "change project" in Johnson City summarizes a nationwide pattern:

> The effort to build a new culture by putting our beliefs, practices and values into written documents and policies that we constantly used as a basis for renewal and growth was crucial. We purged former practices as quickly as possible. . . .[8]

The student outcomes (demonstrated behaviors) sought in the Johnson City experiment were nonacademic, affective results such as self-directed learners, creative thinkers, and group participants who could cooperate with others.

In 1992 the Kansas State Board of Education announced its official plan for change. It explained that "QPA [Quality Performance Accreditation, another name for OBE] is a process which demands new thinking, new strategies, new behavior, and new beliefs."[9] Keep in mind that almost every state has been following suit. They cannot afford to break their link to the national purse strings.

Though most change agents may not take their cues *directly* from the world's occult guides, they follow the same well-trodden track. After all, people everywhere long for solutions to the world's moral decay and collapsing structures. They seek spiritual leaders who can pilot the world through these tumultuous times into the new millennium. More than ever, the noble sentiments of spiritual visionaries offer hope to those who have rejected biblical truth:

- **Noel Brown**, Director, U.N. Environmental Programme, speaking to Minnesota students through a Global Education video: "We need to develop a better sense of connectedness with all of life and when that reverence is developed, I think we'll find ourselves more at home and at ease in this world."[10]

- **The Dalai Lama**: "Today's world requires us to accept the oneness of humanity. . . ."[11]

- **William Smith,** Masonic leader: "God's plan is dedicated to the unification of all races, religions and creeds. This plan, dedicated to the new order of things, is to make all things new . . . a new race, a new civilization and a new religion. . . ."[12]

- **Robert Muller:** "We must feel part of all space and time, of the greatness and wonders of the universe. . . . We must reestablish the unity of our planet and of our beings with the universe and divinity."[13]

Common Paths to Spiritual Power

Reestablishing our unity with earth and spirit is encouraged in classrooms across the country. Multicultural, global, environmental, and arts education teach children the occult formulas that once linked the world's shamans, voodoo priests, and medicine men to their respective spirit guides. While words differ from culture to culture, the pagan practices within earth-centered traditions are similar around the world.

Today most of these religious practices are sweeping into our nation's classrooms. Accepted as an important means to multicultural understanding, they are actually being used to establish earth-centered spirituality. The following practices from the chart on the following page represent only a tiny drop in a rising flood of occult stimuli.[14]

1. *Altered states of consciousness.* Teaching students to alter their consciousness through centering exercises, guided imagery, and visualizations has become standard practice in self-esteem, multicultural, and arts programs. They often encourage contact with spirit guides. For example, the nationwide language-arts curriculum READ is known to captivate students with shocking stories and occult themes. One of READ's audiocassette tapes includes a writing assignment

COMMON PRACTICES OF EARTH-CENTERED RELIGIONS

Ancient religions in—	Trance states	Dreams and Visions	Divi-nation	Spirit-ism	Magic and sorcery	Charms and amulets	Solstice rites	Serpent worship	Sacred sex
Babylon	•	•	•	•	•	•	•	•	•
Canaan	•	•	•	•	•	•	•	•	•
Africa	•	•	•	•	•	•	•	•	•
India	•	•	•	•	•	•	•	•	•
Greece	•	•	•	•	•	•	•	•	•
Rome	•	•	•	•	•	•	•	•	•
Germany	•	•	•	•	•	•	•	•	•
Norway	•	•	•	•	•	•	•	•	•
America	•	•	•	•	•	•	•	•	•
Australia	•	•	•	•	•	•	•	•	

which uses the following visualization to stimulate the students' imagination. A class of Iowa students followed its hypnotic instructions:

> Close your eyes and breathe deeply to relax. Watch the screen inside our mind. . . . You are about to journey to an uncharted land. Picture in your mind a place where there is an opening in the earth. Go and find this place, then wait at the edge. Are you ready? Let yourself fall in. Enter the earth. Let yourself spiral down through the world beneath your feet . . . down through the passage way.
>
> As you become acquainted with your surroundings, ask to meet a guide. An animal, person or being will accompany you and give you whatever power you might need.
>
> Someone or something is coming toward you in a peaceful way. Who is this? Watch what this new companion does or shows you. Listen to what it says. Go wherever this guide wants to lead you. You are safe. You will not be harmed. . . .
>
> The guide who has been with you has a gift for you. Reach out your hands and take what it offers. This gift has special meaning, just for you. What is it?[15]

2. *Dreams and visions.* After studying a pagan myth, students are often asked to imagine or visualize a dream or vision, then describe it in a journal or lesson assignment. For example, Montana fourth-graders read a myth describing how "the Spirits guided" an Indian girl named "Gentle Fawn" by taking the shape of a white deer. The lesson continued: "You have an incredible dream. And just as Gentle Fawn learned from her dream, you also have a vision. 1. Describe your dream. 2. Describe your lesson of truth."[16]

3. *Astrology.* Countless teachers across the country require students to document their daily horoscopes. Others help students discover their powers and personalities through Aztec calendars and Chinese horoscopes.[17] A

Connecticut teacher wrote an award-winning curriculum based on Indian shaman Sun Bear's "medicine wheel astrology." Her students and others who use this program locate their personal birth moons, colors, animal spirits, and spirit keepers on the Indian medicine wheel.[18]

4. *Other forms of divination.* Through palmistry, I Ching, tarot cards and horoscopes students learn to experience other cultures and tap into secret sources of wisdom.[19] Students in Texas were desensitized to occult dangers when told to imitate the wizard pictured behind a crystal ball in their assignment. The instructions told each child to create a vision in his or her own mind and "describe in your best soothsayer tones the details of your vision."[20]

5. *Spiritism.* While pagan myths and crafts *show* students how to contact ancestral, nature, and other spirits, classroom rituals actually *invoke their presence.* California third-graders had to alter their consciousness through guided imagery, invoke or "see" their personal animal spirits, write about their experience for a public bulletin board display, and finally create their own magical medicine shields to represent their spirit helper.[21]

Minnesota students were given this morbid assignment: "Your mother died three years ago. However, she will return briefly. You will have only ten minutes to speak with her and then she is gone for good. What will you talk with her about?" While students only had to pretend to invoke the presence of a dead relative, the exercise made spiritism seem acceptable.[22]

6. *Magic, spells, and sorcery.* Many parents consider magic and spell-casting too bizarre and alien to pose a threat, yet gullible students from coast to coast are learning the ancient formulas and occult techniques. These may seem simple and innocuous to children, but Wiccan leader Starhawk shows how their imagination can open doors to

occult forces. In *The Spiral Dance,* her popular manual on witchcraft, she writes:

> To work magic is to weave the unseen forces into form . . . to leap beyond imagination into that space between the worlds where fantasy becomes real; to be at once animal and god. . . .
>
> Spells [and magic] . . . require the combined faculties of *relaxation, visualization, concentration,* and [mental] *projection.* . . . To cast a spell is to project energy through a symbol."[23] (Emphasis added.)

7. *Occult charms and symbols.* Dreamcatchers, Zuni fetishes, crystals, and power signs like the quartered circle and Hindu mandala are only a few of the empowering charms and symbols fascinating students today (See Symbols and Their Meanings.)

8. *Solstice rites.* After seating themselves "according to their astrological signs," Oregon students who traded Christmas for a Winter Solstice celebration watched the "sun god" and "moon goddess" enter the auditorium to the beating of drums and chanting. "Animal spirits" and "barcode children" followed.[24] Celebrating Winter Solstice with "dance around the Solstice tree" is one of the *Anti-Bias Curriculum's* suggested alternatives to Christmas.[25]

9. *Human sacrifice.* Because of the quieting influence of Christianity over the centuries, almost all ritual human sacrifice around the world apparently ended—for a season. But human nature hasn't changed. As God withdraws His protection from His lands—as He said He would when people turn from Him to other gods[26]—the type of demonic control that originally inspired human sacrifice and torture is likely to return. Death education, assignments like the "Fallout Shelter," and the cultural endorsement of abortion and euthanasia are preparing the new generation to accept

many new forms of human sacrifice at the unholy altar of today's "common good."

10. *Sacred sex.* Sun Bear, whose books are used to teach classroom medicine wheel astrology, writes, "Many native cultures refer to making love as sharing energy or merging energy. . . . [I]n the natural cycle of life, the most powerful thing we can do is to share our energies with each other."[27] Starhawk wrote a similar message: "Sexuality is a sacrament. Religion is a matter of relinking. . . ."[28] Considering today's degrading sex education programs, one might wonder if Planned Parenthood and SIECUS (The Sex Information and Education Council of the United States) authors share this pagan appreciation for the unifying power of promiscuity. Lester Kirkendall, a SIECUS board member, wrote:

> The purpose of sex education is not to control and suppress sex expression, as in the past. . . . The individual must be given sufficient understanding to incorporate sex most fruitfully and most responsibly into his present and future life.[29]

11. *Serpent worship.* Throughout pagan history snakes have symbolized occult power, wisdom, and rebirth. Even if students don't actually worship serpents, their multicultural curriculum and celebrations idealize people who do.

Aldous Huxley was right. In *Brave New World* he showed that a profusion of new suggestions will transform beliefs and attitudes. Just keep the revolutionary stimuli flowing—

> Till at last the child's mind is these suggestions, and the sum of the suggestions is the child's mind. And not the child's mind only. The adult's mind too—all his life long. The mind that judges and desires and decides—made up of these suggestions. But all these

suggestions are our suggestions! . . . Suggestions from the State.[30]

A Strategy for Brainwashing

"How are we to cultivate morality and character in our students without indoctrinating them . . . ?"[31] This provocative question came from a 1988 ASCD (Association for Supervision and Curriculum Development) panel on Moral Education. In his written statement, Richard Paul, Director of the Center for Critical Thinking and Moral Critique, shows how to hide classroom subversion behind misleading labels such as "critical thinking" and "individual moral reasoning skills."[32] Students "discover for themselves" that none of the old ways fit the moral framework of the coming world order. Then they are led to "discover" what *does* fit: earth-centered beliefs and new-paradigm values. Ponder these obvious steps to transformation:

1. Present palatable versions of target beliefs.

2. Dismantle the students' previous beliefs.

3. Blend new beliefs with science to add credibility.

4. Redefine words to fit the new beliefs.

5. Rewrite history.

6. Provide mystical experiences that contradict old beliefs.

7. Immerse students in enticing forms of the new beliefs.

8. Use target beliefs to answer questions traditionally answered by former beliefs.

9. Demand "purity."

1. *Present palatable versions of target beliefs.* The target belief, of course, is the new global spirituality, a pantheistic, monistic, polytheistic blend of the world's earth-centered religions. Any mythical teaching will do, but America's favorite model is the native Indian.

For example, a third-grade social studies text, *From Sea to Shining Sea* (part of the popular Houghton-Mifflin series used from coast to coast), encourages children to personalize the spiritual messages behind Indian myths. One such myth, *The Gift of the Sacred Dog*, is a mythical explanation for the origin of horses, which by then, were extinct in North America. It tells about a boy who asked the Great Spirit to help his famished tribe find buffalo. His answer came through a supernatural vision of a herd of horses. Moments later real horses appeared. The boy joyfully brought them to his tribe. "These are Sacred Dogs," he explained. "They are a gift from the Great Spirit. . . ."[33]

The teacher's guide made sure the students got the point: "Explain that this myth tells about an Indian tribe that could not find buffalo to hunt and how the Great Spirit (God) came to their aid."[34] To personalize the myth, the students had to "imagine being the boy in the story," then record their feelings in their journals before and after receiving their visions.

There is nothing wrong with learning about mythology. Myths can provide valuable insights into other cultures. But when they present the pantheistic Great Spirit as a synonym for God, they distort His character and nullify His message. When they reinforce mythical messages with journaling or "fun" mind-altering rituals, they blur the distinction between reality and fantasy. And when man-made stories such as *The Gift of the Sacred Dog* emphasize *mythical* speculations rather than the *fact* that Europeans reintroduced horses to Indian lands, they sabotage discernment and reason. Without these tools, children will believe anything.

2. *Dismantle the students' previous beliefs.* Houghton-Mifflin's *America Will Be* tells students that "Puritan parents

might beat their children for laziness or disrespect or for running and jumping on the Sabbath. They believed that a child is 'better whipped than damned' by the devil."[35] What does this imbalanced lesson teach children about Christian parents?

The teacher's guide for *The Original Land* prompts teachers to emphasize that the Indians "see the deity as part of themselves, warm and approachable." In contrast, it paints a cold, harsh picture of God based on the sermon "Sinners in the Hands of an Angry God" by the eighteenth-century evangelist Jonathan Edwards: "God's wrath is burning like fire, and he looks upon humans as 'worthy of nothing else but to be cast into the fire. . . .'"[36]

Since teachers must "teach to the test," they are told what students must learn. What do these questions and instructions from the teacher's guide tell you about the planned result of this lesson?

- Does the student explain that God is wrathful and will severely punish those who disobey with eternal damnation?

- Does the student point out that Edwards feels that it is merely God's pleasure, a whim, or his mercy, that keeps sinners from immediate destruction?

- You might want to preface the assignment with a discussion of the Old Testament God and how this deity differs from the New Testament God.[37]

In a group discussion, which deity—the Indian or the Judeo-Christian—do you think students would agree to choose?

Keep in mind that Edwards' message was never intended for today's elementary school-age children. Nor can it be understood by non-Christian adults who have never experienced God's mercy.[38] It seems that the only logical reason for contrasting Edwards' description of God with the idealized images of pagan gods would be to "challenge the students' fixed beliefs," as Professor Benjamin Bloom proposed decades ago. Since few children know enough about God's love to counter the distortions, the educational outcome seems clear: The biblical God will lose the popularity contest.

3. *Blend new beliefs with science to add credibility.* A touch of myth makes classroom science "experiential, relevant, and fun." For example, the elementary text *Floods and Droughts* animate ecology with all kinds of weather gods and earth-centered myths. The result is a subjective mix of reality and fantasy. Will children be able to distinguish between the two?

In an article titled "On a New Vision of Science and Science Education," Jeffrey Kane, editor of *Holistic Education Review,* explains the "difference between the old and emerging paradigms of science." This change seems normal and necessary to him:

> A postcritical model of science is emerging—a model of science that mirrors . . . the principles that both shape and transcend empirical observation.[39]

What happens to the credibility of science when it has license to "transcend empirical observation"? What tools will our children use to stay grounded in reality and reason when fact and science give way to myth and pseudoscience?

One of our more influential leaders, former Governor and Education Secretary Lamar Alexander, wrote a book titled *Steps Along the Way: a Governor's Scrapbook.* In it Alexander makes a revealing statement: "The book that changed my thinking the most during the last ten years: *A God Within* by René Dubos."[40] His admission begs the question, "Just what does Dubos believe?" The answer from Dubos' book displays the same pantheistic/monistic threads we saw in Robert Muller's writings:

Both polytheism and monotheism are losing their ancient power . . . we may instead be moving to a higher level of religion. Science is presently evolving from the description of concrete objects and events to the study of relationships as observed in complex systems. We may be about to recapture an experience of harmony, an intimation of the divine, from our scientific knowledge. . . .[41]

4. *Redefine words to fit the new beliefs.* Since the word *truth* is basic to biblical faith, its meaning must be changed by the change agents, but not through straightforward redefining. The more subtle approach is to simply use the word in a new context. *The Truth About the Moon,* a children's story which is part of a widely used science curriculum,[42] tells how the sun and moon argued over who would shine at night and who would shine during the day. But what does this myth show children about the meaning of truth?

The Truth About Dragons, a politically correct story imbedded in a nationwide language arts curriculum, sounds as credible as an encyclopedia: "We know from ancient records that people in countries all over the world have been seeing dragons for at least 5,000 years. . . . Western Dragons are usually ugly, vicious, and extremely dangerous. . . . Eastern Dragons are beautiful, gentle and friendly. . . ."[43]

Suggestions that demean Western ways and idealize Eastern views are shaping a new, planned, and politically correct set of prejudices. And, like *truth*, the words *Eastern* and *Western* have been cloaked with fresh meanings—cultural definitions that will help mold the envisioned world of the next century. Using the chart on the following page, ponder the characteristics of the two opposing views of reality. Remember, it is written from a new-paradigm or globalist perspective. Discuss it with your children, because if they don't recognize the bias behind this type of teaching, they will probably believe its deceptions.

WESTERN EXPRESSIONS	EASTERN EXPRESSIONS
Competition	Cooperation
Materialism	Spirituality
Violence	Compassion
Division	Wholeness
Dualism	Monism
War	Peace
Nationalism	Globalism
Reason or logic	Imagination
Knowledge from others	Wisdom from within

Since Christianity is equated with Western culture, this anti-Western view discredits traditional beliefs and values along with Western culture. The fact that biblical faith may blossom in any culture—and that American greed and materialism flow from undisciplined human nature, not the biblical God—is ignored.

No culture has escaped the ravages of greed. Former symbols of materialism among American Indians were scalps and horses, not clothes and cars. Accumulation of slaves was a common practice around the world, including pre-Columbian North America and east Africa (where native slave traders sold their neighbors to foreign slave traders). Eastern or Asian history is no less bloody and cruel than Western history. These facts are ignored in today's quest for new models.

5. *Rewrite history.* According to *America Will Be,* when five Indian nations joined to form a single Iroquois nation, their joint rulers "brought an end to the wars and other fights." The inhuman cruelty of Iroquois aggression and intertribal warfare is never mentioned. Instead, the text leaves the impression that, from the 1400s, the Iroquois lived peaceful lives "based on sharing and cooperation."[44] In *Indians of the United States,* respected historian Clark Wissler, who has expressed deep appreciation for Indians,

documents another side: The Iroquois "hated the Huron intensely, like brother against brother. After taking the first town, they massacred its entire population. . . . It is believed that more than 10,000 Huron were killed."[45] Of course this information doesn't fit in the new paradigm.

6. *Provide mystical experiences that contradict old beliefs.* Tammie Kanduch, a Montana mother, read a letter that her fourth-grader had brought from school. "Dear Parents," it began, "in your hands is the Student Guide to HONOR, an historical simulation we are using in your son or daughter's class. . . . Everyone . . . will become a member of the Am Acumwaaa, an imaginary tribe. . . . They all will go on a STRAY, which is a time alone in the wilderness. . . . They will struggle to prove to their tribe that they are worthy of being considered adults."

Would this "simulation of coming of age" be like the traditional Indian Spirit Quest? A family encyclopedia confirmed Tammie's concerns. Like the classroom STRAY, a Spirit Quest is an initiation into adulthood through a wilderness experience. It uses physical challenges and deprivation to alter a person's consciousness and introduce the young initiate to a personal spirit guide—the ultimate goal of the traditional Indian Quest. *That's a demonic spirit*, she thought.

Could the course involve her son in spiritism? Tammie leafed through some of the lessons. Each role-playing exercise seemed designed to draw students into personal identification with Indian culture and pagan beliefs. One lesson introduced a mystical youth from the Modat Tribe, "known to have great shamans." Tammie read the opening story:

> You cannot figure out at first why he seems strange. Then you understand: he will not look you in the eyes. Something about him seems to say that he has secrets that you do not have. . . . As he slowly walks away, you decide to join him. Two days later you arrive at the opening to a deep canyon. . . . Like a slowly rising mist

you feel many spirits rising out of the canyon. Something seems to be calling you to visit this incredible place. . . .What happens to you is so lively and stimulating in the first days that you decide to stay the whole winter. . . .

The assignment, which assumes that students are immediately drawn to the mysterious canyon, now encourages them to *imagine* the fun of occult *experiences*: "Write a long, detailed story of what happens during the time you are with this tribe."

How would this mystical exercise affect Tammie's son's understanding of truth? Would he want to learn the secrets hidden in the Indian boy? Would her biblical warnings seem too narrow? Deeply concerned, Tammie withdrew her son from the class.

7. *Immerse students in enticing forms of the new beliefs*. Multicultural arts, crafts, music, and celebrations have become standard fare in our elementary schools. Children need to understand other cultures and religions, but when teachers tell their captive audience to make pagan masks, use them in ritual dances, sing prayers to Mother Earth, and invoke occult spirits, students are illegally indoctrinated with the global religion designed by contemporary change agents.

The new **whole language** or **thematic learning** immerses students in selected earth-centered cultures for months. Popular themes like ancient Egypt, Medieval Europe, and Southwest Indians may determine the context for math, science, literature, and other subjects for a whole semester. Every lesson must fit the theme and be relevant to the multicultural experience.

8. *Use target beliefs to answer questions traditionally answered by former beliefs*. For example, the question "What happens when we die?" has always been important to Christian families. The biblical answer is based on what

Jesus accomplished for sinners by dying for the people He loved.[46]

Today's multicultural books give different answers. *If You lived with Sioux Indians,* published and distributed by Scholastics, tells young readers that the "Sioux believed that after a man died, he would live with the spirits forever. He would go on doing the same things that he had done on earth."[47]

How do these answers fit into the *old* paradigm? How do they fit the *new* paradigm? How could they alter a student's understanding of truth?

Nothing is more important to our children's future than the beliefs and values transmitted to them. Which paradigm will they choose? Unless parents consciously and conscientiously transmit biblical beliefs and values, most children will drift with their peers into the new paradigm—and the old may never again make sense to them.[48]

9. *Demand "purity."* With America's growing acceptance of the new paradigm comes a decreasing tolerance for the old-paradigm biblical beliefs. When a Wiccan member of the editorial staff at Los Altos High School in California wrote a promotional article about witchcraft based on interviews with other Wiccan students,[49] a Christian editor asked if he could write about Young Life, a Christian group active on their campus. "No," was the response, "because witchcraft is underexposed in our society and Christianity is overexposed." In other words, witches could give public testimonies about the benefits of their religion, but Christians were no longer allowed to express their faith and testimonies.

Regardless of the brainwashing techniques, remember that the battle for the minds of our children is *spiritual* warfare, not an ethnic struggle. God doesn't prefer Caucasians over Indians, nor are Europeans inherently less prone to violence than Asians or Africans. Without Christ and the wise guidelines He offers, *all* people are vulnerable to deception and drift naturally toward spiritual forces that promise power without accountability and peace apart from God.

America's spiritual shift should come as no surprise. Always in the past, when God's people rejected truth they drifted back to earth-centered religions. As humanity once again pits its puny knowledge and strength against the wisdom and power of God, the world follows the same old pattern. Humanism is merely a downward step on the staircase from biblical truth to pagan deception, depravity, and despair.

Resisting the Indoctrination

Monica Grenwich, a perceptive Michigan homeschooler, has noticed that most teens seem to flow with the new teaching. "Hardly any believe in our God," she says. "Some believe in 'a higher being,' but not the God of the Bible. For all they know *it* could be in the hairspray they use every morning. Others have no idea what they believe. They don't believe in anything, really, except their own strength. If parents don't tell their kids about God, who will? It isn't allowed in school."

Monica is right. The greatest challenge facing parents today is training their children to be overcomers in a world that mocks their beliefs. To stay spiritually safe and alert to deception, they need to become competent in each of the following important areas:

- *Know the true God.* When children know God as He has revealed Himself in His Word, they will recognize the seductive counterfeits. Notice in the chart showing God's armor (p. 104), that the main truth we need to "put on" is the truth about God. To do this, memorize the Scriptures that reveal His character, and use them to counter the deceptions of the enemy.

- *Know history's lessons.* Historical and archeological records show that pagan cultures have always been tormented by wars, disease, droughts, and famine. Usually that list included savage torture, mutilation, and human sacrifice. The longing for peace expressed in many pagan myths is an illusion. No pagan hope can offset the horrendous consequences of dealing with demons.

- *Share God's love with everyone.* God's way to multicultural understanding and global unity is essential today. He cares for people in every culture, longs to set them free, and wants to love them through us.

- *Don't apologize for your faith.* Jesus said, "I am the way, the truth and the life. No one comes to the Father except through me" (John 14:7). That sounds exclusive to some, but His loving invitation includes everyone.

- *Remember that God is far greater!* By ourselves we cannot resist "the devil's schemes," but in Christ we are "more than conquerors." Thanks be to God who leads us in His triumph! (Romans 8:37; 2 Corinthians 2:14).

- *Pray.* Only God can slow the massive international movement toward conformity to globalist beliefs and values through educational restructuring.

- *Wear God's armor.* This armor is a set of strategic truths that exposes and counters every deception. When we put on the whole armor, God fills us with His life even as He covers us.[50] Before studying the chart that follows, read the instructions given in Ephesians 6:10-17. Notice that our real enemy is the spiritual hierarchy of occult forces, not globalist educators or well-meaning teachers. Only God's power and protection will enable our children to resist and triumph.

GOD'S ARMOR
OUR DEFENSE AGAINST DECEPTION

	Christianity	Paganism
The belt of truth	Truth is absolute and eternal. It reveals Christ, who is the way, the truth, and the life (John 14:6).	Truth is relative, subject to personal interpretations and evolving myths.
The primary truth to affirm is the truth about God	God is personal, loving, sovereign, and monotheistic (John 3:16; Deuteronomy 4:39).	The universal God is pantheistic, monistic, polytheistic.
The breast-plate of righteousness	Humans are naturally sinful, but freed from sin through Jesus' death on the cross (Romans 3:23,24; Ephesians 2:4-9).	Everything is sacred. Humans are naturally good.
The sandals of peace	We have peace through our union and ongoing relationship with Jesus Christ (Romans 5:1; Ephesians 2:14).	Humans find peace through union with a cosmic god or nature spirits or else through all kinds of occult practices.
The shield of faith	We lift the shield of faith by choosing to trust God, follow His Word, and count on His promises (Mark 11:22; Romans 4:14-21).	Faith grows through trust in inner self, openness to dreams and visions, and readiness to follow spiritual signs.
The helmet of salvation	Our salvation is both daily and eternal in Jesus Christ (Romans 8:37; 1 Thessalonians 4:17).	The salvation of Earth and all its life evolves. Rising human consciousness speeds the process.
The sword of the Spirit, God's Word	We must memorize and speak God's Word to expose and counter deception (Hebrews 4:12).	Spiritual battles are won by speaking affirmations, projecting mental images, and following occult formulas.

5

Saving
the Earth

*I pledge allegiance to the Earth and all its sacred parts,
Its water, land and living things and all its human hearts.*[1]
     —Earth Pledge, Global Education Associates

*By fostering a deep sense of connection to others and to the earth in all
its dimensions, holistic education encourages a sense of responsibility
to self, to others and to the planet.*[2]
     —Global Alliance for Transforming Education

*In searching for a new enemy to unite us, we came up with the idea
that pollution, the threat of global warming, water shortages, famine
and the like would fit the bill. . . .*[3]
     —Club of Rome

*T*o fulfill state requirements for environmental education, California students, like others across the country, participate in weekend or weeklong nature camps. "We were supposed to learn about science, but it's political too," explained eleven-year-old Laura after her off-campus experience. "They told us how terrible it would be if there was any oil drilling off the coast."

The spiritual part was worse. "The counselor led us through the forest," the fifth-grader continued. "He told us to stop to absorb the moment and hug the trees. 'You are the tree,' he told us. 'You are one with all natural things.' He was treating everything as sacred and calling trees 'mother and father trees.' He was really teaching us pantheism."

Laura asked him if he believed in God.

"God is in all things," he told her.

Each student had to collect natural objects "of beauty or curiosity" such as tree bark, shells, or acorns. "Then we had a ceremony, but they didn't call it that. We had to take all our natural objects to a sacred place and put them in a circle. The counselor lit a candle and quoted an Indian saying, 'We're part of the earth and the chain of life. We're of the

107

earth. . . .' Then we sang a Christian song with the names of natural objects instead of the name of Jesus."

"This is an offering to nature," explained the counselor.

Intensely uncomfortable in the pagan setting, Laura asked to be taken home. The counselor called her "a baby" and refused to help. "You'll have to walk," he told her. As far as Laura knew, no telephone was available.

Later she expressed her surprise that more children didn't recognize the deceptions. "When they told us Indian myths, I was the only kid in the class that didn't say, 'Oh, I believe that.'" It hurt when her classmates refused to support her either at the camp or in discussions afterward, but she wasn't discouraged. "I lost some of my friends," she said. "I know we'll face persecution for being Christians, but knowing God is much better!"

Laura's experience is multiplied across the country. Earth Day 1990 flung school doors open to a rising tide of pseudoscience and environmental activism. In the weeks surrounding April 22 (Lenin's birthday), children from coast to coast celebrate nature, give thanks to Mother Earth, and chant prayers to the Great Spirit. Using computers that supposedly "simulate the real world," students re-create environmental disasters and "solve" global problems. Many go home to scold their parents for destroying *their* planet. It's time—they are told—for the world's children to unite, fight, grow in consciousness, and save the earth.

Many children play a game called "Mother Earth, May I?" The book, *Earth Child,* which gained nationwide fame through controversy, explains how to play the game. A student who plays the part of Mother Earth calls out the names of other students one by one. Each child must tell Mother Earth something he or she will do (plant trees, pick up litter, etc.) to make her happy. If pleased, Mother Earth rewards the player by granting one or more steps toward herself. The player who first reaches Mother Earth wins.[4]

Genuine concern for the environment is good and needful. But when environmental education substitutes pseudoscience for factual evidence, it leaves children vulnerable to all kinds of social myths and false solutions. When it makes political activism a requirement for saving the earth, it turns children into puppets serving the global agenda.

With today's emphasis on whole education, thematic learning, and **integrative curriculum**, it is difficult to know where environmental education begins and other studies (math, reading, social studies) end. Drawing inspiration from pantheism and monism, two cornerstones of the new paradigm, educators insist that all things must fit together into a perfect whole. No longer can the spiritual be separated from the physical, math from art, science from politics, etc. Integration is a must! In the spiritual domain, any of the world's earth-centered religions can be used to model this all-pervading oneness.

Sometimes teachers tell me that none of these beliefs have infiltrated their schools. I often ask, "Are you using the Houghton-Mifflin social studies texts?"

"Why, yes," they answer. "Do you see anything wrong with them?"

I do. Look with me at one of our nation's most popular elementary school social studies texts. The primary author is Gary Nash, the same UCLA professor who helped write the proposal for U.S. history standards. His history books are read by children in every state. See what they teach our children about the earth and its people.

Myth and Magic

"Long ago, no rain had fallen on the land for many days. Grass died and animals starved. There was nothing to eat."[5]

Designed to touch the hearts of third-graders from coast to coast, these sad words introduce a lesson titled "The Medicine Wheel" in Houghton-Mifflin's *From Sea to Shining Sea*. What follows is a seductive, uncritical introduction to paganism. The text makes no attempt to differentiate between truth and fiction or reality and fantasy. Instead, the questions and assignments that follow the myth reinforce the impression that the same kind of beliefs and rituals that supposedly brought rain long ago could save plants and animals today. Look at the end of the story.

> . . . a Cheyenne man and woman . . . pushed aside a rock that hid a cave. Inside, they saw an amazing room. . . . In the center stood a tree trunk with a nest of the magical Thunderbird at its top. Then they heard the deep voice of the spirit Roaring Thunder. Roaring Thunder told the man and woman how to perform a dance. The dance would bring life back to the grasses of the earth and would bring herds of buffalo back to the people.

The text identifies the story as a myth but redefines this crucial word to fit the new-paradigm perspective: "A myth is a story that explains something in nature."[6] So does science. Does this mean that myth is the same as science? The text doesn't differentiate.

To encourage critical thinking—a major objective of educators involved in "restructuring" education—the teacher's guide gives the following instruction: "Have students identify Roaring Thunder as one of the powers of nature. Ask what kind of weather usually comes with thunder. . . ."[7] Notice again how myth mingles with science—a process sure to blur the fading line between fact and fantasy.

After the story, Review Question 1 asks, "Why was the Medicine Dance important to the Cheyenne?" The teacher's guide gives the "correct" answer: "The Cheyenne held a Medicine Dance when they needed help from the powers of nature. They celebrated the Medicine Dance to make sure the cycle of nature would continue?"[8] Did the cycles continue because of the occult ritual? The biased selection of facts leaves that impression.

The text never explains that a Medicine Dance is irrelevant to the natural rainmaking process. Nor does it warn students about the devastating consequences of trusting occult forces and inviting help from demonic spirits. When Review Question 2 asks, "How are Cheyenne ideas about nature like Kwakiutl [Indians] ideas about nature?" the text's answer fits: "Both Cheyenne and the Kwakiutl respected nature."[9] The contrasting view that European invaders do *not* respect nature threads through the entire series of Houghton-Mifflin texts.

Notice how—

- children are manipulated into changing their view of nature;

- science has been redefined to include a holistic or spiritual dimension;

- educators use misleading labels like critical thinking to conceal their strategy.

Critical Thinking

Most parents and teachers still believe that critical thinking refers to *factual, logical thinking*. But they have been misled. It actually means the opposite. School fliers explain that this term means teaching students "to think for themselves." Instead, this psychological strategy *limits* factual knowledge and independent reasoning. It encourages myths, imagination, and group synthesis—the tools for manipulating a child's values system.

The fifth-grade Houghton Mifflin social studies text called *America Will Be* defines critical thinking as "reasonable, reflective thinking that is focused on deciding what to believe or what to do."[10] It includes a series of lessons that idealize Native American beliefs and lifestyles, then asks students the following "critical thinking" question: "The Creeks [Native Americans in the Southeast] and the Europeans had different ideas about how the land should be used. Compare the Creeks' ideas with those of the

Europeans. Which ideas do you think are better? Explain your opinion."[11] The teacher's edition shows the *correct opinion,* which is the predetermined outcome:

> Creeks believed land belonged to everyone and couldn't be individually owned. They believed in a respectful use of the land so it would continue to provide food and forest resources. Europeans believed that land was a commodity to be bought and sold and owned by individuals for their own benefit. They cleared forests to make room for farms to make a profit. Students who agree with Creek ideas might cite reasons such as this—clearing forests caused valuable topsoil to be blown away and a loss of trees that produce the oxygen people need.[12]

Since students reading these misleading suggestions usually receive negative information about European settlers and idealistic images of Native American lifestyles, they are hardly equipped to resist the convincing conclusion. Committed to doomsday environmental scenarios that fuel the demand for a global government and earth-centered religions, educators hide the facts that Native Americans often burned forests to expand their cornfields[13] and that forest growth in America today exceeds harvest by a wide margin.[14]

In fact, "U.S. timberlands . . . contain 28% more standing timber volume than they did in 1952." *Forests Today and Forever* reports that "70% of the forests standing in 1600 are still standing today—or some 737 million acres of forests" and that "over one-third of the total forest land is either protected against harvest by law or [is] slow-growing woodland unsuitable for logging."[15]

Before you argue that these facts don't diminish the disturbing sight of clear-cut logging along scenic roads, let me assure you that I agree. When driving through the Pacific Northwest, nothing bothers me more than the ugly clear-cut remnants of once lush forests. But I have to remind myself that by next year there will be young green trees growing in those scarred hills. Other abuses (depleting ocean life through overfishing, soil erosion through unwise farming practices, the destruction of rain forests, all kinds of pollution) are just as genuine. But most *real* problems are local, not global.

Local problems, however, seldom capture the imagination of the world community. They simply don't stir enough emotions to inspire global action. "We must make rescue of the environment the central organizing principle for civilization,"[16] said Vice President Al Gore. But what nation would yield its sovereignty to rescue the earth if the main problems were half a planet away?

Rousing the nations to action and orchestrating a unified call for planetary management requires *global* disasters—the kind of scary scenarios that Al Gore described at the 1992 United Nations conference in Rio de Janeiro: ". . . an enormous hole is opening in the ozone layer," he said, "[and] huge quantities of carbon dioxide, methane, and chlorofluorocarbons are trapping heat in the atmosphere and raising global temperatures."[17]

"But isn't that true?" you might ask.

No, it's not, and later you'll see why. Many of our nation's most distinguished scientists are finally speaking up to counter the astounding public acceptance of the pseudoscientific pronouncements concerning the dire state of the planet. Censored by the liberal media, the voices of respected scientists such as Bruce Ames, Professor of Biochemistry and Molecular Biology and Director of the National Institute of Environmental Health Sciences Center at the Universty of California at Berkeley, are finally being heard. You can study their charts, data, and conclusions in a book aptly titled *The True State of the Planet: Ten of the World's Premier Environmental Researchers in a Major Challenge to the Environmental Movement.*

To understand the global politics behind the environmental movement and the curricula it feeds to our schools, take a look at the social ambitions that drive it. Its agenda was formed during the sixties, when four overlapping anti-establishment groups joined to form the Green Party in Germany: radical feminists, Marxists (the new Left), peaceniks (the antiwar movement), and hippies seeking spiritual enlightenment. Militant U.S. "Greens" formed a similar agenda: radical population control, a global welfare system (eliminating capitalism), planetary governance (including national disarmament), and earth-centered spirituality.

This blend of four counterculture philosophies helps explain why earth-centered spirituality and Marxist economics pervade environmental teaching. Consider the sobering fact that William Reilly, former head of the Environmental Protection Agency, has stated that private ownership of land is a "quaint anachronism."[18] According to former Washington Governor Dixy Lee Ray, Reilly sought the "repeal of the Fifth Amendment to make it easier for government to seize private land."[19]

American Indian spirituality, as you have seen, provides the perfect model for both spiritual oneness and for willingness to give up private ownership of land. Small wonder that Al Gore in his book *Earth in the Balance* presents Native American spirituality and various Mother Earth religions[20] as models for healing our "dysfunctional civilization"[21] and restoring "our feeling of connectedness to the rest of nature."[22] Nor is it surprising that Gore wants to "organize a worldwide education program to promote a more complete understanding of the crisis."[23] But if he has his way, the "solutions" will prove unbelievably costly—both in money and in personal freedom. Look at some of the incredible deceptions.

Ecomyths and Pseudoscience

On a spring day in 1994, Bob Garfield was reading his nine-year-old daughter's writing assignment. Below the title, "What Bugs Me," Allison had written her list. He read the first two items:

"1) Prejudiced people." That was no surprise.

"2) People who kill." Of course. Hatred for homicide would be a fairly predictable sentiment among third-graders.

"3) Lumberjacks." This item startled him. "What lumberjack does my Fairfax County . . . grade-schooler know? And what could this person possibly have done to her to merit this high-ranking grudge? How can burly-but-jolly roughnecks with faded flannel shirts . . . be fundamentally more annoying than 8) Show-offs?"[24]

I wish I could write the father's full response published in the *Washington Post*. Instead, let me share the best of his sobering thoughts. It could be happening in your school.

> It suddenly occurred to me why she should harbor this raging animus: Lumberjacks cut down trees. And in school, young children are being taught—or at least are coming home with the idea—that cutting down trees is the moral equivalent of genocide. . . . And, now that I've regained a proper measure of fatherly solemnity, that bugs me.
>
> "You know, Allie," I continued, "cutting down trees isn't necessarily bad."
>
> At this point, I am gratified to report, she stopped looking at me as if I had cruelly belittled her for the sheer delight of seeing her suffer. Now she looked at me as if I had lost my mind. Her class had spent the last two months fretting about the rain forest. They had celebrated biodiversity, learned to treasure our irreplaceable natural resources, and been invited to contemplate dire scenarios of eco-Armageddon. They had been steeped, in other words, in crisis. She was therefore in no mood to be reassured. . . .

Do you see what is happening? The new worldview is based on a *political ideology,* not facts. It is taught by manipulating a child's feelings, not by feeding his or her rational mind. You can debate an issue through facts and logic, but you can't easily change a person's feelings. When a discussion moves beyond facts and logic, there is no common ground for rational communication.

I'm not telling you to stop guarding and conserving God's resources. As stewards of creation, we don't have license to waste or abuse any part of nature. We should minimize use of natural resources, reuse as much as possible, plant trees, and do all we can to show our gratefulness for the wonders God has created. *Just be aware of the facts,* so that your family can make wise decisions and thereby counter some of the following myths and assumptions taught as truth in our nation's schools.

The Ozone Hole. Do you remember Agenda 21—the action plan for the 1992 United Nations environmental conference in Rio de Janeiro? Today children around the world can catch the U.N. vision through a picture book titled, *Rescue Mission Planet Earth: A Children's Edition of Agenda 21.* Not only is it written *for* children but it is also written *by* children—"in association with the United Nations." One of its well-tutored authors, 14-year-old Rekha Menon from India, blames the "First World" for introducing destructive luxuries like refrigerators: "fluorocarbons from the fridge make ozone holes we cannot bridge. . . ."[25]

The surrounding text is more specific: "The ozone layer is an essential protective filter in the upper atmosphere that surrounds the Earth. As long as human life has existed, it has protected us from the harmful ultraviolet rays coming from the sun. When these rays get through the atmosphere they damage crops, destroy living cells and cause skin cancer. During the last 20 years, ozone levels above Antarctica have decreased by nearly 40% *each* springtime. It's all caused mainly by our use of chlorofluorocarbons (CFCs). . . . The consequences are catastrophic: About 100,000 people die each year from skin cancer. . . . **ALL CFC-use must be stopped immediately!**" (emphasis in the original).[26]

What are the facts? Actually the ozone "hole" is not a hole at all. It is a seasonal thinning discovered back in 1956 by Gordon Dobson,[27] explains Edward Krug, who has degrees in environmental and soil sciences and is listed in *Who's Who in Science and Engineering*. Each spring, after the long sunless Southern winter, the ozone layer thins over the Antarctica. Conversely, it *always* expands after the Southern summer, when ultraviolet radiation once again creates ozone. (The media didn't tell you that the "hole" closes each year, did it?) The annual thinning varies from year to year. In fact, less ozone was measured in 1985 than in 1990 even though more CFC was used.[28] Why? Scientific data indicate a strong and consistent correlation between ozone depletion and major volcanic explosions and other natural factors.[29]

The cost of the ozone hoax defies comprehension. "The ban on CFCs will cost as much as $5 trillion by 2005," says Dr. Krug. "Eight hundred million refrigerators and freezers will have to be replaced worldwide as noncorrosive CFC's will be replaced by highly expensive and *corrosive* chemicals like HCFC. . . . [This ban will] severely undermine efforts to feed millions in the Third World."[30]

Frederick Seitz, past President of the National Academy of Sciences, former Chairman of the Defense Science Board, and recipient of the National Medal of Science, shares those concerns.

> That natural factors may be involved in the variations in the ozone layer is clearly understood by most atmospheric scientists. Unfortunately, this fact was omitted, presumably intentionally, from the summary which accompanied the master report issued by the United Nations Intergovernmental Panel on Climate Change. . . . It was prepared by a special group of participants who apparently had a personal interest in recommending tighter environmental controls. . . . Moreover, the speed with which the Montreal Protocols are being put into effect is entirely unjustified in view

of the enormous price society will pay in cost, convenience, and health. . . .

To summarize, there is reason, based on sound scientific work, to express doubt that we are in immediate danger from either global warming or depletion of the ozone layer as envisaged by some extreme activists in the environmental movement."[31]

Global warming. "Ever walked into a greenhouse?" ask the authors of *Rescue Mission Planet*. "It's steamy, humid and it doesn't let up. That's how our world could be in a few decades in the grip of the 'greenhouse effect.' Gases produced when fossil fuels are burned keep the sun's heat in and don't let it escape back into space. That's good up to a point; it gets to be a problem if we keep too much in. We fry! The main greenhouse gas is carbon dioxide. . . ."[32]

What are the facts? MIT climatologists Reginald Newell, Jane Hsiung, and Wu Zhongxiang tell us that "there appears to be little or no global warming over the past century."[33] The popular belief in global warming is based on computer models that fail to consider a variety of annual and cyclical factors that affect climate: clouds, the 11-year sunspot cycle, the gravitational pull of the moon, volcanic activity, El Niños, the sun's magnetic field, storm tracks, etc. These and other factors interact with each other to create the patterns and cycles of change and turbulence.

Ignoring most of those natural factors, NASA scientist James Hansen told the U.S. Congress during the scorching summer of 1988 that he was "99% confident" the current heat wave demonstrated the greenhouse effect. A 1989 *Forbes* article full of facts that refute the myth of global warming (find it at your local library) describes the media response and its blinding effect on public opinion:

> Even though the vast majority of the climatological community was outraged by Hansen's unproven assertions, environmental advocate Stephen Schneider notes in *Global Warming*, "Journalists loved it.

Environmentalists were ecstatic." . . . By the end of 1988, with Hansen and Schneider's enthusiastic support, global warming was deeply embedded in the public consciousness.[34]

In spite of the world's fear of carbon dioxide, science shows that a rise in CO_2, the major "greenhouse gas," would actually *help* food production. In a CFACT report on the greenhouse effect, Sherwood B. Idso, President of the Institute for Biospheric Research, explains that "a simple doubling of the air's CO_2 concentration increases the productivity of essentially all plants by about one-third, while decreasing the amount of water they lose through evaporation by an equal amount. These effects essentially *double* the water use efficiencies of all plants, making them more productive and drought resistant."[35] (Notice, that *all* green plants, not just trees, use CO_2 for photosynthesis.)

The editors of *The Economist* seem to agree. "Environmentalists are dismayed," they wrote in an April 1995 issue. "Their efforts to scare the world over global warming seem not to have worked. . . . Some areas of the world would benefit from a warmer climate."[36]

So why are government and media scientists so insistent that our world will roast? Because many care more about funding and their political agenda than about genuine science and the enormous costs involved in ignoring true science. "There's a selective use of facts," said S. Fred Singer, atmospheric and space physicist at the University of Virginia. "Nobody tells an untruth, but nobody tells the whole truth either. It all depends on the ideological outlook. . . . A lot of scientists promote the greenhouse effect because of increased funding."[37] Steven Schneider's admission adds more insight:

On the one hand, as scientists, we are ethically bound to the scientific method, in effect promising to tell the truth, the whole truth, and nothing but—which means that we must include all the doubts, the caveats, the ifs, ands, and buts. On the other hand, we are not just scientists but human beings as well. And like most people, we'd like to see the world a better place, which in this context translates into our working to reduce the risk of potentially disastrous climatic change. To do that, we need to get some broad based support, to capture the public's imagination. That, of course, entails getting loads of media coverage. So *we have to offer up scary scenarios, make simplified, dramatic statements and make little mention of any doubts we might have. . . .* Each of us has to decide what the right balance is between being effective and being honest.[38] (Emphasis added.)

Melting ice caps will raise sea level. Our Troubled Skies, one of the texts in *Our Only Earth Series, A Curriculum for Global Problem Solving,* tells students that—

scientists predict that various forms of air pollution may cause global temperatures to rise, the oceans to expand and flood coastal lowlands, interrupting natural food chains, and cause widespread skin cancer among humans.[39]

Since such a global catastrophe is sure to evoke strong feelings, it is taught often and with variety. In *Rescue Mission Planet Earth,* José Luis Bayer, from Chile tells the world's children that the "use of fossil fuel (coal, oil, gas) results in acid rain and the greenhouse effect: hurricanes, floods and the rising of the sea level. . . . The sea level is rising at ten times its natural speed. This can result in whole countries disappearing!"[40]

What are the facts? For a moment, let's pretend that global warming is a reality and that the earth warms by 3 to 8 degrees—the maximum that even the most dramatic doomsayer is likely to predict. Would the oceans rise and flood the land?

The reason given for this frightening scenario is a major meltdown of the polar ice caps. But the temperature around Antarctica usually hovers around 50 degrees Celsius *below* freezing. A 5-degree reduction would still leave the ice intact at a chilly minus 45 degrees. No meltdown!

What about the Arctic icebergs to the north? Wouldn't all those icy peaks melt into the ocean and add to its volume? A simple family experiment would disprove that myth. Put some ice cubes in a glass of water. Mark the water level. Let the ice melt. Check the water level. Did it change? Of course not! Since ice expands when it freezes, it contracts when it melts. The ice only fills the space it originally replaced. Melting ice has no effect on ocean level.

If anything, rising temperatures would *lower* the ocean level and widen seashores. Think about it: Warm air causes evaporation and in turn brings rain, fills reservoirs, helps farmers, and shrinks deserts (which are dry because they get little rain, not because they are hot).

"Extreme global warming," says Dr. Krug, ". . . would probably induce a modest *drop* in sea level as more water gets stored on land. . . . Not only would the world's great desert be greened, but marginal dry lands would also be transformed into moister pasture plus cropland."[41]

So when the media tell you that a rising ocean level proves global warming, don't believe it! That's called political "spin control." If indeed there was a temporary minimal rise (a few millimeters or a fraction of an inch), it was *probably* caused by decreased evaporation due to *cooling* temperatures over large masses of water, not by warmer temperatures.

Supported by the media and global politics, this new breed of scientists seem determined to prove that *man,* not nature, is the culprit. After all, you can mobilize global support for controlling *human behavior,* but you can't do much to stop the *natural forces* that affect global climate and the skin of an apple.

Columnist George Will doesn't mince words. "Whose interests are served by [such] exaggerations?" he asks in a 1992 column on the environmentalist attacks on pesticides. "The answer often is: The people whose funding or political importance varies directly with the perceived severity of the problem."[42]

Global Activism

Ecology books and curricula undoubtedly help raise that level of "perceived severity." Full of scary scenarios, many of such books blame parents for the disasters. After all, says Captain Eco, the high flying superhero of a large picture book called *Captain Eco and the Fate of the Earth:*

> Your parents and grandparents have made a mess of looking after the earth. They may deny it, but they're little more than thieves. And they're stealing your future from under your noses.[43]

It gets worse. Captain Eco takes two children on a soaring tour of the damaged earth. After showing them all the well-known abuses in the worst possible light—and blaming everything on rich, self-centered Westerners—the noble captain points them to the final megaproblem: "and that's YOU."

"We're not that bad, are we?" they respond.

"Not you personally, but the whole human race. There are so many of you, it's getting harder and harder to meet everyone's needs—and harder for other creatures to find breathing space. . . ." The solution, of course, is global welfare and intense family planning.

Finally the Captain gives his final orders: "You young ones have got to speed things up. Keep the pressure on. . . . work toward a better world . . . Grown-ups just haven't been able to make that choice . . . but there's a new force at work in the world. Things are changing very fast, and it's time for you young earthlings to make peace with the earth. Will you help me?"[44]

Lots of children are willing to help. They plant trees and clean riverbanks—which in itself is commendable. They join Kids for Saving the Earth, Kids for a Clean Environment, Kids in Nature's Defense, the K-12 Network, and all kinds of other organizations that help them save the planet. They become vegetarian peace activists and Enviro-Cops who receive badges and recite an oath to "protect the environment and arrest waste."[45] They write letters by the thousands—to the White House, to their senators, and to their local newspapers. (That's not so great, since most young eco-warriors can only echo the politicized messages they have been told.)

Determined to change their world, they join worldwide environmental networks through global computer links, which can tap into advocacy groups like PeaceNet and EcoNet. Nearly 300 schools in 21 countries are linked through the International Education and Resource Network (I*LEARN) which formed in 1991 when the Copen Foundation expanded its New York/Moscow project. "It empowers people to become active learners,"[46] says Ed Gragert, program manager for the network.

Clean Sweep, an environmental curriculum published by the Iowa Department of Education, is full of fun cartoons and creative classroom exercises. But it demonstrates the same biased information and politicized solutions found in environmental curriculum elsewhere. Take a look at one of the lessons.

The "learners" divide into two groups. One group, the people of the Earth, sit on chairs in a circle representing the Earth. The others, the "unborn" people of the world, wait on the sidelines "to be born." In the center of the circle the learners have piled up things like aluminum cans, foil, plastic bags, paper clips, and glass bottles.

When the music plays, the children mill around looking for natural resources. When it stops, the children sit down and collect stickers that represent consumption of a particular resource. To demonstrate the rising world population, new children are "being born" and added to the group using the dwindling resources. When all the stickers on a chair are taken, the chair is removed. Learners without a chair must find someone willing to share their chair or lap. Guess what happens—the world runs out of resources.

Like the computer models used to predict climate change, the game doesn't match reality. This exercise is designed to *change attitudes,* not show real life. Therefore it teaches neither scientific facts nor social statistics. What it *does* accomplish is far more dangerous than what it omits: It gives children a new exaggerated and alarming view of an imagined reality—one designed to stir fear and anger. The children *felt* the imagined dangers. They *wanted* to do something about them. Here's how the "Questions" manipulate those feelings:

1. What would happen if the game continued . . . ?

2. Was it sometimes difficult finding someone to share a chair or lap? (Do countries have difficulty sharing resources?)

3. How did it feel to be crowded on one chair?[47]

To make sure the learners understand that America is the villain of the world, this variation and question is added: "The U.S.A. uses over 20% of the world's resources, so the U.S.A. could always have first chance at a chair and would not have to share. How do the others feel toward the U.S.A. in this game?"

Do you wonder what global and economic alternative to capitalism the Iowa Department of Education might be advocating?

Resisting the Myths

To withstand the classroom and peer pressures to accept the scary environmental scenarios and their global "solutions," your children need to do each of these things:

- Know science *facts* that 1) provide evidence against false scenarios and 2) show *genuine* problems and practical solutions. In addition to the ecomyths listed earlier, they need to know that we are *not* running out of natural resources, that farmers *can* produce far more food than they do today, and that "we even have a national glut of landfill capacity."[48] (For more facts that counter ecomyths, yet expose genuine concerns, contact CFACT and their team of respected scientists at P.O. Box 65722, Washington, D.C. 20035 or Dr. Edward Krug at P.O. Box 1161, Winona, MN 55987.)

- Understand some of the political visions which fuel the environmental movement.[49]

- Remember that classroom computer models don't simulate the real world. At best they match the standard environmental philosophy. The programmers determine what the computers will demonstrate.

- Realize that the U.S. government is manipulating science to fit political purposes. "Executive Order 12498 allows scientific research to be skewed 'for conformity with administration policy.'" One result: researchers are "forbidden to collect data on a range of sensitive topics."[50]

- Get environmental education curricula from:

  1. HIS CREATION, P.O. Box 785, Arvada, CO 80001-0785.

  2. CFACT (See address above).

One final myth prompts our scrutiny. Though evolution has never been proven, classrooms still teach it as absolute truth. Since much social and environmental dogma is based on faith in evolution, our children need to know some of its serious flaws as expressed by well-known and respected secular scientists.

For example, Sir Frederick Hoyle, Professor of Astronomy at Cambridge University, compared the absurdity of believing that life could result from time, chance, and properties in matter with believing that "a tornado sweeping through a junkyard might assemble a Boeing 747 from the material therein."[51] Listen to some of the other credible voices of science:

> The extreme rarity of transitional forms in the fossil record persists as the trade secret of paleontology. The evolutionary trees that adorn our textbooks have data only at the tips and nodes of their branches; the rest is inference . . . (Stephen Jay Gould, Professor of Geology and Paleontology, Harvard University).[52]
>
> One problem biologists have faced is the apparent contradiction by evolution of the second law of thermodynamics [entropy]. Systems should decay through time, giving less, not more order (Dr. Roger Lewin, a well-known evolutionist).[53]
>
> The origin of life appears to be almost a miracle, so many are the conditions which would have to be satisfied to get it going (Francis Crick, Nobel Prize winner for DNA discovery).[54]
>
> We now have a quarter of a million fossil species, but the situation hasn't changed much. . . . Ironically, we have even fewer examples of evolutionary transitions than we had in Darwin's time. By this I mean that some of the classic cases of Darwinian change in the fossil record, such as the evolution of the horse in North America, have had to be discarded . . . (David Raup, Curator of Geology, Field Museum of Natural History, Chicago).[55]
>
> Evolution became in a sense a scientific religion; almost all scientists have accepted it and many are

prepared to "bend" their observation to fit with it. . . . To my mind, the theory [of evolution] does not stand up at all (H.S. Lipson, a British physicist).[56]

Faith in evolution was essential to America's *paradigm shift*. First, it provided an alternative to biblical truth. Second, it built a much-needed "scientific" foundation for today's leap of faith into the new-paradigm view of the future. Many of today's most outspoken visionaries—Al Gore, Robert Muller, Marilyn Ferguson, etc.—base their hopes for the next century on the spiritual evolution first popularized by the controversial Catholic priest and scientist Teilhard de Chardin. Notice how he fits *everything* into the context of his cosmic evolution:

[Evolution] is a general postulate to which all theories, all hypotheses, all systems must henceforward bow and which they must satisfy in order to be thinkable and true. Evolution is a light which illuminates all facts, a trajectory which all lines of thought must follow.[57]

Quoting de Chardin, Al Gore writes, "'The fate of mankind, as well as of religion, depends upon the emergence of a new faith in the future.' Armed with such a faith, we might find it possible to *resanctify the earth*. . . ."[58]

René Dubos, a board member of the futuristic organization Planetary Citizens, carries Gore's thoughts a step further. In *A God Within* (the book Lamar Alexander said "changed his thinking the most")[59] Dubos writes:

The earth is literally our mother, not only because we depend on her for nurture and shelter but even more because the human species has been shaped by her in the womb of evolution. . . . Our salvation depends upon our ability to create a religion of nature. . . .[60]

Dr. Thomas Sowell, economist and senior fellow at the Hoover Institution at Stanford University, would disagree. Piercing the hollow visions of Utopian dreamers, he writes:

> Dogmatic environmentalism, like fascism, communism and eugenics, appeals to the frustrated egotism of intellectuals who burn to tell lesser people how to live. . . . Nothing as mundane as mere evidence can be allowed to threaten a vision so deeply satisfying.[61]

To avoid compromise with the kind of mythical thinking and earth-centered environmentalism that brings destruction, rather than healing, children should watch out for each of these:

- Songs and poems that encourage earth worship.

- Classroom exercises or rituals that "empower" children to connect with Mother Earth, hear her voice, learn her wisdom, and visualize her healing.

- Environmental programs that promote the lifestyles of pagan cultures.

- Native American chants and prayers to the Great Spirit.

- Buzzwords like *connectedness*—referring to spiritual oneness rather than biological interdependence— and *reverence* (suggesting a response toward nature rather than toward the Creator).

- A pledge of allegiance to the Earth. Many versions are in use.

To help your children understand both the national and the personal consequences of worshiping nature instead of God, read Romans 1:18-32, Deuteronomy 11:13-19, Isaiah 24, and Jeremiah 14:22 together. Take time to think about each message. Talk about the ways God shows His love by giving us these warnings.

Remember, God told man to take care of His beautiful planet.[62] To do our part, we need to heed the Maker—not earthy spirits. When He put humans in charge of His creation,[63] He wanted us to love and care for it as He would, and not abuse it. He wants us to see the world through His watchful eyes and value all life as He does. His Word tells us how. It warns us against mistreating animals, wasting trees, and squandering His resources. Before the watchful eyes of the world, we need to model grateful appreciation for God's gifts. "For from him and through him and to him are all things. To him be the glory forever" (Romans 11:36).

6

Serving
a Greater Whole

. . . all students will be involved in activities that demonstrate community service.

—Goals 2000: Educate America Act

As young people mature we must help them develop . . . a service ethic . . . the global servant concept in which we will educate our young for planetary service and eventually for some form of world citizenship. . . . [I]mplicit within the global servant concept are the moral insights . . . that will help us live with the regulated freedom we must eventually impose on ourselves.[1]

—Harold G. Shane, *Phi Delta Kappan*

A really efficient totalitarian state would be one in which the all-powerful executive of political bosses and their army of managers control a population of slaves who do not have to be coerced because they love their servitude. . . .[2]

—Aldous Huxley
Brave New World

*L*aura's fourth-grade teacher was reading a new book called *The Giver*. The story seemed sort of strange and spooky, but most of her classmates at Adams Elementary School in Davenport, Iowa, liked it. After all, it had won the 1994 Newbery Medal and was dedicated to "all the children to whom we entrust our future."[3] Therefore it had to be good—didn't it?

The book told about a special community where every child felt safe, ate plenty of food, took pills to stop any pain, and lived in a family no larger than four. Overpopulation was no problem since new babies were limited to 50 a year in the whole community. Born to professional "birth mothers" instead of real mothers, the newborns were placed in Nurturing Centers where older children helped care for them during volunteer hours. To keep people comfortable and free from stress, handicapped babies and low-weight twins were "released" to go to a mystical "Elsewhere."

Each December all the children advanced into the next age group. At the Ceremony for the Ones, all the healthy babies born during the year were assigned to selected families. Jonas, one of the Elevens, still remembered when his sister Lily was a One and came to live in his family. Next

December she would become an Eight and receive her first voluntary service assignment. On the same day all the Nines would get their first bicycle, and the Tens would get special haircuts. The new Elevens would soon have to take daily pills to quench the strange "stirrings" that came with puberty.

Each group of children—up to Twelve—learned to follow the rules for their age, succeed in school, complete their service assignments, and share their dreams and feelings with their designated family. Sometimes Jonas preferred to hide his feelings, but that was against the rules.

As they neared December once again, Jonas and the other "young adults" waited anxiously for the Ceremony for the Twelves. This year they would receive their permanent Assignments—their place to work during their productive years. These Assignments were chosen by the Committee of Elders, who had been observing every child. Jonas, who had intuitive power to "see beyond," was selected to be the Receiver of Memories. The former Receiver—who now became the Giver—would place his hands on Jonas' back and psychically transfer all kinds of past experiences and distant memories to the boy. Eventually Jonas would become the community's source of wise counsel and secret wisdom—similar to a tribal shaman.

Laura's class never discussed the readings. The children simply listened, imagined, absorbed, and pondered. They were expected to draw their own conclusions. Sometimes Laura felt uncomfortable—as when Jonas had to bathe a frail, slippery old woman during his volunteer hours at the House of the Old. But the worst part came when Jonas' father, a Nurturer, had to "release" the smaller of two newborn twins.

As the teacher read from the book, Laura pictured the scene she heard: Jonas and the Giver were watching the *Release* on a video screen. They saw a small, windowless room with a table and scale—the same room Jonas had seen during his volunteer work at the Nurturing Center. "It's just an ordinary room," he said to the Giver. "I thought maybe they'd have it in the Auditorium, so that everybody could come. All the Old go to Ceremonies of Release. But I suppose when it's just a newborn, they don't . . ."

Suddenly Jonas saw his father enter the room with a tiny newchild. He put it on the scale and noted the weight. ". . . [Y]ou're only five pounds ten ounces," he said. "A shrimp!"

A shrimp? Laura could identify with the tiny infant. She too was a low-birth-weight twin. Feeling shaky, she listened closely as the teacher continued to read:

> His father turned and opened the cupboard. He took out a syringe and a small bottle. Very carefully he inserted the needle into the bottle and began to fill the syringe. . . . [Then he directed] the needle into the top of newchild's forehead, puncturing the place where the fragile skin pulsed. The newborn squirmed, and wailed faintly.
>
> "Why's he—"
>
> "Shhh," the Giver said sharply.
>
> His father . . . pushed the plunger very slowly, injecting the liquid into the scalp vein until the syringe was empty. . . .
>
> As Jonas continued to watch, the newchild, no longer crying, moved his arms and legs in a jerking motion. Then he went limp. His head fell to the side, his eyes half open. Then he was still. . . .
>
> His father tidied the room. Then he picked up a small carton that lay waiting on the floor, set it on the bed, and lifted the limp body into it. . . . He opened a small door in the wall. . . . It seemed to be the same sort of chute into which trash was deposited at school.
>
> His father loaded the carton containing the body into the chute and gave it a shove.
>
> "Bye-bye, little guy," Jonas heard his father say before he left the room. Then the screen went blank.[4]

Stunned, Laura stared at her teacher. Would they really kill a baby if it didn't weigh enough? The horrible image of the tiny infant, murdered and thrown down a chute like a piece of garbage, made her sick. Her thoughts raced on. How could the kind Nurturer kill it? What if it had been her? She was just as tiny when she was born! And she had already been thinking about death already, since only weeks earlier her own grandmother had died.

She rushed home from school and burst into the house. "Mom, Mom," she cried. "Guess what my teacher read today!" She poured out her story, while her mother, Elaine Rathmann, listened quietly.

The next day Mrs. Rathmann, a member of the local school board, visited the school. When she suggested that *The Giver* might be inappropriate reading for fourth-graders, the principal indicated his reluctance to "stifle academic freedom."

Next, she told the teacher how the book had affected her daughter.

"But I didn't tell the class what I believed," he answered. "I let them come to their own conclusion. My children know fiction from nonfiction."

But that doesn't matter, thought Mrs. Rathmann. *Sometimes an exciting story can transmit horrible images and socialistic messages more easily than a history lesson.*

The New Community

The Giver fits into the flood of classroom literature that force children to think the unthinkable and reconsider the values they learn at home. It also models the perfections and pitfalls of the Utopian community envisioned by today's change agents:

- State surveillance and control of wealth, attitudes, beliefs, values, and behavior.

- State-controlled child care, health care, training of parents, and vocational guidance and licensing.

- Constitutional rights and personal freedoms conditioned on compliance.

Hard to believe? Read the Chronology (1946–1970) on page 223. Listen to Chester Finn, Professor of Education and Public Policy at Vanderbilt University and Director of the Educational Excellence Network in Washington, D.C. At the top echelon of education policy-making, he helped President Bush and Lamar Alexander market America 2000 to the public. He wrote these words in *We Must Take Charge,* a book showing the perceived importance of ensuring that local learning matches the *right* national outcomes:

> Perhaps the best way to enforce this standard is to confer valuable benefits and privileges on people who meet it, and to withhold them from those who do not. Work permits, good jobs, and college admission are the most obvious, but there is ample scope here for imagination in devising carrots and sticks. Drivers' licenses could be deferred. So could eligibility for professional athletic teams. The minimum wage paid to those who earn their certificates [Certificates of Initial Mastery][5] might be a dollar higher. . . .[6]

Is this freedom—or social engineering?

Teachers as therapists and surrogate parents are vital to the new socialization process. So is early control of child development. "I suggest we create a brand-new American school," says Lamar Alexander, who was invited by Newt Gingrich, Speaker of the House, to "send him my most radical thoughts."[7] This "school would probably start with babies and go through the eighth grade. . . . It would be open 6 A.M. to 6 P.M. . . . Every child would have a team of teachers that would stay with that child until graduation."[8]

In the envisioned community, a team of professional "experts" replaces parents as ultimate decision-makers in the lives of children. They will make sure parents are trained to follow the prescribed guidelines for parenting, so that "every child starts school ready to learn," fulfilling the first national/international goal. Those who refuse to conform will find their parental authority usurped by school-based community leaders. The voices of noncompliant parents will be stilled by all kinds of strategies designed to ensure consensus.

A sensational fantasy? Not at all, as you will see in Chapter 7. Since many of the specific strategies are hidden behind sugar-coated promotion and misleading labels, few people see the danger. Many refuse to even look. Some are silenced by the politically correct notion that discernment results in intolerance. Others simply don't believe that America could really change all that much. After all, we have our Constitution!

Could we have become a nation of listless frogs, drifting blindly in cultural waters that are nearing the boiling point? Laura's mother, a school board member, would probably answer yes. She saw the blind drifting both in her daughter's classmates and among the other parents.

"*The Giver* desensitized students to the new values," she told me. "Though the last part showed the downside, the book helped make the futuristic community seem normal. The children were free to form their own conclusions, but their conclusions would be based on the biased information they were given."

"Did other parents share your concern?" I asked her.

"I don't think so. They didn't want to be disturbed. No one else was willing to say, 'I won't let you teach this to my child.'"

The educational establishment would be pleased. They hope that parents will be either too apathetic to resist the transformation or supportive enough to help quench opposing voices. To win supporters to their side, they design innovative programs that appeal to the majority and conceal their new-paradigm teaching. Few programs have proven more sucessful than community service—or "service-learning," as some call it. Praised by parents and educators alike, it has spread quickly across the country.

Why shouldn't it? Since the turn of the century, leading educators have been fine-tuning their skills in psychosocial manipulation. Many of today's parents were yesterday's guinea pigs, and they see nothing wrong with classroom encounter groups and global oneness. Trusting "experts" who promise happy, healthy, self-confident, and productive children, parents blindly applaud the latest techniques in behavioral psychology. Endorsing the new-paradigm reality, they add credibility to Huxley's fantasy:

> The most important Manhattan Projects of the future will be vast government-sponsored inquiries into . . . "the problem of happiness"—in other words, the problem of making people love their servitude. . . . The love of servitude cannot be established except as the result of a deep, personal revolution in human minds and bodies.[9]

Do you recognize this vision? We saw its fruit in Nazi Germany, Soviet Russia, and other twentieth-century totalitarian states. Most gained their initial power base by winning popular support through seductive but misleading promises. Some of those nations, especially the USSR, pioneered the psychological strategies now mandated in American schools (see the Chronology). In the end, the masses were persuaded to trade individual freedom to think or act for the noble purpose of serving a greater whole.

In order to make this chapter easier to understand, I have outlined the main points:

- Voluntary service is becoming a normal part of public education.

- Service sounds good, but there are reasons for concern.

- National service has been used to force free people into involuntary servitude in other countries and cultures.

- To avoid deception, you must know the true meaning of voluntary service.

"Voluntary" Service

Anne Mecham loves her community service class. "It's kind of cool," said the seventh-grader at Standford Middle School. "It's a school class, but you're not stuck in a class learning; you actually get to go out and do something."[10]

Anne and her friends do volunteer service four days a week. They may be sent to a daycare center, to a housing complex for the elderly, or to a local elementary school. To them it's more fun than class. To educators it's a hands-on way of teaching compassion, responsibility, citizenship, and teamwork. To busy parents, it offers children a simple path to positive, character-building experiences.

"In California, we encourage service learning as a highly effective tool for teaching students the true meaning of citizenship and caring for one's community and people,"[11] said Linda Forsyth, an education programs consultant.

It sounds almost too good to be true. Could anything be wrong with such noble motives and selfless service? There could be—when service supports a hidden agenda, or when it ceases to be voluntary. Involuntary service involves coercion, and coercion can take many forms. Peer pressure, implied social obligations, and classroom assignments are subtle ways of coercing students to postpone their studies or change the emphasis of their education. In addition, when "volunteer" service is planned by the government, assigned by educators, and required for high school graduation or college admission, it borders on violating Constitutional rights.[12]

"Community service is a mandatory part of the curriculum in more than 200 public and private schools nationwide," wrote Lori Aratani in a 1994 article titled "Out of the Classroom, into the Community." Basing her observations on a New York research program called the National Center for Service Learning in Early Adolescence, she continued, "Thousands more support voluntary community service projects, and some even make it a graduation requirement."[13]

"Volunteer" service is required for graduation in Woodside, California. Thirteen-year-old Ayelet Arbuckly spends some of her weekends folding curtains and doing chores at a homeless shelter. Eliott Butler, also 13, helps build houses for the needy. "It's hard work sometimes," says Eliott, "but when you're finished, you feel really good about what you've done."[14]

Most people *feel* good about service. Back in 1988, when President Bush first shared his vision of a Thousand Points of Light shining as beacons into needy neighborhoods, our nation *felt* good and noble. When his Points of Light Foundation began to plan national service as an antidote to hunger and homelessness, expectations grew. But when we heard that the Points of Light payroll had tripled to $4.1 million and the Foundation "may have misspent millions,"[15] we learned a sobering lesson: Big government and big foundations are easy targets for human greed and big ambitions.

"I challenge a new generation of young Americans to a season of service," said President Clinton in his inaugural address five years later. "There is so much to be done—enough, indeed, for millions of others who are still young in spirit to give of themselves in service, too."[16]

Vice President Al Gore echoed Clinton's message. "This is the beginning of national community service in our country," he told 1500 young adults selected to launch the National Youth Service Corps at Treasure Island Naval Base in California. "And you are the first. . . . I expect you to change the world!"[17]

Change the world? Keep in mind that there is nothing new about voluntary service. Long ago Jesus demonstrated it to His followers. Earlier yet, Old Testament prophets taught it to ancient Israel. Throughout much of its history the United States has led the world in voluntary service to its own poor as well as to distant victims of war, famine, plagues, and floods. So what does today's "voluntary" service offer that past service didn't?

The Hidden Agenda

The present student service movement began with the 1983 report by the Carnegie Foundation for the Advancement of Teaching (CFAT).[18] The following year David Hornbeck, State Superintendent of Maryland's Public Schools and a member of the Carnegie Foundation Board, testified before the Maryland State Board of Education concerning the need to "mandate community service at state-approved places."[19] He quoted from the much-acclaimed book *High School* by CFAT President Ernest Boyer:

> The goal of service in the schools is to teach values—to help all students understand that to be fully human one must serve.[20]

To understand the meaning behind Boyer's statement, let us look at the history and philosophy of the Carnegie foundations. Together with the Carnegie Corporation and the Carnegie Endowment for International Peace, CFAT has been funding futuristic and globalist causes for nearly a century.[21] Their combined wealth has bought astounding and alarming political favors. "All three organizations are so well-heeled financially that they are entrusted by nearly every administration, Republican and Democrat, with performing all sorts of vital functions, from negotiating foreign treaties with the Soviet Union to setting policy in education,"22 wrote Beverly Eakman in *Educating for "The New World Order."*

Long before our government became involved, CFAT and other globalist foundations were importing Soviet strategies for training youth and organizing centralized communities. Along with welcome grants from the same traitorous foundations, these psychological strategies began to infiltrate our public school, tax-funded educational laboratories, and teacher training centers. Now they are a vital part of the community-wide transformational system being implemented by the educational establishment.

How did the funding for this Soviet-based behavioral psychology shift from private foundations to tax-payers' pockets? A part of the answer is obvious. In 1985, our U.S. Department of State gave the Carnegie Corporation, "Authority to negotiate with the Soviet Academy of Sciences, which is known to be an intelligence-gathering arm of the KGB, regarding 'curriculum development and the restructuring of American education.'"23

Why, you might ask, would our government give the Carnegie Foundation this kind of authority? How could a tax-exempt organization with its eye on global socialism be allowed to act on *our* behalf without any accountability to American voters?

Charlotte Iserbyt, a former Senior Policy Adviser in the U.S. Department of Education, believes American parents deserve an answer. In her exposé of the seditious U.S.-Soviet Agreement, she quotes the response given by Carnegie President Dr. David Hamburg, chief negotiator for the Soviet exchange. His astounding admission gives us a glimpse of the hidden power behind the scenes:

> Privately endowed foundations can operate in areas government may prefer to avoid.24

When CFAT president Ernest Boyer wrote that "the goal of service in the schools is to teach values," the emphasis was on *changing* a student's values, not on encouraging loving service. The values he promotes are the new-paradigm values—those that will replace what Christian students learn at home. These objectives have characterized the Carnegie foundations for decades.

In 1989 the Carnegie Council on Adolescent Development issued a report titled "Transforming the Education of Young Adolescents." Reprinted from *Turning Points: Preparing American Youth for the 21st Century,* it emphasized not the needs of those who are served—but the *new attitudes* to be developed in students through service:

> Every middle grade school should include youth service—supervised activity helping others in the community or in school—in its core instructional program. . . . Teachers will need to provide opportunities for students to reflect on and learn from their service experience, arrange student placements, coordinate with site supervisors, and oversee students' service activities on campus.[25]

So far it doesn't sound too bad, does it? Perhaps a 1994 article in *Teaching Sociology* will help us look beyond the innocuous facade. Titled "Community Service-Learning: Promises and Problems," it describes the Joint Education Project (JEP) at the University of Southern California which offers experimental learning by "placing students in community volunteering positions."[26]

The "fundamental goal" of JEP is "the enhancement of academic learning," wrote the authors, Pierrette Hondagneu-Sotelo and Sally Raskoff. "Sociological concepts come alive when they are complemented by firsthand experiences and guided reflections."[27]

Notice the words *experiences* and *guided reflections.* In this project students are not free to think for themselves. The experiences and conclusions of the 32,000 students who have passed through the program were carefully planned by new-paradigm sociology teachers determined to convert students to their beliefs.

Even so, some students refused to see community problems through the new-paradigm perspective, nor would they embrace the politically correct outcomes. Using facts, observation, and reason (remember the old-paradigm tools?), these students drew *independent* conclusions, causing great consternation to their teachers. The authors shared their dismay:

> The most serious and frustrating problem . . . is the tendency to reach unwarranted, often racist conclusions based on selective perceptions. In these cases, observations are made through the prism of prejudice and *individualism.* This tendency reflects both U.S. racist ideology and the legacy of viewing social problems as the product of individuals' character deficiencies. Such a view is antithetical to the goals of sociology. . . .[28] (Emphasis added.)

Did you hear what they said? *Society, not individuals, are responsible for behavior.* Humans, like animals, are conditioned by their circumstances. This anti-Christian social philosophy (based on B. F. Skinner's behavioral psychology) is the basis for today's Mastery Learning, Outcome-Based Education, Performance-Based Education, and any other temporary label identifying our international world-class education.

In case you are wondering if the noncompliant students above were actually racist, let's put the authors' comments into the new-paradigm context. In Chapter 3 I wrote that only the *right* kind of thinking will transfer students from the old to the new paradigm. Only the new-paradigm context will give the *right* meaning to words and experiences. The *context* determines the meaning of words. In the old context, racism meant racial prejudice: judging a person by skin color. In the new context, it refers to *everything* tainted by Western culture or Christian beliefs. No matter how many multiracial friends you have, *you would be called racist if you considered America or Christianity better than any other nation or religion.*

To see the absurdity of this reasoning, read *Illiberal Education* by Dinesh D'Souza. He quotes Donna Shalala, then Chancellor at the University of Wisconsin, saying, "I would plead guilty to both racism and sexism. The university is institutionally racist. American society is racist and sexist. Covert racism today is just as bad as overt racism was thirty years ago. . . ."[29] You can't win—unless you join the march into the new paradigm!

If you are still not convinced, may I suggest that you read the JEP report containing the concerned, caring statements by those accused of being racists. You should be able to find it in any university library. Then read *Illiberal Education*. It opened my eyes to the astounding new socialization process at our politicized universities. For example, the American emphasis on *individual* rights and freedoms is now considered a racist principle by pacesetting educators:

> When the University of Pennsylvania recently announced mandatory "racism seminars" for students, one member of the University Planning Committee voiced her concerns about the coercion involved. She expressed her "deep regard for the *individual* and my desire to protect the freedoms of all members of society." A university administrator sent her note back, with the word "individual" circled and the comment, "This is a RED FLAG phrase today, which is considered by many to be RACIST. Arguments that champion the individual over the group ultimately privilege the "individuals" who belong to the largest or dominant group."[30] (Emphasis added.)

In the Joint Education Project, written observations and conclusions that disagreed with the teachers' politically correct values were not acceptable. To encourage greater conformity to the new-paradigm values, the authors suggested that future teachers help students "place their community service-learning experience in a sociological framework." In other words, first teach students new-paradigm sociology (introduce the new *context*). Later, explain the experience in light of that context or "sociological framework."

To prevent a student's "lapse into racist, culturally deterministic, individualistic views," wrote the authors—

> we suggest that an initial orientation session on diversity—which has already been instituted. . . . and the [instructors'] vigilance. . . . Unless students already are speaking and thinking within a sociological framework, placing them in a community where they work with individuals may encourage them to reify [treat as real] rather than dispel stereotypes.[31]

Did you get the point? Students who view reality from a traditional "individualistic" perspective will draw conclusions that reinforce their old beliefs. That would undermine the strategy for change. Teachers can avoid that pitfall by "integrating the curriculum more closely with the student's community experience."[32] In other words, *more indoctrination before the experience and more surveillance during the experience.*

Genuine voluntary service doesn't need a government mandate. Practical training would help, but manipulation and mandates undermine both motivation and personal rewards. True service flows from hearts moved with love for people and compassion for the needy. Service-learning, on the other hand, is a strategic tool for transformation.

You have seen the goal: to produce world-class citizens ready to serve a greater whole, whether the community, the state, the Earth, or a pantheistic union. Capitalism, nationalism, individualism, and biblical truth are major obstacles to that goal. Could we be staring at Huxley's programmed Utopia?

Brave New World?

Most high school graduates have read Huxley's futuristic fantasy. To some students it sounds as frightening as George Orwell's *1984*. To others it inspires Utopian visions that seem both plausible and fun. After all, Huxley's revolutionary world promises what change agents demand: socialist security, spiritual meaning, global oneness, and vast opportunities for free sex and fun "feelies."

In this brave new world, parents can no longer set limits on sensual thrills or government indoctrination. The family has ceased to exist. Children are born in laboratories, programmed through daily behavior modification exercises, and conditioned to enjoy sexual experimentation, group consciousness, unquestioning service, and the right ways to think. Peace, order, and conformity have won the day. But the trade-off hurts. Tracked by the watchful eyes of the state and peer informers, few people dare challenge the prescribed boundaries of worldwide political correctness.

The official promotion of sensual indulgence serves a social purpose. "As political and economic freedom ... diminishes, sexual freedom tends compensatingly to increase," writes Huxley. "And the dictator ... will do well to encourage that freedom. In conjunction with the freedom to daydream under the influence of dope, movies and the radio, it will help to reconcile his subjects to the servitude."[33]

Compliant servitude is essential to Huxley's world. Together with an all-inclusive global spirituality marketed under the banner of unity, it sets the stage for a peaceful transition to a new world order:

> A really efficient totalitarian state would be one in which the all-powerful executive of political bosses and their army of managers control a population of slaves who do not have to be coerced because they love their servitude. To make them love it is the task

assigned . . . to ministries of propaganda, newspaper editors and schoolteachers. . . .

If persecution, liquidation and the other symptoms of social friction are to be avoided, the positive sides of propaganda must be made as effective as the negative.[34]

Compare Huxley's totalitarian world to twentieth-century dictatorships for a moment. Both Nazi and Communist regimes believed that individual people, young and old, belonged to the state. Both used positive propaganda, nice-sounding notions like *service* and personal *sacrifice,* to hide their totalitarian controls and sadistic cruelty. Both used the threat of intense persecution and "liquidation" to back up the negative side of their propaganda.

Coming from Hitler and Stalin, who showed nothing but hatred for their own poor and handicapped, the word "service" became meaningless. Their purpose for youth service was *social transformation,* not charity. The bottom line was *control.* The children belonged to the state, not the parents.

In her article "Mandatory National Service Is a Tool to Indoctrinate Youth into Socialism," Maxine Shideler shows that parental resistance meant nothing to Hitler. In a 1933 speech the Nazi leader told the spellbound crowd:

When an opponent says, "I will not come over to your side," I calmly say, "Your child belongs to us already. . . . What are you? You will pass on. Your descendants, however, now stand in the new camp. In a short time, they will know nothing else but this new community."[35]

"All totalitarians, whether Nazis or Fascists or Communists, consider national service and the nationalization of education to be extremely important," wrote Dr. Dennis Cuddy. His conclusion is confirmed by an interesting book prepared through the Department of History and Archaeology at the University of Exeter titled *Nazism: A History in Documents and Eyewitness Accounts.* "Service learning" was a major part of the Nazi indoctrination:

> The purpose of labor service was partly practical—to ... provide a source of cheap labor—but mainly ideological. It was a part of the cult of community current in the youth movement now manipulated by the Nazis for their own end. Students would be confronted with Real Life and, by being forced to mix with the less privileged sections of the community, would be reminded that they were all [national comrades] together.[36]

Hitler's occult connections are no secret, and his life showed the consequences. His blend of seductive words and social manipulation created a political monster with a global appetite. Because the gullible masses believed his grandiose dreams and promises, they chose to trade their individual freedom for national servitude.

Sobered by the inhumaneness of slavery, our 1865 Congress saw the dangers in national service. To guarantee our safety from the abuses of involuntary service, they wrote Article XIII of the U.S. Constitution:

> Neither slavery nor involuntary servitude, except as punishment for crime whereof the party shall have been duly convicted, shall exist within the United States. . . .

History's record of successes and disasters offer a storehouse of wisdom—if only we would remember and take it to heart. But unless we can identify with the event, we quickly forget. Since I was born in Norway during the Nazi occupation, I still remember how fast a nation can shift from freedom to tyranny. I also know that America's two centuries of freedom from persecution is an anomaly in the history of mankind. If that doesn't sober you, read some of the Bible passages showing what happens when God withdraws His hand of protection from nations that reject His truth.[37] For we too, like ancient Israel, are blindly chasing every false god and seductive Pied Piper that offer counterfeit morsels of God's eternal promises.

Like Hitler's enticing talks, the writings of contemporary occult leaders are salted with deceptive phrases. Positive labels such as World Servers, Goodwill, Points of Light, and global oneness flow through the writings of Alice Bailey, the medium for "spirit guide" Djwhal Khul. They permeate Robert Muller's books and his World Core Curriculum, who based his philosophy on Khul's occult messages. They enchant the disciples of the Dalai Lama, the world's best-loved ambassador for Buddhism, who exudes the hollow promises of *love, unity,* and *compassion.* Few in his worshipful global audience realize that the Tibetan leader represents cultures based on karmic passivity that historically have ignored the suffering of its poor and maimed. Rich in noble sentiments, Buddhist communities are poor in the practical demonstrations of self-giving love.

Remember that truth, facts, and logic fade in significance as America drifts into the new paradigm. But most old-fashioned Americans still trust that people will speak truth and facts. That makes us more gullible. The noble words that sugarcoat educational philosophy and occult visions have blinded Americans to the transformation.

We need to consider with caution and prayer what globalist and occult change agents are really saying. If Germans had read Hitler's *Mein Kampf* before the Holocaust began, perhaps his devilish ambitions and cruelty would have rallied enough opposition. Remember that the Old and New Testament prophets didn't hesitate to warn God's people about the nature of demonic deception.

The apostle Paul warned us that "in latter times some will depart from the faith, giving heed to deceiving spirits and doctrines of demons" (1 Timothy 4:1 NKJV). Today's "doctrines of demons" expose some of the world's most seductive schemes. They are spread through high-tech channels unimaginable to former generations. Never has it been more urgent for God's people to be "wise as serpents and innocent as doves." If we don't know truth, we will love deception. Millions of people already do.

Most people have never heard of Alice Bailey. It doesn't really matter. Her message is everywhere—not because people read her books, but because Satan whispers the same message through most of today's self-focused, New Age, neopagan, and mystical literature. You will find his popular deceptions in school libraries and curricula as well as in your major bookstores. In our post-Christian culture, Satan's seductions are everywhere. Alice Bailey summarized one of his most seductive lies in *Education in the New Age.* Notice again the noble words that hide totalitarian intentions:

> Through education . . . self-consciousness must be unfolded until man recognizes that his consciousness is a corporate part of a greater whole. . . . Self-interest becomes group interest. Such should be the major objective of all true educational endeavor. Love of self (self-consciousness), love of those around us (group consciousness), become eventually love to the whole (God consciousness). Such are the steps.[38]

That "self-interest" leads to "group-interest" and eventually to God is a cunning demonic lie that appeals to today's self-focused masses. That man's consciousness can be part of a greater whole when all members follow the same spiritual source, applies only to the body of Christ, the true church. There is no genuine unity among those who follow demons.

According to God's Word and the historical record, hatred, divisions, segregation, and oppression are the norm in cultures that reject God's love and enabling strength.[39] And now we are beginning to see this in America. The quest for justice and equality apart from God has brought the opposite: rising violence and division. In spite of the nice-sounding words and promises, today's educators seem to be pulling our children toward an end that looks strangely similar to an occult prophecy from the *World Goodwill Newsletter* (from Lucis Publishing Company, started by Alice and Foster Bailey):

> People in the world at this time can be divided into four groups:
>
> First the *uninformed masses*. . . . They are, however, enough developed to respond to the mental suggestions and control of more advanced people.
>
> Second, the *middle classes*—both higher and lower. . . . Because they can read and discuss and are beginning to think, they form the most powerful element in any nation.
>
> Third, the *thinkers* everywhere. . . . They are steadily influencing world affairs—for good and sometimes for selfish ends.
>
> Fourth, the *New Group of World Servers*. These are the people who are building the new world order. . . . They recognize no authority save that of their own souls.[40]

The last line brings the deception full circle—back to Bloom's Taxonomy and Outcome-Based Education. Dr. Bloom showed educators how to disarm and shape a nation of servers naive and malleable enough to flow with the revolution. Purged of absolutes, children "recognize no authority save that of their own souls." Without solid convictions, they cannot resist the tempting visions of peace and oneness. The most "intuitive" students will be molded into tomorrow's leaders through programs for the gifted. The rest will be programmed to fit their slot in the global economy—just like the mindless masses of human capital in Huxley's *Brave New World*.

In this nightmarish novel, people were programmed from their test-tube conception until the time when their usefulness ended. Conversations, beliefs, and attitudes were tracked, documented, and—if the people deviated from the plan—corrected, sometimes by banishment to remote regions.

A far more sophisticated system of controls threatens us today. Europeans are already using "smart cards"—little plastic cards that store personal information. "Seeking convenience and security, Americans may soon be persuaded to accept a new ID system," says Roy Hanson, Jr., founder of Family Protection Ministries. "One or more of several brewing crises could be the final catalyst. This crisis could come in the area of health care, education, banking and finance, gun control, drug traffic or delinquent parents. An implanted microchip with a transponder for tracing any person anywhere at any time would sound wonderful to many parents concerned about baby switching or missing children."[41]

Since people lose things, and since loss of a "smart card" would cause endless confusion, it may not be long before the biomedical technology available today and already used to track animals would be used to insert a tiny "smart" microchip through the skin of every person. According to Revelation 13:16,17, something like this will happen one day. By that time service will be involuntary, and it will serve an agenda that opposes everything that true Christianity represents.

Keep in mind that service itself is good. God tells us to "serve wholeheartedly." No one demonstrated the role of a servant more perfectly than did Jesus Christ Himself. The real issue is: *Whom do we serve?* God makes it very clear that we cannot "serve two masters. Either [we] will hate the one and love the other, or [we] will be devoted to one and despise the other" (Matthew 6:24). We see this choice today. Those who serve the mastermind behind the globalist agenda will more and more hate God and His followers. Conversely, when children and adults know and serve God, they will recognize and resist deception.

As Jesus began His three-year ministry, Satan tried to divert His course. He offered Jesus "all the kingdoms of the world and their splendor" (the very riches he would eventually give the Antichrist) for a moment. The condition: Jesus had to worship him. Centuries later the coming Antichrist would win that dubious reward by bowing to the global mastermind and serving his purpose. But Jesus refused. His answer ended the temptation: *"Away from me, Satan! For it is written: 'Worship the Lord your God, and serve Him only.'"*[42] What a perfect response to the seductive voices that beckon American students to serve an illusion of global oneness!

7

Silencing
the Opposition

It takes a whole village to raise a child.
— A much-quoted allegedly African proverb

*. . . try to identify resisters before they become vocal and committed
on this particular innovation. Resisters, like innovators, should be
judged for relative sophistication and influence.*[1]
— Ronald G. Havelock
*The Change Agent's Guide
to Innovation in Education*

*If persecution, liquidation and the other symptoms of social friction
are to be avoided, the positive sides of propaganda must be made as
effective as the negative. . . . To bring about the revolution, we require,
among others . . . a greatly improved technique of suggestion through
infant conditioning and . . . a fully developed science of human differences, enabling government managers to assign any given individual to his or her proper place in the social and economic hierarchy.
Round pegs in square holes tend to have dangerous thoughts about
the social system and to infect others with their discontents.*[2]
— Aldous Huxley
Brave New World

I am making a hag doll," announced Michelle after school a few weeks before Halloween.

"What's a hag doll?" asked her mother.

"It's like a witch."

"Oh!" Concerned, Grace Rhie added quietly, "I don't want you doing that."

Michelle's smile faded. "Why not?"

When her mother explained that hag dolls were used in pagan harvest rituals, Michelle tearfully agreed to say no to the hag project. She hated to be different, but neither did she want to displease God.

Michelle's teacher agreed to let her do an alternative project: Create the figure of an alien. But she refused to let the sixth-grader escape the embarrassment of giving an oral report in front of the whole class. Michelle was forced to show her classmates that she and her family lived by a different standard than the rest. That hurt.

In a world that values conformity rather than truth, biblical obedience becomes costly, and the change agents know that fact well. The more Christianity is vilified and ridiculed, the more embarrassment children face when forced to admit being Christian. On the other hand, the more children experience the fun rituals and empowering myths of idealized paganism, the more willing they are to embrace the pantheistic/global paradigm.

Based on B.F. Skinner's behavioral psychology, this manipulative system of rewarding conformers and punishing resisters characterizes the new world-class education. Educators assume that children, like laboratory animals, will—with enough time and stimuli—accept what gives pleasure and reject what causes pain. Naturally, the more pain associated with traditional loyalties, the more quickly children will discard the old ways and embrace the new.

Children who refuse to conform may be considered handicapped. "Although they appear to behave appropriately," explains a NTL (National Training Labs, Institute for Applied Behavioral Science) Teacher Training Manual, "and seem normal by most cultural standards, they may actually be in need of mental health care in order to help them change, adapt, and conform to the planned society in which there will be no conflict of attitudes or beliefs."[3] Notice that the criterion for mental health follows the guidelines of new-paradigm sociology, not the accepted standards of psychiatry.

Nonconformists, whose beliefs clash with global standards, simply won't fit the envisioned next-century world. Remember what Chester M. Pierce told the Association for Childhood Education International in his 1972 keynote address:

> Every child in America entering school at the age of five is insane because he comes to school with certain allegiances toward our founding fathers, toward his parents, toward a belief in a supernatural being. . . . It's up to you, teachers, to make all of these sick children well by creating the international children of the future.[4]

The blueprint for "creating the international child of the future" would end parents' freedom to transmit Christian beliefs to their children. From the globalist perspective, *our* freedom to raise *our* children blocks *their* freedom to train *all* children. To them the needs of the *whole*—the Earth as well as its people—would transcend the rights of the *individual*.

Kathy Collins, former Legal Counsel to the Iowa Department of Education, typifies the growing hostility toward Christian parents. Ponder her assertion in the article "Children Are Not Chattel":

> Children . . . are not "owned" by their parents. . . .
> The Christian fundamentalists who want the freedom
> to indoctrinate their children with religious education
> do not understand [that] the law that prevents them
> from legally teaching their kids prevents someone else
> from abusing theirs.[5]

In simpler words, training your children according to biblical truth is equated with child abuse. From the new-paradigm perspective, the *old* beliefs are handicaps which block their evolution into a global citizen and hinders the mission of the "brand-new American school."[6]

To save children from the hands of uncooperative parents, the change agents have devised a clever plan: Place them in the hands of the "local community." Fred Newmann, Director of the Center on Organization and Restructuring of Schools, explains a small part of that strategy in his article "School-wide Professional Community." Where do you think parents fit into his picture?

> "It takes a whole village to raise a child." The much-
> quoted African proverb says it can't be done by an indi-
> vidual teacher, or even by several teachers working
> independently. Instead, it requires communal effort of
> many adults, in a variety of roles, who share a unified
> common purpose, and who help one another to teach
> and socialize their youth. . . .[7]

Newmann's article ignores the part that parents play in the socialization of their children. Other change agents simply transfer parental responsibility to everybody—especially trained professionals. "Roots and Wings," one of the New American Schools Development Corporation's "design teams," is a federally funded model for Outcome-Based Education. It states that—

> . . . all persons, agencies and institutions with whom 0–6-year-old children interact should be *held responsible* for enhancing their development, thus contributing to their preparedness for school. This requires collaboration with representatives from the health and medical, child/care . . . education communities. . . . [8]

Other change agents do mention parents, but in a more sinister way. The Iowa Roundtable, a state branch of a growing nationwide partnership between schools and the business sector, shows how schools will be compelled to take charge of entire families. It has developed "eight principles that must guide the transformation of today's Iowa schools into the world-class schools of tomorrow." The first five items suggest that local schools will be forced to transform their students or face punishment. The last three deal with parents. Ponder the shocking assumptions behind the positive words.

> 1. Iowa's world-class education system should be based on results. The success of schools in the new system should be judged on how well students master a clearly defined, measurable core of learning. . . . [This is typical Outcome-Based Education language.]
>
> 2. Student performance should be measured with a variety of tools that reflect what students are expected to learn. Setting high expectations for students who can think, understand ideas, and solve problems will require the creation and use of equally complex assessment

strategies. [National student assessments will test whether or not schools did their assigned job.]

3. Successful schools, judged on the improvement of student achievement, should be rewarded, unsuccessful schools should be helped to improve, and consistently inferior schools should be penalized. [Schools, not students, are held responsible for a student's failure.]

4. Staff in individual schools must have the authority to make decisions affecting student achievement and must be accountable for results. . . . **Site-based management** and shared decision making must replace the current more-authoritarian system of managing education. [Private professional management will replace elected school boards. They can better silence the opposition.]

5. Educators must have the training, knowledge, and leadership skills to help students succeed. . . . [This refers to retraining and certification for teachers.]

6. Schools must be responsible for seeking the full involvement of parents as partners in the education of children . . . [and] for seeking parent involvement in all facets of children's education and development. When parents cannot or will not become involved, schools must help the child overcome that difficulty. [What will they do? Punish the parents? Remove the child?]

7. Readiness for school is critically important. Providing a stimulating environment early in a child's life can prevent problems in the future. . . . Schools in the new system must provide the option of prekindergarten opportunities. [Educators want early access to the minds of all children.]

8. Schools in the new system must be responsible for ensuring collaboration with health and human services agencies to reduce barriers to student learning. Children of all ages must be physically, mentally, and emotionally healthy if they are to learn. . . . Hunger,

stress, or illness will keep students from school success. Schools must be responsible for eliminating those barriers to success. . . .[9]

The last point calls for partnerships between schools and the various health services. Words like "stress" and "mentally and emotionally healthy" are being defined and measured against the new mental and emotional ideals for raising "the international child of the future." Later you will see how deviation from these norms—such as refusing to let go of traditional attitudes about right and wrong, sin and guilt—could put children "at risk," induce charges of child abuse, and cause the child's removal from the home.

Sounds scary, doesn't it? It's not supposed to. Every effort is made to give restructuring a positive image, one that is palatable to the public. "Couch the language of change in the language of the status quo," wrote Massell Smith in *Social Change,* a newsletter from the NTL Institute for Applied Behavioral Science. "Use the stated objectives of the status quo. They are almost broad enough to encompass innovation."[10]

The Myth of Local Control

Since both Republican and Democratic change agents know what American parents want, they speak glowingly about parental involvement, high standards, and the other misleading ideals of Outcome-Based Education. Few tell us what they really mean. Chester Finn, who helped Lamar Alexander and President Bush market America 2000 to the public, promised early in 1995 that the new Republican leadership was determined to "straighten out" public education and "repair the damage" done during the Clinton administration. He offered what parents want: "local control," "quality results," and "decentralization."

The problem is that Finn's own vision of "local control" doesn't fit the nice images he paints. In an article titled "Reinventing Local Control," Finn suggests that the state would specify the "ends" (based on national standards or outcomes) of education, while local schools determine the "means" (the classroom strategies) of learning. In other words, local districts must figure out *how* to carry out the bidding of the state. What each of their students learn, *must* match the predetermined national outcomes, which deal primarily with the beliefs, mental attitudes, and group thinking supposedly needed for global citizenship and work. If students fail, the schools will face dire consequences.

In other words, "local control" means control over *how* to teach, not *what* to teach. The question still remains: *Who* at the local schools would make the decisions?

Finn has a ready answer: "We need change agents in charge of those schools," he explains, "not preservers of entrenched interests and encrusted practices. . . . Local control is dead. Long live local control."[11] Could he mean "*out* with parents and school boards that might resist change, and *in* with our professional 'change agents'?"

Finn's 1991 book *We Must Take Charge: Our Schools and Our Future* puts local control squarely into the hands of professional educators. He writes, "[M]any conservatives have a charming but antiquated devotion to 'local control' of schools that bears scant relationship to contemporary reality. . . . If we want revolutionary changes in American education we have to overhaul its power structure and its ingrained practices."[12] He continues:

> [T]hough the ends [outcomes] of education are the responsibility of society in general to prescribe through the familiar processes of democratic government, the means by which we reach those ends are the province of expert professionals. . . . The school is the vital delivery

system, the state is the policy setter and nothing in between is very important.[13]

The "nothing in between" includes parents and elected school boards—the main barriers to "learning." Finn calls them "superfluous" and "dysfunctional."[14]

Where in this new system would there be public accountability to parents whose children will be forced to participate in the new system? True, there will be local partnerships—carefully planned alliances with selected parents and community leaders who support the new agenda. But parents who oppose Outcome-Based Education would be excluded—or included as an insignificant minority.

Already, facilitators in communities across the country are training local committees to operate by the rules of consensus. They will recognize no dissenting voices. After all, from the new-paradigm perspective, Western culture and Christian values represent intolerance. Those who perpetuate these obsolete views must be ignored or intimidated into silence. Gen Yvette Sutton, Educational Analyst with the Pennsylvania Coalition for Academic Excellence, describes her experience with local attempts at building consensus:

> Minority opinions are totally ignored. Having participated in the preliminary hearings for Outcome Based Education in this state [Pennsylvania], I can tell you how it works. You can stand up in a meeting and say anything. You can disagree . . . but all that is recorded is the consensus . . . the agreement, so that it looks like they reached a consensus. When this is done regionally, the state sends secretaries to record these meetings. . . . They don't transcribe . . . they only record what they choose, censoring anything that doesn't fit. Several superintendents raised very legitimate concerns, but these concerns were ignored in the state reports. It was a sham and scam.[15]

Parents As Teachers

The popular slogan "It takes a whole village to raise a child" ignores the vital question: What part is left to the parent? If globalists have their way, parents may have little choice outside the guidelines provided by the new school-based "village."

The village idea has been brewing in the minds of international change agents for decades. Back in 1967 an experimental daycare center had opened at the University of North Carolina. Founder and psychologist Hal Robinson, who served on a Presidential task force charged with recommending improvements and innovations in young children's education, sought to find the best possible mix between the family and the society as child-rearing institutions. Funded by the Carnegie Corporation as well as the U.S. government, the project was named after United Nations mediator Frank Porter Graham.[16]

A few years later Kurt Waldheim, Secretary-General of the U.N., said in an address to the Executive Board of UNICEF:

> Until fairly recently, in most societies, the responsibility for child development rested entirely with parents. . . . This is still largely true, but it is changing. . . . The process of child development has to be the concern of society as a whole—on the national and international level. From the very beginning, the leaders of UNICEF . . . clearly understood this. . . .[17]

In 1981 American educators began to implement UNICEF's vision. The Missouri Department of Education launched the first government program to actually tell parents how to raise their children. Under the misleading title Parents As Teachers (PAT), it was introduced as a voluntary project to help disadvantaged children. That the state mandated PAT for *all* children in *all* schools in 1985 came as no surprise. Five years later it had been introduced in 40 states and "at least eight foreign countries,"[18] according to Laura Rogers, a mother whose research exposed the horrendous deception. Her report, "In Loco Parentis," explains how PAT works: A "parent educator" bonds herself to the young family through home visits. Then—

> Once that bond. . . . is established, the children and parents are eased into school programs that deliver a battery of services. First, under the guise of educational screening, parents and children are evaluated, the child is given a personal computer code number, and a computer record is initiated that will enable Missouri to track each child for the rest of his life. . . .
>
> The next step of the PAT program is to change and usurp the relationship parents have with their children. The change agent, the "significant other," will be working with the children in a "mentoring program" or perhaps as a "certified parent educator." This new "certified parent educator" delivers free medical care, free nutrition counseling, free mental health services and free food—all things formerly provided by the parents.
>
> As time goes on, children spend more time at school than at home. Services are increased . . . the schools will provide free daycare, free overnight care, and free camps, as well as free education.
>
> All these free services come, however, at the price of sometimes significant interference in family life. One young mother, Gabrielle Copp, reports that she was outraged at the arrogance of the "state certified parent" who told her husband he could not spank their children. . . . [19]

The parent educator is responsible to the state, not the parents. She functions as a child abuse investigator as well as a parent trainer, and must report suspected abuse or neglect to the child-abuse hotline. In Missouri, failure to report carries a punishment of a thousand dollar fine or a year in jail.[20] The definition for child abuse is broad enough to include actions that many parents consider normal, such as spanking or "yelling" at a rebellious child. Restricting television viewing became grounds for child abuse in Florida, and the parents of a learning disabled boy were found guilty of child abuse for allowing their son to miss a week of school while competing in a newsmaking cross-country run.[21]

The Parents As Teachers National Center has developed a set of "Risk Factor Definitions" to identify possible child abuse or hindrances to a child's early social development and learning. Open to interpretation by the parent educator or social workers, they include—

- Low birthweight and other "handicapping conditions";

- "Inability of parent to cope with inappropriate child behavior";

- "Low functioning parent";

- "Negative or hostile behavior toward child" [which could include biblical disciplines];

- "Undue stress";

- "Other"[22]—the boundless catchall word for any unspoken obstacle to the state's plan for our children.

PAT has been promoted as voluntary. Yet "if the parent refuses the recommended services, the state can remove the child from the home, place it in a residential treatment center, and force the parent to take psychological counseling for an indefinite period,"[23] says Laura Rogers.

Funded by the Carnegie, Danforth, Ford, Rockefeller, and New World Foundations, as well as the federal government, PAT became the law of the land in 1994 as part of Goals 2000. Though many believed that PAT fit under the umbrella of the U.S. Department of Education, "the Danforth Foundation in concert with the Missouri Department of Elementary and Secondary Education exclusively control the Parents As Teachers National Center."[24]

As a private tax-exempt, not-for-profit corporation directed by powerful people like Christopher Bond, U.S. Senator from Missouri (R), Richard Gephardt, U.S. Congressman from Missouri (D), and Ed Ziglar, Yale University early childhood education specialist, it can easily be manipulated for political purposes with no accountability to parents. Ziglar's "total childcare plan is aimed for 'full service schools' that would transform schools into the central delivery point for the cradle-to-grave socialism. . . ."[25]

Laura Rogers asks some discerning questions that challenge the astounding power granted to PAT and other privatized programs accountable, not to parents, but to globalist organizations like the Carnegie and Ford Foundations:

> Why does a tax-exempt state department need a tax-exempt, not-for-profit private corporation? How can we have taxpayer-controlled public schools if they are run by a private corporation whose director the taxpayers cannot vote out of office?[26]

As the last of the eight goals of Goals 2000, PAT has ranked high on the list of mandated *musts* by the year 2000. Since it is cloaked in promotional literature that defuses criticism, most parents welcome the promised aid and are happy to follow the new child-raising guidelines. Besides, most of PAT's parent educators have seemed friendly and helpful. But that may change. According to Missouri Secretary of State Roy Blunt, a new brand of "Certified educator parents" is being trained at the Danforth Foundation's Teachers Pre-Service Institute. When the program is fully in place, they will replace the current "nice grandmothers from local churches."[27]

To win public support for PAT and for countless other pieces of the global transformation puzzle, educators have begun a massive nationwide campaign to promote their vision, win supporters, and silence opposition. Nothing illustrates this "social marketing"[28] effort better than the

Community Action Toolkit, prepared by the National Education Goals Panel led by Education Secretary Richard Riley. It provides local change agents with such transformational strategies as identifying other potential change agents, building a leadership team, expanding their base of support, winning the media to their side, and responding to opponents. Like most educational literature today, the suggested arguments for "influencing the attitudes and behaviors" of community leaders and followers are based on deceptive words and misleading euphemisms, and rarely the actual facts.

Call it "propaganda" if you will. The process bears an alarming likeness to the mental manipulation of the German people under Nazi leadership.

The Power of Propaganda

Webster's Dictionary defines propaganda as "information and opinions (esp. prejudiced ones) spread to influence people in favor of or against some doctrine or idea."[29] Hitler knew well how to use this tool for transformation to accomplish his purpose.

"The most striking success of a revolution," wrote Adolf Hitler in *Mein Kampf,* "will always have been achieved when the new philosophy of life as far as possible has been taught to all men, and, if necessary, later forced upon them."[30] This "philosophy of life" was taught through propaganda, which was first designed "to fill a small nucleus of men with the new doctrine, and so prepare the material which could later furnish the first elements of an organization."

Since Hitler's scheme proved so successful—and since similar strategies are evident in the current transformation of American schools and culture—you may want to consider some of its parts below. View them as both timeless and timely, not sensational or irrelevant. Remember that behind the visible scenes lurks the spiritual master-mind of Satan. According to 1 John 5:19, "The whole world is under the control of the evil one." All except those who follow Christ are susceptible to his timeless suggestions. The deceptive schemes that worked in the past will probably succeed again, for neither human nature nor Satan's hatred for God's people ever change. If contemporary Americans were better equipped with God's Word and the lessons of history, we would not be so easily duped.

Compare what Hitler wrote in 1925 to what is happening today:

> When a movement harbors the purpose of tearing down a world and building another in its place, complete clarity must reign in the ranks of its own leadership with regard to the following principles:
>
> Every movement will first have to sift the human material it wins into two large groups: supporters and members.
>
> The function of propaganda is to attract supporters, the function of organization is to win members. A supporter of a movement is one who declares himself to be in agreement with its aims, a member is one who fights for them. . . .
>
> Understanding in its passive form corresponds to the majority of mankind which is lazy and cowardly. Membership requires an activist frame of mind and thus corresponds only to the minority of men.
>
> . . . the organization must take the greatest care only to make the most valuable elements among the supporters into members. . . .
>
> The first task of propaganda is to win people for subsequent organization. . . . The second task of propaganda is the disruption of the existing state of affairs and the permeation of this state of affairs with the new doctrine, while the second task of the organization must be the struggle for power. . . .[31]

Like Hitler, today's change agents know that propaganda is key to their success. Remember what North Carolina school superintendent Jim Causby said in his 1994 speech at the *Second Annual Model Schools Conference*[32] in Atlanta: "We have actually been given a course in how not to tell the truth. How many of you are administrators? You've had that course in public relations where you learn to put the best spin on things."[33]

You saw in Chapter 4 how words have been redefined. They must appeal to the public, reflecting what parents want to hear while concealing their true meaning. Without the corresponding facts and truths, most people are likely to be deceived by the propaganda. They will believe the words and phrases that describe the very system designed to take control not only of our children's education but of their entire lives.

New Partnerships

To win grass-roots supporters in every community, the U.S. Department of Education prepared a report called "Organizing Your Community to Reach the National Education Goals." Matching the earlier definition for propaganda, it opens with a reminder that "there is much ground to cover, and the year 2000 seems just around the corner. . . . Goals 2000 calls for partnerships across local, state and federal levels—partnerships for mustering the support it'll take to help communities and local schools do what only they together can do. . . ."[34]

You saw that education has bridged the gap between Republicans and Democrats. Both sides agree that the ultimate goals—what communities *must* accomplish in the end—are determined by the national and international goals. To achieve those goals, "a state panel of teachers, principals, parents and others, including the governor and chief state school officer, would evolve a standards-driven reform plan" which would be communicated to each local community. After all, explains the above report, it "wouldn't make sense for communities to go off by themselves and create their own standards from scratch, especially if they're to be *internationally competitive* standards . . ."[35] (emphasis in the original).

As Chester Finn suggested earlier, *only* the final, practical implementation is left to the local school. It can use its own ingenuity to find creative ways to teach the required national curriculum content. It can create its own corresponding curriculum and teaching programs, but if it fails to produce the required change in its students, it will be punished. Since the goal is a new type of student with a new set of attitudes and behaviors, the transformation of our children will require total community participation. And since everyone will apparently be tested through national assessments, there will be no hiding place from group conformity.

To help each community accomplish its part, Riley's report described various model communities. Each had planned its own programs and communication links, and "almost all of them found it necessary" to "identify" and organize "key individuals in the community."[36] These vital "partnerships" were also emphasized in a list of warnings. It encouraged local school planners to "involve key players who could easily block what the collaborative hopes to do. Whenever possible, try to make allies out of adversaries."

In order to "make allies out of adversaries," the educational establishment has formed some surprising partnerships that bridge the ideological chasms rarely crossed in our separation-between-church-and-state culture. Local schools are sometimes even linked to community churches. Considering the growing hostility toward biblical truth, this makes little sense. Yet it's part of the plan.

To help communities test their rate of progress, Riley and the congressmen who prepared the Community Action Toolkit provide questions local leaders can ask themselves: "Are we creating 'a whole community' partnership to improve teaching and learning? Are we enlisting partners throughout the community . . . churches and media, social service agencies and law enforcement, and others?"[37]

Remember, the social transformation could not succeed without general consent from the public, however uninformed that consent might be. And what strategy could better win support among the opposing forces than a friendly invitation to cooperate and seek "common ground"?

The strategy works because few people dare suspect what the change agents plan to do to parents. Lured by pride or propaganda, leaders in every field are accepting the invitation to join hands with a kind of deception that few people could even imagine. Many Christian leaders, who should be a parent's prime defender, have become part of the horrendous betrayal. Left behind are countless Christian parents who find no church support in their attempt to raise godly children God's way.

A few years ago U.S. Senator Christopher Bond, one of the Missouri leaders of Parents As Teachers, told Laura Rogers that he was trying to recruit churches to support the PAT program. On December 16, 1994, his dream came true. The U.S. Department of Education issued the official "Statement of Common Purpose of Religious Leaders." Education Secretary Riley made the announcement: "The religious communities standing with me represent some seventy-five percent of all religiously affiliated Americans. . . . Our meetings led to the clear recognition that our nation's religious community can play a more active and positive role in helping parents in the education of their children."[38]

It sounds just as promising as Parents As Teachers, doesn't it? Would you like to know who signed it? The "religious communities endorsing the statement" included the Assemblies of God, Association of Christian Schools International, Council of Jewish Federations, Evangelical Lutheran Church in America, Lutheran Church (Missouri Synod), National Council of Churches, National Association of Evangelicals, National Baptist Convention, Christian Life Commission of the Southern Baptist Convention, National

Church of God, Presbyterian Church U.S.A., United Methodist Church, U.S. Catholic Conference, United Synagogue of Conservative Judaism, Church of Jesus Christ of Latter-day Saints, and many others.

If you are wondering who still shares *your* concern, you are not alone. Across the country, Christian parents have sought help in their churches only to be told not to worry or rock the boat. "But I can't let my child participate in Native American rituals or make those occult medicine shields," said a heartbroken mother in Ohio. Her pastor and church friends simply couldn't understand why not. They had already embraced the popular vision of the human family holding hands around the world—a vision that mocks the gospel but approves all "other gods."

The Statement of Common Purpose never mentions God. It ignores His warnings about spiritual compromise. Look at what it does mention:

> It is imperative that religious communities join together with governments, community organizations, businesses, and public and private schools in striving to provide families, parents, grandparents, foster parents, guardians, or extended family members with the information, skills, tools, and opportunities that will encourage their participation in the total education of their children, including **character education**. We are committed to working together to improve children's learning through family involvement partnerships.
>
> We call upon all citizens, religious communities, community organizations to do their share.[39]

Perhaps, as Jesus said on the cross, "They do not know what they are doing." Maybe the religious leadership simply believes the propaganda and has joined a movement they don't understand, just as many German churches did during the Nazi rise to power. Perhaps they really do believe that the educational establishment wants to support, not control, Christian parents. The vision looks so tempting—until its deceptive claims turn to calamities that can no longer be denied.

Dealing with Resisters

In addition to the "members" and "supporters" gathered through propaganda, Hitler counted two other groups of people: the ignorant masses and the stubborn resisters. The first he considered too "lazy and cowardly" to take a stand. The second he viewed as enemies of good, deserving no mercy.

Now as then, resisters who challenge the revolution are considered enemies of progress. "Religious Right groups and their local affiliates are conducting an unrelenting campaign of harassment and intimidation against public education all over the nation,"[40] writes Dr. Richard Manatt, Professor of Education at Iowa State University, in a book full of strategies for combating "fundamentalists."

The labels help to discredit the opposition. Most of us have seen those labels: the Radical Right, Christian fundamentalists, book-burners. The flier on the following page illustrates how these hostile tags are used to identify a common enemy ("the radical right") and to join community "partners" in a joint attempt to quench opposition. Notice the strategic mix of participants: politicians from both parties, lawyers, a pastor, a writer, Planned Parenthood, and other nongovernmental organizations. Where do you see the tolerance they proclaim?

Similar combat sessions are springing up everywhere. In 1993 a series of seven-day conferences was planned for presentation throughout the U.S. One such conference took place in Greensboro, North Carolina, in December. Called "Responding Democratically to Opposition Groups," it taught supporters how to identify opposition groups, their arguments and tactics, and how to plan the action needed to counter their efforts.[41]

WHO ARE THE RADICAL RIGHT
AND WHAT ARE THEIR PLANS FOR YOU?

The Advocates of Santa Clara County Planned Parenthood
present an important informational community forum on:

THE THREAT OF THE RADICAL RIGHT
featuring: **Senator Tom Campbell**
California State Senator
and Co-founder of the Republican Majority Coalition

Tom Conry, President of the Vista Teachers Association (Vista
was the first school board in California to be taken over by the Radical
Right)
Dr. Ignacio Castuera, United Methodist Church Minister and board
member of People for the American Way
Ken Yager, Ph.D., first openly gay elected official in Santa Clara County
Janis Schechter, Chair, Intellectual Freedom Committee of the
California Library Association
Tracey Labbe-Renault, author of *Without Justice for All: A Report on
the Christian Right in Sacramento and Beyond.*

Forum co-sponsors: National Organization for Women; Santa Clara
Valley National Lawyers Guild: AAUW; Peninsula P-FLAG; Santa Clara
County Democratic Party; Democratic Activists for Women Now
(DAWN)
Friday, October 14 from 1-5 p.m.
Silicon Valley Conference Center, 985 Stewart Drive, Sunnyvale

---

In a report titled "Primer on the Extremist Attacks on
Public Education," selected educators in Mountain View,
California, learned to do just that and more. Designed to prepare teachers to respond to complaints from the Radical Right,
it listed the issues and buzzwords "used by extremists," some of
the active "Extreme Right Groups," and their key leaders:
Robert Simonds, Phyllis Schlafly, etc. A checklist of ways to
combat extremist attacks included:

- Does your contract [with your school] have
  an academic freedom clause?

- Does your association report information on the Extreme Right to your Primary Contact Staff, Regional Organizer, Political Action Consultant, or the Human Rights Department?

- Has your association conducted, or does it plan to conduct, an awareness program for members about the Extreme Right censorship targets, strategies and activities?[42]

Prepared by the California Teachers' Association, the report included "Watchdog Guidelines" and interview questions for school board candidates. "The purpose of watchdogging school boards," it explained, is to alert "the community's mainstream" to the "influence of extreme radicals" so that "the majority's moderate, more inclusive values may be promoted and protected. . . ."[43]

Ignoring the fact that most of those dreaded "extremists" are actually the parents of their students, the CTA "condemns the philosophy and practices of extremist groups and their efforts to recruit students in our schools and . . . censor curriculum." To whom do they think the children belong?

You have seen some of the answers: The children belong to the community, to the world, to the professionals trained to prepare them for the global workforce of the next century. Many of these professionals have distorted God's timeless guidelines for families to fit a new world order where "good" is synonymous with "global" and "sin" means refusing to join the march to planetary oneness.

Seducing the Children

One of the most disturbing tactics for change incites children to turn against their parents. You have seen examples of how multicultural and environmental education are used as vehicles for change. The various strategies for sex and AIDS education are being just as effective in confusing a child's values and fueling rebellion against traditional authorities.

When Kim Shaw signed a permission slip allowing her daughter to attend an AIDS-awareness seminar at Hale Middle School, she had no idea that her 12-year-old would be exposed to explicit descriptions of sex acts. If she had known that the seventh- and eighth-graders would learn practical ways to apply condoms in order to enjoy premarital sex without consequences, she would never have signed. Worst of all, the seventh- and eighth-graders were coached to hide their sexual activity from their parents and reject their home-taught values.

"I felt it went too far in giving graphic details," Shaw said, "but what I was most upset about was how they taught them to cheat and lie to their parents. They told them how to hide their condoms and their wrappers after they were done with them. They said, 'You want to make sure your parents don't find them.'"[44]

Two pamphlets were given to the students. One showed how to use condoms. The other was titled "100 Ways to Make Love Without Doing It."

This particular seminar, provided throughout the huge Los Angeles Unified School District, was led by health workers from a county clinic. Similar programs operate across the country, as Phyllis Schlafly documents in her excellent exposé, *Child Abuse in the Classroom.*

That premarital sexual freedom should be encouraged as part of the new-paradigm education program should come as no surprise. As I have documented in *Under the Spell of Mother Earth,* sexual activities played a vital part in the "sacred" fertility rituals of earth-centered cultures around the world. While most change agents find sex education a valuable tool for severing a student's ties to home, many also view free sex as a needed vehicle for raising humanity's consciousness of its spiritual connectedness.

"Sexuality is a sacrament," writes Starhawk, founder and priestess of the Covenant of the Goddess, in her Wiccan manual, *The Spiritual Dance.* "Religion is a matter of *relinking,* with the divine within and with her outer manifestations. . . ."[45]

Separation Prohibited

We shouldn't be surprised at the success of today's cultural revolution. The new-paradigm message began to take root soon after prayer and Bible reading were outlawed in our schools in the early sixties. The youths who led the counterculture became mainstream pacesetters in the seventies and eighties. Some became professors and mentors for today's young teachers, while others wrote the books and music that helped establish the new values.

Politicians as well as media leaders *have* joined the march. Al Gore summarized their growing vision well. "Seeing ourselves as separate is the central problem in our political thinking,"[46] he told his audience at the 1991 Communitarian Conference in Washington, D.C. *A World Goodwill Newsletter* put it another way:

> The day is dawning when all religions will be regarded as emanating from one greater spiritual source; all will be seen as unitedly providing the one root out of which the universal world religion will inevitably emerge. . . . They will seek unitedly to co-operate with the divine Plan. . . .[47]

Those who belong to God can neither condone this dangerous illusion of unity nor the religions that support it. "What harmony is there between Christ and Belial?" asked Paul. "What does a believer have in common with an unbeliever?

What agreement is there between the temple of God and idols? For we are the temple of the living God. As God has said, 'I will live with them and walk among them, and I will be their God, and they will be my people. Therefore come out from them and be separate'" (2 Corinthians 6:15-17).

Such an attitude of separation is no longer permitted in American classrooms. Students who love God will surely face increasing persecution. The NEA's well-organized opposition to Christian interference shows the growing hatred for contrary opinions. All critics must be censored, expelled, or intimidated into consensus, for when imagined *unity* is the dominant goal, objective criticism becomes an intolerable offense.

Amara Essy, President of the United Nations General Assembly, articulated this double standard well: "Let us vow to attack intolerance and discrimination wherever they occur. . . . Intolerance is unacceptable."[48]

Recent totalitarian rulers have relied heavily on intimidation and persecution. History shows that persecution took cruel turns in pagan cultures where human nature—animated by occult spirits—had free rein. With today's explosion of occult teaching and pagan rituals throughout the Western world, can we count on anything less?

Yet this is no time to sit on the sidelines or be afraid. As God's people we fight on the winning side. Jesus told His disciples, "As long as it is day, we must do the work of him who sent me. Night is coming, when no one can work" (John 9:4). Our work is first and foremost to allow Christ to live His life through us, so that His transforming wisdom and love can touch the multitudes who are being deceived. Remember, "Salvation is found in no one else, for there is no other name under heaven given to men by which we must be saved" (Acts 4:12).

Do you still feel shocked by the immensity of the battle? Then don't stop here. The next chapter will help and encourage you. As a dear friend keeps telling me, "Nothing is hopeless until God abdicates His throne. And we know

He will never do that!" What He promised His people long ago through Moses is just as true for His followers today:

> Be strong and courageous. Do not be afraid or terrified because of them, for the Lord your God goes with you; he will never leave you nor forsake you (Deuteronomy 31:6).

8

What
You Can Do

*Never, anywhere in the Holy Bible will you find God giving civil government any authority to rear or direct the rearing of children. . . .
God told parents, not the government, to "train up" their children.[1]*
— Laura Rogers, Missouri mother and researcher

*If . . . God is denied, all obligations and responsibilities that are
sacred and binding on man are undermined. A Christian has then no
other choice but to act, to suffer and—if it has to be—to die.[2]*
— G. Leibholz commemorating Dietrich Bonhoeffer,
who gave his life resisting totalitarianism

*Communists invented brainwashing too late! Christ had already
invented the opposite to brainwashing—heartwashing. He has said:
"Blessed are the pure in heart, for they shall see God."[3]*
— Richard Wurmbrand
Romanian pastor persecuted for his faith

*E*lizabeth Franklin listened in silence as her classmates at Mountain View High School discussed *The Crucible,* an assigned book about the Salem witch trials. She had felt uneasy when she read it. The story about the horrible accusations and hangings made Christians seem really bad. Sure, the Puritans had made some cruel and irrational decisions back then. But all Puritans weren't like that, were they? It just didn't seem fair that her English teacher would use that one awful event to put down all of Christianity.

The discussion ended and the teacher told someone to close the door. Then he invited everyone to gather around his desk. He showed them a deck of tarot cards, held up one of the cards, and said, "Focus your energy on the card."

Elizabeth refused. She stepped back, found a place at the far end of the room, and sat down to wait and pray. Sensitized to occult dangers through years of Scripture reading and warnings from her parents, she refused to participate in the lesson on witchcraft.

Wayne and Jan Franklin were not surprised by Elizabeth's experience. They had seen the rising tide of occult teaching, and they had prepared their two daughters well.

Concerned about the spiritual safety of other students as well, they began to invite neighborhood families to join them in prayer. Eventually Jan helped form a local Mom's In Touch[4] group. Each week she meets for an hour with other moms committed to prayer for their children and schools. Month after month, God's answers encouraged them to keep trusting.

These praying moms are fighting for the spiritual safety of their children. They know that, without God's intervention, the national/international new-paradigm training and cradle-to-grave surveillance system will affect every American family, whether their children attend public, private, or home schools.

Laura Rogers, the courageous Missouri mother who first exposed the intrusive plans of Parents As Teachers, explains God's pattern for a healthy society. "In His infinite wisdom," she writes, "God established three main structures for society: the home/family, the church, and civil government."[5] To each He gave a specific set of responsibilities and corresponding authorities:

1. Home and family—the raising or training of the children. God gave parents both the responsibility and the authority to bring up their own children in the nurture and admonition (under the authority) of the Lord.

2. The church—spiritual guidance of the community. It has limited responsibility for training children. It's up to parents to exercise discernment, follow God's leading, and make wise choices on behalf of their children.

3. Civil government—enacting and enforcing laws and maintaining peace. It has no God-given right to force families to submit to antibiblical training. When the government usurps parental authority or when parents surrender that authority, they violate God's order. This violation leads to rampant immorality

social disorder, and totalitarian controls.[6] When the government opposes parents' rights to train their children to follow God, Christian parents can only say as Peter did, "We must obey God rather than men!" (Acts 5:29).

When the government controls the children, no one will be free. When earth-centered beliefs and global values become standards for graduation certificates (CIM), Christian children will become social outcasts. Painfully aware of these dangers, the Franklins formed the Citizens Alert Connection, a community forum to encourage and equip local parents. Their links to researchers across the country keep them in touch with nationwide plans as well as community strategies. From their home they encourage families to stand together against the forces of the paradigm shift. No longer can a local principal dismiss a parent's concern with the standard response: "You're the *only* one who has *ever* complained about this."

The Franklins model a Christian response that brings success. They may not turn the tide, but they demonstrate practical ways to bring families together, fight for what they believe, communicate vital facts, and show the kind of love only possible for those who follow God. Their action plan includes six vital steps:

- *Pray.* Jesus said, "Apart from me you can do nothing" (John 15:5).

- *Prepare yourself.* Before you can outfit your children for spiritual warfare, you need to know and apply everything God provides for spiritual victory.

- *Prepare your children.* Equip your children to face an increasingly hostile world in God's strength.

- *Play.* The fun times help keep the door open for serious talks.

- *Partnerships.* Work together, encouraging, helping, and informing each other.

- *Persuasion.* Inform and equip your community.

Pray!

"Pray continually; give thanks in all circumstances, for this is God's will for you in Christ Jesus" (1 Thessalonians 5:17,18). You have seen the plan for global oneness. Unless God turns the tide and restrains the spreading evil, Christians will be the persecuted outcasts of a totalitarian global society. Since the forces arrayed against us are far stronger than any of us can face in our own finite strength, we can't join the battle without prayer. Therefore:

- Pray that you and your children will have discernment to recognize deception, strength to follow truth, and faith to persevere through every kind of opposition.

- Pray for a devotion to God that will surpass all pressures to conform to a world that has turned from truth to myth.

- Pray that God will bring together those who love Him and want His best for their children.

- Pray that God will open the eyes of educators to the deceptions they are trained to teach.

- Praise God for the victory He promises those who follow Him. He says, "I send you out as sheep in the midst of wolves. Therefore be wise as serpents and harmless as doves" (Matthew 10:16). When we seek His wisdom to fight His battles in His way, we will win His victory in His time.

Prepare Yourself

We may never see the armies that assault God's people, but we are all engaged in a spiritual war. This war grows more intense each year as America drifts further away from her biblical foundations. Many people are blind to the current battles, for our "struggle is not against flesh and blood, but against the rulers, against the authorities, against the powers of this dark world and against the spiritual forces of evil. . . ."[7] There is no way we can resist those powers with mere human strength.

David, God's faithful shepherd-king, knew the secret of winning tough battles: *Trust in God's strength, not your own.* "The Lord is my rock, my fortress and my deliverer," he sang; "my God is my rock in whom I take refuge. He is my shield and the horn of my salvation, my stronghold. I call to the Lord, who is worthy of praise, and I am saved from my enemies" (Psalm 18:2,3).

We too can know God as our strength and deliverer. Using a soldier's armor as a visual aid, Ephesians 6:10-17 outlines the main steps to victory over our enemies. They include not only the demonic forces that attack us from the outside, but also inner enemies such as weakness, fear, discouragement, and anger—which Satan manipulates for his own destructive purposes. To win each battle, here is what you can do:

> . . . be strong in the Lord and in his mighty power. Put on the full armor of God so that you can take your stand against the devil's schemes. . . . Stand firm then, with the belt of truth buckled around your waist, with the breastplate of righteousness in place, and with your feet fitted with the readiness that comes from the gospel of peace. In addition to all this, take up the shield of faith, with which you can extinguish all the flaming arrows of the evil one. Take the helmet of salvation and the sword of the Spirit, which is the word of God (Ephesians 6:10-17).

This armor of God brings victory because it is far more than a protective covering. It is the very life of Jesus Christ Himself. "Put on the armor of light," wrote Paul in his letter to the Romans; ". . . clothe yourselves with the Lord Jesus Christ."[8] When you do, He becomes your hiding place and your shelter in the storm, just as He was to David. Hidden in Him, you can count on His victory, for He not only covers you as a shield but He also fills you with His life.

"I am the vine; you are the branches," said Jesus. "If a man remains *in me* and *I in him,* he will bear much fruit; apart from me you can do nothing" (John 15:5).

Since living in the safety of the armor means oneness with Jesus, we can expect to share His struggles as well as His peace. Remember, God has promised us victory in the midst of trials, not immunity from pain. So "do not be surprised at the painful trial you are suffering, as though something strange were happening to you. But rejoice that you participate in the sufferings of Christ" (1 Peter 4:12,13). Christian heroes who have been tortured for their faith continue to testify to the supernatural strength—even joy— that enables them to endure unthinkable pain. They affirm with Paul that—

> in all these things we are more than conquerors through him who loved us. For I am convinced that neither death nor life, neither angels nor demons, neither the present nor the future, nor any powers . . . will be able to separate us from the love of God that is in Christ Jesus our Lord (Romans 8:37-39).

This life in Christ begins with learning, affirming, and trusting in each part of the armor. The first part is *truth*— God's revelation of all that He *is* to us, all that He *has done* for us, and all that He *promises to do* for us in the days ahead. This enduring truth is written in the Bible, revealed by the Holy Spirit, and realized through Jesus Christ. It cuts through all the world's distortions, deceptions, and compromises. When you study, memorize, live, and follow truth, it enables you to see the world from God's high vantage point. Putting on the first piece of the armor means feeding on truth through daily Bible reading and making it part of yourself.

PARTS OF THE ARMOR	KNOW THE TRUTH ABOUT	KNOW AND AFFIRM KEY SCRIPTURES
Belt of truth	God	Deuteronomy 4:39; Psalm 23; 18:1-3
Breastplate of righteousness	Your personal righteousness	Romans 3:23,24; Galatians 2:20,21; Philippians 3:8-10
Sandals of peace	Inner peace and readiness	Romans 5:1; Ephesians 2:14; John 14:27; 16:33; 20:21
Shield of faith	Living by faith	Romans 4:18-21; Hebrews 11:1; 1 Peter 1:6,7
Helmet of salvation	Salvation through Christ today and forever	Each day Psalm 16; 23; Hebrews 1:3-6. For eternity: 2 Corinthians 4:16-18; 1 John 3:1-3
Sword of the Spirit, God's Word	Countering spiritual deception	Hebrews 4:12; Matthew 4:2-11; 1 Peter 3:15; Psalm 119:110-112

© 1996 Berit Kjos

To put on the full armor and enjoy a daily and eternal love-relationship with Jesus Christ, thank Him for what He has shown you in His Word. *Know* the Scriptures behind your prayer so that your words and faith are grounded in the authority of the Bible. (Some of those verses are listed in the chart above.) Then pray through each piece of armor. You can use the following prayer as an outline.

- *The belt of truth:* Thank You, my Lord, for showing me the *truth* about Yourself: Thank You for reminding me that You are the only God, the Creator of heaven and earth, the King of the universe, my Father who loves me, and my Shepherd who leads me. You are my wisdom, my counselor, my hope, and my strength. You are everything I need each day.

- *The breastplate of righteousness:* Thank You for showing me the truth about myself: that on my own I could never be good enough to live in Your presence. Thank You for taking my sins to the cross and offering me Your righteous life. Lord, show me any sin I need to confess right now, so that nothing will hinder me from being filled to overflowing with Your Spirit. [Take time for confession.] Thank You for forgiving me and for filling me with Your *righteous* life.

- *The sandals of peace:* Thank You for the *peace* You give me when I trust and follow You. Show me how to help others find that peace.

- *The shield of faith:* Thank You for helping me have *faith* in You. I choose to count on everything You have shown me about Yourself; and everything You have promised me in Your Word.

- *The helmet of salvation:* Thank You for promising me *salvation* both for today's battles and for all eternity.

- *The sword of the Spirit, the Word of God:* Thank You for the Scriptures You have given me to memorize. Please show me which one(s) You want me to use to cut through deceptions and gain Your victory in any battle I may face today.

Filled with His life, you are ready to equip your children. Now you can use each daily opportunity to establish in their minds a mental framework or worldview based on biblical *truth*. When they know God's Word and are trained to see reality from God's perspective, they too will recognize and resist deception.

Prepare Your Children

The educational net has been spread around the world in order to ensnare *all* children, including homeschoolers. The only safe place is in the arms of the Shepherd, so train your children "in the way [they] should go and when [they are] old, [they] will not depart from it" (Proverbs 22:6). Consider these practical suggestions.

1. *Let your family conversations communicate your trust in God.* Deuteronomy 6:6,7 reminds us to talk about God and His ways when we sit, walk, lie down, and get up. When your daily conversations demonstrate *your* confidence in God's faithfulness and your love for His Word, your children begin to see reality through the filter of truth. When you show your gratefulness for answered prayer and God's constant care, your children learn that God is more real than today's endless parade of counterfeits. Start early. If the Christian worldview is being formed in your children's minds, they will see New Age practices from God's perspective. But if games and cartoons with occult themes mold their worldview, they may reject truth, since it won't fit their perception of the supernatural.

2. *Help your children put on the full armor of God.* Read Ephesians 6:10-18 together with them, then review the chart at the end of Chapter 4. It shows why the parts of armor will expose and resist all the main lies of New Age and neopagan religions. Memorize Scriptures that show the truth about God and His righteousness, peace, faith, and salvation. Explain that these verses are Scripture *swords* that counter the main lies of the enemy. Remember, when children know the truth about God, they won't trust popular counterfeits. Knowing the source of their righteousness, they won't believe sanctification without the cross. Knowing God's way to peace and salvation, they won't choose occult paths.

Remind your children that the armor is not like a magic shield which they can casually slip on in order to be safe anywhere they want to go. One day my youngest son asked if he could see a popular movie with some friends.

"No, I'd rather you didn't," I told him.

"Why not?" he asked.

"Because it makes occultism seem both fun and right.

"But I'll put on the armor."

"It won't help. When you go somewhere that you shouldn't, you disobey God and lose the breastplate of righteousness. You're never safe if you go somewhere Jesus wouldn't want you to go."

David got the message and stayed home. He knew that by himself he was no match for occult forces. But with God he was on the winning side.

To help your children put on the armor, follow the Scriptures and outline shown in the previous section of this chapter. Make sure they *know* the Scriptures behind the prayer so that their words will be based on God's Word. Then pray through the pieces of the armor, simplifying each part to fit the ages of your children.

3. *Teach your children to examine today's culture in the light of God's Word.* As a family, read Isaiah 5:20 and compare it with today's values. Discuss Deuteronomy 18:9-13 and guard against the occult practices listed. Talk about the problems mentioned in 2 Timothy 3:1-13 and 4:2-5. Follow the guidelines in Ephesians 5:1-21. Thank God for the timeless relevance of the *whole* Bible.

4. *Discuss the seductive vision of global oneness.* The new education system means that children will be tested for global citizenship and work skills which involve "respect" for *all* lifestyles and openness toward New Age beliefs that supposedly promote unity. Help them understand the danger behind the tempting illusion of planetary harmony through occult "oneness." The following questions can help you get started:

- How does this vision line up with God's Word? (See John 17:14-16 and 2 Corinthians 6:14-18.)

- What happened in Old Testament days when God's people imitated their pagan neighbors? (See Deuteronomy 8:7-20 and Psalm 106.)

- What will happen to us if we conform to the beliefs of the world around us? (See Romans 1:18-32; 1 Corinthians 10:6-12; 2 Kings 17:7-22.)

- How can we live among pagans and still follow God without compromise? (See Galatians 2:20; Romans 12:1-3; 2 Corinthians 12:9,10.)

Throughout the Bible God promises to care for His people—those who trust and follow Him. In Old Testament days He told His people that they were different and special—set apart from all the rest. But their special privileges ended when they stopped reading and following God's Word. Proud of the power and prosperity God had given them, they ignored the Giver and mocked His truth. Like their pagan neighbors, they turned to other gods—and lost their uniqueness. Finally God allowed strong enemies to invade the land and enslave His people. The ancient Jewish historians, who carefully recorded the bad along with the good, explained:

> All this took place because the Israelites had sinned against the Lord their God. . . . They worshipped idols, though the Lord had said, "You shall not do this . . ." But they would not listen. . . . They imitated the nations around them although the Lord had ordered them, "Do not do as they do. . . ." They bowed down to all the starry hosts. . . . They practiced divination and sorcery. . . . So the Lord was very angry with Israel . . . and gave them into the hands of plunderers (2 Kings 17:7,12,14-20).

5. *Teach your children Scriptures that counter accusations.* God tells us to avoid corrupting influences, which is

difficult when New Age or neopagan classroom assignments require participation. Your children need to know
reassuring Scriptures when accused of violating the new
social standards. The following chart was adapted from
Under the Spell of Mother Earth:

ACCUSATION	WHEN PEOPLE SAY . . .	REMEMBER GOD'S TRUTH
Intolerant	"You should be more toler-ant of different beliefs and lifestyles."	**Ephesians 5:11** (cf. 5:3,11,15,17): "Have nothing to do with the fruitless deeds of darkness."
Judgmental	"You think we're sinners because we don't want your God."	**Romans 3:23** (cf. Isaiah 53:6): "All have sinned and fall short of the glory of God."
Arrogant	"You believe your religion is better than ours."	**John 14:6:** "Jesus said, 'No one comes to the Father except through me.'"
Narrow-minded	"You're not open to other spiritual traditions."	**Deuteronomy 4:39:** ". . . the Lord is God in heaven above and on the earth below. There is no other."

6. *Don't compromise.* Psalm 1:1 shows a downward pro-
gression that traps many children today.

The vast majority of students learn to—

- follow the counsel or advice of teachers and peers
  with contrary values;

- condone the beliefs and imitate the behavior of the
  crowd;

- join those who mock God and truth.

Compare those steps with the Scripture below:

Blessed is the man who does not—

- *walk* in the counsel of the wicked or
- *stand* in the way of sinners or
- *sit* in the seat of mockers.

But his delight is in the law of the Lord, and on his law he meditates day and night. He is like a tree planted by streams of water, which yields its fruit in season and whose leaf does not wither. Whatever he does prospers. . . . For the Lord watches over the way of the righteous, but the way of the wicked will perish (Psalm 1:1-4,6).

7. *Prepare your children to face persecution.* Through most of church history, persecution has been part of the normal Christian life. As Jesus told His disciples: "If they persecuted me, they will persecute you also" (John 15:20). The 200 years of religious freedom in America is an anomaly in the history of time, and it may soon end. When nations turn from truth to myth, persecution of nonconformists naturally replaces justice. First John 5:19 explains why Satan and his demonic forces hate God's people: "The whole world is under the control of the evil one." But for those who refuse to conform to the world's values, God will more than make up for the pain.

Persecution seems remote to most children. When they face it in their schools, many of them feel confused, hurt, and angry. To help them understand how God uses suffering to strengthen their faith, discuss Scriptures such as 2 Corinthians 1:3-9; 1 Peter 1:6,7; and 4:12-15. Remember that "it has been granted to you on behalf of Christ not only to believe on him but also to suffer for him" (Philippians 1:29).

To help your children appreciate the courage, faithfulness, and godly vision of past believers who were persecuted for their faith, you may want to read some books and stories together. All of us would be enriched by a deep look at the lives of biblical men and women who were willing to give their lives rather than betray or dishonor the God they loved: Joseph, Daniel, Esther, Ruth, Paul, and Stephen. Some of their stories have happy earthly endings, but many of the heroes and heroines in God's hall of fame died for the One they loved. (Look at Hebrews 11, especially the last two verses.) They and other giants in the faith have, throughout history, modeled an *eternal perspective* that puts far greater value on eternity with Jesus than on temporary riches here on earth.

"Blessed are you," said Jesus to His friends, "when people insult you, persecute you and falsely say all kinds of evil against you because of me. Rejoice and be glad, because great is your reward in heaven" (Matthew 5:11). Are you willing to walk with Jesus in the hard places here on earth so that you may share His happiness for all eternity?

Cathy Warncke, a teenager from Oregon, asked herself that question. Confident that her answer is yes, she says:

> When I consider the possibility of Christians being persecuted in this generation, it's a little frightening. But in a way it's also exciting and adventurous. Whenever I start feeling scared, the Lord reminds me that He's in control. He's planned it all from the beginning. He determined that I would be born and live in this age. He chose me in Christ before the foundation of the world, and He lives in me to accomplish His purpose for my life. I can wait and trust in Him, looking forward to the day when His work on earth is finished and I stand before Him complete and pure, able to truly know, love, and worship Him for eternity.[9]

8. *Share God's love with everyone.* Jesus provided the only way to oneness across cultural and racial barriers: the cross. Pray with your children that His life in them will touch the hearts of the needy in their school. When they

become His special missionaries, they won't become a mission field for the New Age.

Play with Your Children

Demonstrate the excitement of being God's children together. Sure, the warfare continues, but that's all the more reason to set aside plenty of time for family games, sports, reading, and other fun activities. Some, such as hiking and fishing, are great for relaxed, heart-to-heart communication. But when those are not viable options, an after-school snack of fresh cookies may work just as well.

Stand Together

The more opposition we face, the more we need to stand together, encourage each other, and demonstrate God's wisdom and love to others. The Greek word for both partnership and fellowship is *koinonia*. Whenever it refers to communion, community and intimate relationship, it is translated *fellowship*. When it means working together or joint participation, the word *partnership* may be used.

"I thank my God every time I remember you," wrote Paul. "In all my prayers for all of you, I always pray with joy because of your *partnership* in the gospel from the first day until now, being confident of this, that he who began a good work in you will carry it on to completion until the day of Christ Jesus" (Philippians 1:3-6).

Partnership means far more to Christians than to others. First, it should remind us that our *partnership* or *fellowship* is primarily with Jesus Christ,[10] our Lord Himself, who understands all the problems we face far better than we do. Second, it means fellowship with other believers who know Him and share His concerns. Pray that God will lead you to them. When we are joined together in a biblical unity based on His Word, inspired by

His love, and strengthened by His power, we are ready to reach out into our schools and community.

Persuade Other People

Help your community understand by sharing your information about our schools with parents, local newspapers, educators, pastors, business leaders, and everyone else that God puts in your path. These facts open doors to sharing our only real hope for peace and safety: Jesus Christ. He said, "As long as it is day, we must do the work of him who sent me. Night is coming, when no one can work" (John 9:4).

Many educators will hate you for resisting *their* plans for *your* children. Since Christian politeness and courtesies have faded in society along with moral standards, don't expect gentle criticism and polite discussion. Today, as in earlier times, human nature reigns without disciplined restraint, so be ready for slander, malicious vandalism, overt hatred and persecution. Some educators will ignore you, and some will hate you, but a few will believe and support you. Together in Christ, we may be able to slow the spreading tide of totalitarian controls and lengthen our time of freedom—if God so wills.

Consider these practical steps:

1. *Know the facts.* Some of the agencies and newsletters in operation at the time of this writing may have been replaced by the time you read this book. With that warning in mind, try to take advantage of the following sources of information:

- *Your state and county office of education.* At the time of this writing, your county office of education must make current frameworks and curricula available to parents upon request.

- *Other concerned parents and researchers.* Exchange information across the country. Since some states have implemented certain parts of the new system ahead of others, we need to share information across state lines. (To connect with distant researchers write to The Iowa Research Group, Inc., P.O. Box 17346, Des Moines, IA.) To keep up on monthly changes across the country, subscribe to the monthly magazine *Christian Conscience,* available at the above address.

2. *Be involved with your children's school.* Whether your children attend public or private schools, do your best to know what is happening in their classroom. If possible, help the teacher on a regular basis. Even so, the new classroom computer technology and individualized learning programs will hide many of the teaching strategies. In the end, your main source of information may be your own children and their peers, so take time for daily after-school talks. (Good snacks usually help.)

Remember, many of today's teachers are trained to be parent substitutes. They know strategies for making classroom discussions more intimate and revealing than do most parents. Many of their classroom group sessions end with the admonition, "Don't tell your parents!" According to your children's maturity, warn them that this could happen in their classroom. As simply as possible, explain to them the new goals of education. Help them to understand some of the deceptive tactics and misleading promises. Then, when it happens, they will recognize and resist the classroom strategies. You could compare these deceptions to the tempting promises made to Pinocchio and his friends: Come to Pleasure Island and play all day! No more drills and homework. Eat all the cake and ice cream you want.

Remember what happened? The boys turned into donkeys, just like the rest of the gullible children on Pleasure Island. They had become the frightened slaves in the tyrannical master's workforce. Pinocchio, who grew long ears and an embarrassing tail, barely escaped with his life.

Be careful that you don't yield to the new deceptive terminology used to bring parents into the planned community partnerships. Don't forget that the promising words used by the educational planners in your community are designed to win supporters, not tell the truth.

3. *Know who serves on your local school board.* Become familiar with their stand on key issues and be ready to share facts with them in a nonconfrontational way.

4. *Serve on local committees.* If that is not God's place for *you,* perhaps another member of your local team can serve on one of these: curriculum committee, school board, site council, or new community partnerships. But, as you saw in Chapter 7, these committees are usually led by a facilitator trained to ignore opposing voices in order to demonstrate consensus. So be wise—and careful.

5. *Avoid demeaning labels and emotional appeals.* While such dishonest and irrational tactics are often used in educational propaganda, we need to build our answers on factual foundations.

6. *Remember the enemy behind the scenes.* Our ultimate battle is not against teachers, principals, superintendents, or the national educational establishment. As you saw in Ephesians 6:12, the real battle rages in the spiritual realm ". . . against the authorities, against the powers of this dark world and against the spiritual forces of evil. . . ." Few change agents know whose purpose they serve. "Forgive them, for they do not know what they are doing" (Luke 23:34).

God tells us to "fight the good fight, holding on to faith and a good conscience" (1 Timothy 1:18,19). Our main weapons are truth, faith, love, and prayer. Perhaps you want to join a nationwide army of Christian parents and teachers who pray—counting on God's promises—each Friday for their children, schools, government, and nation. Many fast until 3 P.M. and call this special day each week the Fabulous Fasting Friday.

7. *Stand on God's victory promises.* Remember, as our world grows increasingly hostile to God and His truth, our

only safe place is in Christ. He doesn't promise to make us any more comfortable than He was here on earth, but He will make us "more than conquerors" when we choose to walk with Him. To find peace in the middle of the coming storms, memorize encouraging Scriptures like the one below. Make sure you and your children are ready to hold them up as the "swords of the Spirit" whenever the battle gets tough. Remember, with God you are on the winning side!

> Be strong and courageous. Do not be terrified; do not be discouraged, for the Lord your God will be with you wherever you go (Joshua 1:9).

SECTION A
Making a Difference

Anita Hoge

Anita Hoge, a native of Pennsylvania, is no stranger to concerned parents or to the educational establishment. While her story has encouraged thousands of parents across the country, it has also brought anxiety to the change agents who hoped to conceal their strategies until they accomplish their purpose. Anita's courageous search for answers to mystifying school practices have given us a glimpse of an educational process designed to conform all children to the new, politically correct version of "appropriate mental health."

Anita's journey will take you through a maze of white papers and technical documents and expose the true nature of contemporary education: social engineering. It will give you an inside look at the deceptive testing mechanism designed to measure the attitudes and values of our children and make sure every student will demonstrate the preplanned nonacademic "outcomes." Unwilling to give up in the face of overwhelming opposition, Anita has become a living demonstration of the hope that "one person can make a difference."

The Journey Begins

The journey began when my son as an eighth grader was given a "state assessment,"[1] supposedly to test academics. A four-year ordeal pitting an ordinary Pennsylvania housewife against the education elite followed.

The test was the Pennsylvania Educational Quality Assessment or EQA. My son said it was the "weirdest" test he had ever taken. One test question in the Career Awareness section asked, "The prospect of working most of my adult life depresses me." Possible answers: yes, no, or sometimes.[2]

A question in Citizenship presented this challenge: "A girl has a term paper due in several days. The book she needs most is not permitted to leave the library. If I were this girl I would SNEAK THE BOOK OUT OF THE LIBRARY when I knew (a) I would be late with my paper if I couldn't get the book. (b) I could return it without anyone knowing. (c) I didn't have time enough to complete my work in the library. The child was told to respond yes, maybe, or no.[3]

A question on tolerance asked, "Your sister wants to marry a person whose religion is much different from yours and your family." The possible answers were "I would feel very comfortable, comfortable, slightly uncomfortable, very uncomfortable.[4]

The controversy began when I was denied access to see the test my son had taken. I discovered after many months of research and continual follow-up that 370 of its questions "measured" the attitudes, values, beliefs, opinions, and home-life of the children. It had only 30 questions on math and 30 questions on reading. I followed the paper trail to Washington, DC, where I learned that the Pennsylvania test was connected to a national test called the National Assessment of Educational Progress or NAEP.[5] I also found that in the name of "educational reform," our trusted educators were de-emphasizing the main components of learning:

knowledge and comprehension, which were now called "lower order thinking skills."

I discovered that the Pennsylvania children were being used for psychological research for the federal government. The traditional method of teaching—directing students toward individual achievement and independent thinking—was not only being set aside but methodically replaced with psychological techniques. The new goals were taking our child "beyond text"[6]—beyond traditional understanding into a higher level of thinking called "higher order thinking skills" or "critical thinking skills and analysis." Children's attitudes, values, and beliefs would be tested, then molded, through behavior modification techniques. This new model of education trains teachers to view themselves as facilitators using behavior modification strategies to train students in group conformity.[7]

I learned that in order to conform a child to a specific government goal, the test must measure "the development of the whole child."[8] This meant that a sophisticated personality profile was needed to describe a child's social, emotional, intellectual, and behavioral development. It also meant that children were scored to a "minimum positive attitude"[9]—a term used to identify the level of change in attitude needed to meet government goals. Individual children were scored on their opinions and personality traits, or in scientific terms, "thresholds of compliance," "locus of control," or adaptability to change,[10] without the knowledge or consent of their parents.

The national objectives or standards tell us what information must be gathered about the controlling influences in a child's life. Was the child internally or externally motivated? Would he or she conform to group goals? To what extent would the student be willing to change his attitudes or values? What situation or factors will cause the child to comply with directives from authority figures?

Scientific analytical research[11] was done on the "scored data" to produce teacher methodology and specific validated national curriculum or software that would guide the process of conforming the child to the new global values. This "guinea pig" social experimentation continued for 20 years in Pennsylvania. Meanwhile, other states were developing other aspects of the overall planning, programming, and budgeting system (PPBS).[12]

Why Did the Government Want this Personal and Sensitive Information?

When I realized the state had lied to me about the tests, I determined to expose the entire process. In 1986 I filed a complaint against the Pennsylvania Department of Education. In 1990, after a four-year investigation by the U.S. Department of Education, the tests were stopped. The Pennsylvania EQA was withdrawn because of major privacy violations and violations of a federal law that protects children from psychological testing, treatment, and illegal psychological abuse.[13]

But NAEP, the national test, remains. So do all the test objectives that Pennsylvania children had validated for the NAEP "banks" of test items or questions. States use these test-item banks to design their own state assessments.[14] For example, if a state decides to test self-esteem, it can go to NAEP test-item banks to retrieve test questions that have received the "government stamp of approval," confident that those questions would measure the attitudes and values they are supposed to measure.

If you are shaking your head in disbelief at this point, I'm not surprised. The impossibility of any fair or objective standard for what a child must believe should cause mass objections and raise all kinds of questions: How can government score the attitudes of its citizens? What is happening to American freedom?

Although the EQA was stopped in Pennsylvania, almost every state was already preparing similar tests. The EQA was the national pilot for this huge social experiment, and as the rest of the nation followed in its wake, the same vague and subjective outcomes appeared in state after state.

Tracking and Privacy

In Pennsylvania, a child's belief system, not his academic knowledge, was tested. His score was permanently recorded on a computerized dossier[15] which could indicate his political leanings, personal problems, family finances, medical records, and personal background data. This information would then be merged into federal computer networks through the Department of Education, the Department of Labor, and the Department of Health and Human Services. This system was part of an electronic verification system that used a Social Security number[16] to identify the child for funding and services.[17]

Eventually, this information would be used in high-stake decision-making to control who would graduate, who would work, and what type of health care services the school would provide. The school would be used as a model for administering a national agenda.[18]

Unacceptable attitudes—as defined by the new, politically correct standards—would be changed through remediation. Children "at risk" of not meeting health or mental health outcomes would be identified and targeted through special education,[19] then funneled into a service delivery system of mental health rehabilitation funded through Medicaid.[20] Any child not meeting subjective and vague outcomes outlined by Outcome-Based Education (OBE) would be candidates for remediation.

To open the new system to *every* student, poverty guidelines were dropped. "All children" would be screened for eligibility in a seamless web of partnership activities. This complex plan would be piloted in Pennsylvania under a waiver for health care reform approved by the federal government.[21] Yet the state legislature, which represented the interests of parents, knew nothing about this subversive plan.

The Controversy Begins

In 1991, as the Pennsylvania State Board pushed education restructuring and reform onto its citizens, parents began to awaken to the deception. Confronted with new data that proved the academic failures of reform, they demanded immediate answers to their questions. The Board, preparing to vote for radical changes that would introduce OBE graduation requirements, refused to answer.

Public meetings cropped up all over the state as parents challenged bureaucrats who could not explain their own reform package. The debates turned into hotly contested battles about parents' rights, local control, psychological testing and manipulation, privacy, and social engineering. To defend their unproven, faulty, and illegal techniques, the change agents labeled parents "extremists" and began spouting slanderous "hate" remarks about religious people to create fear. This battle tactic has been effective in many states, but in Pennsylvania it made the bureaucrats look ridiculous.

A well-informed research group called "PARENTS" used common sense, facts, and knowledge to inform a public that now refuses to accept slogans or marketing techniques as sound educational practice. Consequently, education reform in Pennsylvania is now torn by controversy even as the state Department of Education continues to push the national agenda.

In the spring of 1995, the Pennsylvania House of Representatives passed Resolution 37[22] and created a committee to investigate the Department of Education, its nonacademic standards, and its Medicaid connection. The Resolution won by an astounding vote of 175 to 25—a grand victory for parents.[23] Now the select committee can use the hearings as a means to pursue legislation that protects children and families from state intrusion. The key: Return education to true local control.

How to Debate the Issues

As Outcome-Based Education becomes law in state after state, the National Education Goals legislated in Goals 2000 and Title I refine the process of ensuring that "ALL" children meet government goals in order to graduate. Outcome-Based Education (under any of its names) is designed around performance of specific behavioral outcomes controlled by the state graduation requirements. Children will be forced to meet the government outcomes in order to earn the Certificate of Initial Mastery. Without this credential, they will not graduate, get a job or go on to college.

To gain their Certificate of Initial Mastery, which was developed by **SCANS** under the Department of Labor during the Bush administration, students must master the "new basics." These are the SCANS standards, but they also include the same vague outcomes and personal qualities measured in the EQA, the NAEP, the New Standards Project,[24] and the planned goals of restructuring in the states.

I have devised five questions to debate the issues on values and attitudes that can guarantee your success in winning the fight against vague and subjective outcomes:

1) How do you measure that outcome? For example, if an outcome states, "All children must make ethical decisions, have honesty or integrity," what exactly will be measured? How do you measure a bias in a child in order to graduate? Must children be diagnosed? Will they be graded by observation or pencil and paper test? How will behavior be assessed?

2) How is that outcome scored or what is the standard? What behavior is "appropriate" and to what degree? For example, how much self-esteem is too much or not enough to graduate? Can government score the attitudes and values of its citizens?

3) Who decides what the standard will be? The state has extended their mandated graduation requirement or exit outcomes down to the individual child. This bypasses all local autonomy. What about locally elected school

directors —will they become obsolete? Are we talking about a state or government diploma?

4) How will my children be remediated? What are you going to do to my children to change them from here to here in their attitudes and values in order to graduate? How do you remediate ethical judgment, decision making, interpersonal skills, or environmental attitudes? What techniques will be used? What risks are involved to change personality? What justification does the state have to change my children's attitudes and values?

5) What if parent and state disagree on the standard or how it is measured in the classroom? Who has the ultimate authority over the child . . . parents or the state? What about privacy? Can parents opt out of a graduation requirement mandated by the state?

The challenge is upon us. The moral upbringing of our children is being taken from us. The STATE is moving in.

The parents in Pennsylvania believe that it will be parents who will make the decisions regarding their children . . . not the government. We believe in the basic principles that are guaranteed to us. We stand by those principles and invite others to stand with us by providing vital information to anyone who wants to protect their children and our future.

Our children belong to us. We must take a stand.

Remember, you can make a difference, too.

SECTION B

SCANS

Outcome-Based Education's School-to-Work Manual

Pamela Hobbs Hoffecker
Recognized OBE authority

June 16, 1994. 7:30 PM. Connie Chung's "Eye on America" camera crew focuses on high school sophomores parading across Oregon's Cottage Grove High School stage. Students who proved they mastered Outcome-Based Education's (OBE's) outcomes are handed a Certificate of Initial Mastery (CIM)—OBE's new "diploma."

Earlier that day, CBS-TV had filmed more than 100 people protesting. "Frankly, I find it difficult to be proud of this piece of paper [the CIM]," said tenth-grader Nicole Doggett, "because I did not receive the education I deserved."[1]

Another student, Renee Cook, told reporters that although outcome skills sound good, they're "hung up on political correctness. Fundamentals such as reading and writing are no longer being taught." Grades are eliminated, except *A*, *B*, and *I.P.* (*In Progress*). Renee quoted a teacher who said he was only teaching his students one-fourth of his normal curriculum.[2]

One student's mother, Janice Kincaid, explained to the producer of "Eye on America" that by 1996-1997 all Oregon schools must abandon the old system of awarding diplomas based on the accumulation of 22 course credits. OBE reform mandates that every student must earn a Certificate of Initial Mastery based on 11 outcomes such as "work with others on team projects" and "understand diversity."[3]

In 1991, *Education Week* headlines warned, "Oregon Bill [creating the CIM] Would End Traditional Schooling After the Tenth Grade."[4] Since then, like a summer forest fire, the CIM has been silently flashing across America. Today in Pennsylvania, the Certificate of Initial Mastery is called CAP (Career and Academic Passport); Mississippi calls it Certificate of Employability; Indiana's name is Gateway Certificate; in Maine it's CCM (Common Core of Mastery); Massachusetts legislated a Competency Determination; and Washington mandates a Certificate of Mastery.[5]

"Would I sound too negative," Mrs. Kincaid shyly asked the "Eye on America" producer, "to say on camera that my daughter—who received a CIM with a 4.0 (straight A) average—didn't even know the president who freed the slaves was Abraham Lincoln?"

"That's dynamite. Say it!" replied the concerned producer. "I want this to be a wake-up call to America."[6]

Wake Up, America

But is America waking up? No.

You probably never heard of the SCANS with its Certificate of Initial Mastery. Yet, it's no secret. Who is pushing this rapidly spreading "OBE diploma" idea? The U.S. Department of Labor. That's right. *It's federal.* And it's from *labor,* not education. The Labor Department published manuals for schools called SCANS (Secretary's Commission on Achieving Necessary Skills), which say, "It is society's *obligation* to provide each student with multiple opportunities to achieve the CIM" (emphasis added).[7]

In other words, Labor's SCANS manual tells American schools about "reinventing K-12 education"[8] around one "universally" recognized standard—a Certificate of Initial Mastery.[9] Why? To develop "human resources."[10] That's dangerous. When labor tells schools how to educate, then business becomes the customer, parents are demoted to partners, and children are seen as human resources—commodities, like coal.

SCANS Scam

This manual tells educators, "The Federal Government should continue to bridge the gap between school and the high-performance workplace, by advancing the SCANS agenda."[11] Besides the Certificate of Initial Mastery, SCANS recommends:

1. *"Teachers and students . . . change their traditional roles."* Teachers become coaches, while technology "dispenses information" and "monitors" learning.[12]

Objection: Teachers—not technology—should teach. Allowing technology to teach is experimental, pricey, and potentially dangerous. "Precious little research on their [computers as instructors] effectiveness has been done," says a Senior Fellow at Colorado's Independence Institute. He adds, "And what little there is suggests caution."[13]

Outcome-based education requires both retesting and moving students at an individual pace. Proposed plans include tying each student to a computer where individualized programs will serve up "Learning Nuggets." To create individual lesson plans, the computer will access "biographical data, assessment criteria, [and] learning styles" on each pupil.[14]

Learning Nuggets access a youngster's learning style (background, values, and how he or she learns). Then it determines the most efficient way to change behavior and serves it back to the child.

"Can Computers Teach Values?" an article in *Educational Leadership,* states, "The computer is ideally suited to the role of facilitator in values education."[15] Psychologist

B.F. Skinner, an early OBE architect,[16] called educational computers "teaching machines." And he said, "What we need is a technology of behavior"[17]—a systematic and scientific program to alter the nature of man.[18]

And what will this shift from human-teachers to machine-teachers cost? SCANS projects a one-year technology budget for 1400 students would total $2,100,000.[19]

2. *"Schools . . . reinvent themselves to teach the* **SCANS competencies.***"*[20]

Objection: This is workforce education. It's primarily attitudinal, not academic. It will create sociable, compliant workers. But will it produce individualists or poets? Look at some required SCANS competencies:

- Participates as a member of a team
- Negotiates to arrive at a decision
- Works with cultural diversity
- Mental visualization
- Self-esteem
- Decision making
- Integrity/Honesty
- Sociability

Many states such as Wisconsin, Florida, and Oregon admit their outcomes are from these exact attitudinal SCANS competencies.

Why does OBE shift away from academics into attitudes? One of the SCANS Commissioners, Thomas G. Sticht, shed light on that question in 1987 when he said:

> What may be crucial . . . is the dependability of a labor force and how well it can be managed and trained—not its general education level, although a small cadre of highly educated creative people is

essential to innovation and growth. Ending discrimination and *changing values* are probably *more important than reading* in moving low-income families into the middle class (emphasis added).[21]

3. *Implement the three P's: student projects, portfolios, and performances.*[22]

Objection: The three P's can't accurately measure the three R's. But they can assess attitudes—how students feel about birth control, homosexuality, or finiteness of the environment. OBE portfolios are stuffed with information proving a child has met OBE outcomes. That's how the Oregon students mentioned in this chapter qualified for their CIM. They presented portfolios to a "Board of Review." However, unlike traditional tests with right and wrong answers, the grading of portfolios is subjective. A well-researched Rand Corporation study of portfolio scoring called it "unreliable."[23]

In Pennsylvania, an OBE school exchanged final and midterm exams for projects and performances. In humanities, one sophomore glued sugar cubes together to form a pyramid. Another student received a grade for juggling.

4. *Students follow "a single track, until they are about 16."*[24]

Objection: The death of "general education" will track young people into career choices too early. In Oregon, as soon as the CIM is earned, students must choose among six occupational paths. Should a child be forced to decide his or her career at age 16? A *Newsweek* article calls the new tracking system "undemocratic."[25]

5. *A cumulative resume [report card].* Beginning in middle school, this resume would follow students throughout school—and into their working place.

Objection: Page 65 of the SCANS displays a hypothetical resume/report card for Jane Smith (age 19). Her resume lists Jane's workplace skills and the proficiency level she mastered. In "honesty" Jane earned only a 6. But she scored a perfect 10 in "self-esteem" and "sociability." How do you test, score, and retest these personal qualities? What business would hire Jane with only a 6 in honesty?

This resume—a prototype for all schools—also shows whether a student has earned the CIM. Although SCANS states that "most students will earn their certificate of initial mastery by age 16,"[27] the hypothetical Jane Smith has only earned *300* points out of a required *500*.[28] Jane, at age 19, is still in tenth grade.

According to Hillary Rodham Clinton, "Possession of the certificate [of Initial Mastery] would qualify the student to choose among going to work, entering a college prep program, or studying for a Technological and Professional Certificate."[29] Where does that leave Jane Smith? What message is SCANS giving Americans?

6. *"WORKLINK, an electronic information system linking local schools and employers."*[30]

Objection: Keep in mind that "Jane Smith" would have a hypothetical WORKLINK resume. The *New York Times* reports that China keeps a resume/file, called a *dangan,* on citizens. This resume/file starts in elementary school and "shadows the person throughout life." It moves directly from school to employer. "The *dangan* contains political evaluations that affect career prospects and permission to leave the country."[31]

Today, in New Jersey, 40 districts now use the WORK-LINK system. It includes "confidential teacher ratings of work habits."[32] How secure is the information highway? Should a cumulative resume follow American citizens?

Just a Fad?

Lest you think all of the above is simply an education fad, consider:

• Education is buying it. OBE schools throughout the country parrot much of the SCANS report, verbatim. One major education magazine calls SCANS the "most important document to come out of the federal government since the Bill of Rights."[33]

• Non-profit organizations, like the Carnegie Foundation, are buying it. One newsletter states that the primary job of schools is to "enable all students to attain the CIM. Anything else is a distraction, or worse, a hindrance."[34]

• Business is buying it. A report by the Business Coalition, whose scope of members includes the National Alliance of Business, the Business Roundtable, and all U.S. Chambers of Commerce, says, "SCANS was correct." It says that SCANS workplace know-how (including the CIM concept) will produce "a more complete human being."[35]

But are parents buying it? They're the largest stakeholder in education. And ninety-six percent want more emphasis on reading, writing, math and science.[36]

Speaking for that majority, Virginia A. Miller, researcher for Public Education Network and mother, explains, "I don't like labor telling us how to 'reinvent' grades K-12. . . . SCANS directives shift the mission of schools from educating thinkers to training workers." Mrs. Miller refers to a *Wall Street Journal* article which pointed out that under China's centrally planned economy, the State assigned students jobs—for life. Instead of teaching students how to think, they taught children what to think.[37]

CBS coverage on the CIM ended with producer Wyatt Andrews concluding, "Many Cottage Grove parents worry their children were used more like guinea pigs than pioneers. Which is why so many of these pioneers [students] want the expedition turned around."[38]

SECTION C

Chronology of Events
Leading to International Education

If you have read the preceding chapters, you will recognize the three themes flowing through the next few pages:

- Purge the beliefs, values, individualism, independence, and free enterprise that made this nation unique.

- Promote global beliefs and a **collective** society where individual rights must yield to the "rights" of a "greater whole."

- Implement the psychosocial strategies of Mastery Learning to modify beliefs and behavior to match the needs of a global economy.

The massive effort to accomplish these three goals through public education has made a difference; America has changed. We were once "a nation under God, indivisible, with liberty and justice for all." We have now become a divided nation with many gods and eroding liberties for those who refuse to conform. The seeds for this transformation were planted long ago, but few people saw the warning signs. Now that the evidence is too profuse to deny, it may be too late to stop the process. I hope not. Perhaps this chronology will help you persuade others to seek truth and freedom, not myths and illusions.

As you read, notice the powerful people, organizations, and foundations that inspire, plan, and fund the transformation. Follow their names and see their links to other groups. By the time you reach the eighties, the names will become more familiar: President Bush, Lamar Alexander, President Clinton, Ted Turner. . . .

I want to thank Dr. Dennis Laurence Cuddy, former Senior Associate in the U.S. Department of Education, for providing most of the following quotations from his extensive *Chronology of Education*.[1] I also thank Charlotte Iserbyt, former official with the U.S. Department of Education, for her many contributions and her concluding summary. These two discerning educators noticed the trend toward internationalism long before most of us sensed the danger.

• • •

1905. The Carnegie Foundation for the Advancement of Teaching (CFAT) was founded. Together with other Carnegie organizations, it has been a major promoter and funder of socialistic, global education projects.

1919. The Institute of International Education was established with a grant from the Carnegie Endowment for International Peace. Edward R. Murrow became the IIE's Assistant Director and John Dewey served on its National Advisory Council.[2]

1933. John Dewey, "father of progressive education" and honorary president of the National Education Association (NEA), coauthored the Humanist Manifesto I. Its introduction warned against identifying "religion" with existing doctrines which "are powerless to solve the problems of human living in the Twentieth Century. . . . Any religion that can hope to be a synthesizing and dynamic force for today must be shaped for the needs of this age."[3]

1934. National Education Association (NEA) former Executive Secretary Willard Givens warned that ". . . all of us, including the 'owners,' must be subjected to a large degree of social control. . . .

An equitable distribution of income will be sought. . . . the major function of the school is the social orientation of the individual. It must seek to give him understanding of the transition to a new social order."[4]

1934. The Carnegie Corporation funded the American Historical Association's Report of the Commission on Social Studies. Like most of today's social studies curricula, the report called for a shift from free enterprise to collectivism:

> . . . the age of individualism and laissez faire in econ-omy and government is closing and . . . a new age of collectivism is emerging. . . . It may involve the limiting or supplanting of private property by public property or it may entail the preservation of private property, extended and distributed among the masses . . . Almost certainly it will involve a larger measure of compulsory as well as voluntary cooperation of citizens in the context of the complex national economy, a corresponding enlargement of the functions of government, and an increasing state intervention in fundamental branches of economy previously left to individual discretion and initiative. . . . [5]

1942. The editor of the *NEA Journal*, J. Elmer Morgan, wrote an editorial titled "The United Peoples of the World." In it he explained a world government's need for an educational branch, a world system of money and credit, a world police force, "a world bill of rights and duties."[6]

1946. In his NEA editorial, "The Teacher and World Government," J. Elmer Morgan, wrote, "In the struggle to establish an adequate world government, the teacher . . . can do much to prepare the hearts and minds of children. . . . At the very top of all the agencies which will assure the coming of world government must stand the school, the teacher, and the organized profession."[7]

1946. Five decades ago, in February 1946, Canadian psychiatrist and World War II General Brock Chisholm, M.D., head of the World Health Organization (WHO), promoted the behavior modification processes now used in our schools. Compare *his* vision with today's Mastery Learning (Chapter 3) and planned control of the family (Chapter 7):

> We have swallowed all manner of poisonous certainties fed us by our parents, our Sunday and day school teachers. . . . The results are frustration, inferiority, neurosis and inability to . . . make the world fit to live in.
>
> The re-interpretation and eventually eradication of the concept of right and wrong which has been the basis of child training . . . these are the belated objectives of practically all effective psychotherapy. . . .
>
> Psychology and sociology . . . the sciences of living, should be . . . taught to all children in primary and secondary schools, while the study of such things as trigonometry, Latin, religions and others of specialist concern should be left to universities. Only so . . . can we help our children carry their responsibilities as world citizens. . . .
>
> . . . it has long been generally accepted that parents have a perfect right to impose any points of view, any lies or fears, superstitions, prejudices, hates, or faith on their defenseless children. It is, however, only recently that it has become a matter of certain knowledge that these things cause neuroses. . . .
>
> Surely the training of children in homes and schools should be of at least as great public concern as are their vaccination . . . for their own protection and that of other people. . . . [Individuals with] guilts, fears, inferiorities, are certain to project their hates on to others. . . . Any such reaction now becomes a dangerous threat to the whole world. For the very survival of the human race, world understanding, tolerance and forbearance have become absolutely essential. We must be prepared to sacrifice much. . . . Whatever the cost, we must learn to live in friendliness and peace. . . . putting aside the mistaken old ways of our elders if that is possible. If it cannot be done gently, it may have to be done roughly or even violently. . . .[8]

1948. The NEA, funded in part by the Carnegie Corporation, produced a set of international guidelines called *Education for*

International Understanding in American Schools—Suggestions and Recommendations. It included this statement:

> The idea has become established that the preservation of international peace and order may require that force be used to compel a nation to conduct its affairs within the framework of an established world system. The most modern expression of this doctrine of collective security is in the United Nations Charter. . . . Many persons believe that enduring peace cannot be achieved so long as the nation-state system continues as at present constituted. It is a system of international anarchy.[9]

1962. An editorial in the *Chicago Sun-Times* gave an insightful glimpse into the NEA's plan and power: "For control—real control over the Nation's children—is being shifted rapidly to the NEA. That organization has about completed the job of cartelizing public school education under its own cartel. . . . It is extending that control over colleges and universities. In the NEA scheme of things it will be a simple matter to extend control over whatever Washington agency handles the funds."[10]

1965. The U.S. Congress passed the federal Elementary and Secondary Education Act (ESEA). Months later, it decided to fund *Citizens for the 21st Century,* a book by UCLA Professor John Goodlad. This respected leader in international education wrote,

> Although the conduct of education and especially the clientele have changed . . . the school is perceived very much as it was then: a partitioned box where boys and girls come to sit still for six hours a day and to be told about some fragmentary pieces of "knowledge" thought to reflect the rudiments of their "culture." This image must be shattered, violently if necessary—and forever. The future of mankind may rest upon it.[11]

1968. Professor John Goodlad reported that Professor Benjamin Bloom [called Father of OBE] "was invited by UNESCO in 1968 to submit a proposal for a six- to nine-week training program which would partially fulfill recommendations made at UNESCO's Moscow meeting dealing with the formation of national centers for curriculum development and research. . . ." Bloom's "program was ultimately approved by the UNESCO General Council. . . ."[12]

1970. The Association for Supervision and Curriculum Development (ASCD), the curriculum arm of the NEA, published *To Nurture Humaneness: Commitment for the '70's.* The visionary statements of its authors are coming true in our times:

> The old order is passing. . . . The controls of the past were sacred. . . . Social controls cannot be left to blind chance and unplanned change—usually attributed to God. Man must be the builder of new forms of social organizations. . . . Here education must play a stellar role.[13] (Dan W. Dodson, Professor of Educational Sociology at New York University).
>
> The school will need to be supplemented by neighborhood family centers which provide infant care and developmental activity. . . . Education may well begin at birth in cooperative family centers[14] (Francis Chase, Professor Emeritus of the University of Chicago).
>
> Many daily decisions and value judgments now made by the individual will soon be made for him. . . . How to plan for one's children's education will be partially taken out of his hands[15] (John Loughary, Professor of Education at the University of Oregon).
>
> Vital questions of values, beliefs, feelings, emotions and human interrelationships in all forms must be integral parts of the curriculum[16] (Arthur Combs, Professor of Education at the University of Florida).

1973. Global Education Associates (GEA) was founded. A publicity brochure for its 1989 conference at Wichita State University described it as "an international network of men and women in over 70 countries who collaborate in research and educational programs aimed at advancing world peace and security, cooperative economic development, human rights and ecological sustainability." That may sound good, but the book *Toward a Human World Order,* written by GEA founders Gerald and Patricia Mische a few years later, put their noble intentions into the new-paradigm context of a world government and global socialism. "It examines the strait-jacket of the present nation-state system and . . . explores world order alternatives. . . ."[17]

1974. Alvin Toffler (Newt Gingrich's mentor), Willard Wirtz, and other futurists wrote a report issued by the Institute for Chief State School Officers and titled "Man, Education, and Society in the Year 2000." Other CSSO participants were George Bush, James Baker, and Edmund de Rothschild. Funded by HEW's Office of Education, the report concluded that "the 50 states should organize a commission to establish the values that are significant in approaching problems (e.g., population) that must be faced in the future." The summary explained that—

> The home, the church and the school cannot be effective maintainers [of society] since the future cannot be predicted. . . . The traditional cluster of knowledge, skills, values and concepts will not help our young face the future in their private life, the international situation. . . . Perhaps there is a need for the clarification of new values needed to solve future problems.[18]

1976. Phi Delta Kappan printed "America's Next 25 Years: Some Implications for Education" by Harold Shane, Project Director for the NEA Bicentennial Committee. Notice that Shane used the same buzzwords that characterize Outcome-Based Education today:

> Rather than adding my voice to those who urge us to go "back to basics" I would argue that we need to move ahead to the *new* basics . . . the arts of compromise and reconciliation, of consensus building, and of planning for interdependence, a command of these talents becomes "basic.". . . As young people mature, we must help them develop . . . a service ethic which is geared toward the real world . . . the global servant concept in which we will educate our young for planetary service and eventually for some form of world citizenship.[19]

1976. The Russian book *The Scientific and Technological Revolution and the Revolution in Education,* translated and imported to the United States, helped lay the foundation for the philosophy behind Outcome-Based Education. Its cover jacket explains that the book "examines the fundamental directions that the revolution in education will take: introduction of teaching machines, instruction from a younger age, linking instruction with productive labor, 'continuous' education. . . . Under socialism, education has become not only the personal affair of every individual, but also a concern of society as a whole." In the book, Vladimir Turchenko wrote:

> One of the most important functions of education today is . . . the preparation of a skilled labour force for the national economy. . . . A second task . . . is to *ensure the socialisation of the younger generation.* . . . A child at the moment of birth is but a biological organism that turns into a person . . . [through] socialisation. . . . Actualisation [of education] involves shifting the focus of instruction from memorisation to teaching how to think. . . . In many countries, practical steps are being taken to begin education from earliest childhood. . . . The upbringing of the younger generation will become the affair of all.[20]

1978. According to *Project Global 2000: Planning for a New Century,* "Robert Muller and Margaret Mead challenged the people of the world to prepare for the year 2000 by a 'worldwide collaborative process of unparalleled thinking, education and planning for a just and sustainable human world order.'"[21]

1981. Together, the UNESCO, the World Bank, and the Office of Economic Cooperation and Development (OECD) were researching *Critical Thinking Skills.* (You may want to review the true meaning of Critical Thinking.) The World Bank planned to "increase the Bank's lending for education and training to about $900 million a year."[22]

1981. Professor Benjamin Bloom explained that the International Association for Evaluation of Educational Achievement (IAEEA) "is an organization of 22 national research centers which are engaged in the study of education. This group has been concerned with the use of international tests. . . . The evaluation instruments also represent an international consensus on the knowledge and objectives most worth learning."23

1983. The Institute for 21st Century Studies was founded by Gerald O. Barney, ex-director of the U.S. Government's Global 2000 Report (President Carter, 1980) and funded by the Rockefellers, the World Bank, and UNESCO. Its mission is "to provide support for the growing international network of 21st Century Study teams," and to "engage participation of communities of education and others . . . in *exploring alternative national futures* . . . examining education and other key areas . . . adopting a global perspective."24

1984. The Robert Muller School in Texas, which uses Muller's World Core Curriculum, was accredited by the Southern Association of Colleges, despite Muller's acknowledgment that his philosophy is based on "the teachings set forth in the books of Alice Bailey by [her spirit guide] the Tibetan teacher, Djwhal Khul." The review team "was so impressed with the Robert Muller School that they recommended that information of the school's educational processes be shared with educators everywhere as much as possible."25

1985. The New Age/globalist book *New Genesis: Shaping a Global Spirituality* by Robert Muller, who directed the U.N.'s powerful Economic and Social Council, was published. Within a year it would influence many leading educators around the world.

1985. The U.S. Department of State gave the Carnegie Corporation "authority to negotiate with the Soviet Academy of Sciences, which is known to be an intelligence-gathering arm of the KGB, regarding 'curriculum development and the restructuring of American education.'"26

1985. At a 12-nation international-curriculum symposium held in the Netherlands in November, Gordon Cawelti, President of the Association for Supervision and Curriculum Development (ASCD), the curriculum arm of the powerful NEA, urged representatives of ten other Western nations and Japan to develop a "world core curriculum" built on knowledge that will ensure "peaceful and cooperative existence among the human species on this planet." It would be based on "proposals put forth by Robert Muller, Assistant Secretary-General of the United Nations, in his recent book *New Genesis: Shaping a Global Spirituality.*"[27]

1987. Robert Muller was one of the "distinguished lecturers" at ASCD's 42nd Annual Conference and Exhibit Show, "COLLABO-RATION." Muller's topic: "Government and Global Influences on Educational Policy."[28]

1987. In a *Washington Post* article titled "Experts Say Too Much Is Read into Illiteracy Crisis," Willis Harman and Thomas Sticht (Senior Scientist, Applied Behavioral and Cognitive Sciences, Inc., San Diego, and a member of SCANS: Secretary's Commission on Achieving Necessary Skills) explain that—

> many companies have moved operations to places with cheap, relatively poorly educated labor. What may be crucial, they say, is the dependability of a labor force and how well it can be managed and trained—not its general educational level, although a small cadre of highly educated creative people are essential to innovation and growth. Ending discrimination and changing values are probably more important than reading in moving low income families into the middle class.[29]

1987. Among the notable members of the Study Commission on Global Education were (then) Governor Bill Clinton, AFT president Albert Shanker, Professor John Goodlad, CFAT (Carnegie Foundation for the Advancement of Teaching) President Ernest Boyer, and Frank Newman, president of the Education Commission of the States. (In 1995, Newman's commission plays a central role in the implementation of Outcome-Based Education.) Together they prepared a report titled *The United States Prepares for Its Future: Global Perspectives in Education.* In the Foreword to the report, New Age networker Harlan Cleveland, author of *The Third Try at World Order,* wrote:

> A dozen years ago . . . teaching and learning "in global perspective" was still exotic doctrine, threatening the ortho-doxies of those who still thought of American citizenship as

an amalgam of American history, American geography, American lifestyles and American ideas. . . . It now seems almost conventional to speak of American citizenship in the same breath with international interdependence . . . and the planetary environment.[30]

1988. At a Soviet-American Citizens' Summit during February 1-5, the education task force recommended that the NEA "guide a global computer program." New Ager Barbara Marx Hubbard was one of the summit organizers.[31]

1988. Ted Turner and Robert Muller shared a platform at the Peace Through Education Conference in Arlington, Texas, sponsored by United Nations University for Peace and the Robert Muller School.[32]

1989. Robert Muller spoke at the ASCD's 44th Annual Conference in Florida during March 10-14. Title: "Educating the Global Citizen: Illuminating the Issues."[33]

1989. Eugene, Oregon, School District 4J published its "Integrated Curriculum K-5" in July. Page 11 in this public school curriculum acknowledged that "the three curriculum strands are adapted from the World Core Curriculum by Robert Muller. . . ."

1989. UNESCO's Peace Education Prize was awarded to Robert Muller on August 7.

1989. President Bush called the nation's governors together in September. Education secretary Lamar Alexander, together with governors Bill Clinton and Richard Riley and others, planned the six goals of America 2000.

1989. Speaking at the Governors' Conference on Education in November, Shirley McCune, Senior Director with MCREL (Mid-continent Regional Educational Laboratory, which develops curriculum), said:

> What's happening in America today . . . is a total transformation of our society. We have moved into a new era. . . .

I'm not sure we have really begun to comprehend . . . the incredible amount of organizational restructuring and human resource development restructuring. . . .

What the revolution has been in curriculum is that we no longer are teaching facts to children. . . . [34]

1990. In *The Keys of This Blood: The Struggle for World Dominion,* Malachi Martin described the transnationalists' goal that "ideally the same textbooks should be used all over the world in both the hard sciences and the soft curricula. And sure enough, a concrete initiative in this direction has been under way for some years now, undertaken by Informatik, a Moscow-based educational organization, and the Carnegie Endowment Fund. . . ." Martin then explained the new values they will promote:

> "Good" will no longer be burdened with a moral or religious coloring. "Good" will simply be synonymous with "global." Else, what's an education for? . . . The emphasis is on homogeneity of minds, on the creation and nourishing of a truly global mentality. . . . We must all become little Transnationalists.[35]

1990. The "flagship effort of the new spirit of sharing in education" became reality at the WCEFA (The World Conference on Education for All) in Jomtien, Thailand, during March 5-9. Organized by UNESCO, UNICEF, World Bank, and other international agents, it established six goals that matched the six goals of America 2000. Echoing promotional literature for America 2000/Goals 2000, the follow-up promotion indicated that the strategies for meeting these goals must be prepared in one package "by year 2000," for they "cannot be implemented successfully on a piecemeal basis."[36]

1990. Project Global 2000 was founded by Global Education Associates (see 1973) in response to the 1978 challenge by Robert Muller and Margaret Mead to prepare for the year 2000 by "a world-wide collaborative process of unparalleled thinking, education and planning for a just and sustainable human world order. . . ." It is made up of "sixteen leading international non-governmental organizations and four United Nations Agencies" which work together to establish "Transcultural Dialogue, a Holistic Perspective; A Spiritual Renaissance; Environmental Security; Economic Security and Disarmament."[37]

Linking the U.S. Goals 2000 to the international Global 2000, Dennis Cuddy explains that—

> its Education Council works with educators to integrate World Order Perspectives into [American] curriculum and teacher education. UNESCO and UNICEF, which are Partners with Global 2000, are putting into action the initiatives developed at the World Conference on Education for All [WCEFA], the largest educational conference ever held. . . . It is very evident that Goals 2000 is only one phase leading to Project Global 2000.[38]

1990. A cross-section of the educational community gathered in Chicago to explore holistic education, resulting in the formation of GATE (Global Alliance for Transforming Education), with Phil Gang as Executive Director and Dorothy Maver on the Steering Committee. In 1991, GATE printed *Education 2000: A Holistic Perspective,* which emphasizes multiple intelligences, experiential learning and other facets of Outcome-Based Education. The document calls for "Educating for Participatory Democracy . . . for Global Citizenship . . . for Earth Literacy. . . and Spirituality. . . ."[39]

GATE now networks with educators across the country, various United Nations organizations, government leaders, citizen groups for social change, the media, and others.

1990. Dorothy Maver, a Steering Committee member of GATE, presented a workshop in Sydney, Australia, in October titled, "Creative Esoteric Education." She spoke of "bridging esoteric principles into mainstream education. There's a paradigm shift happening in education . . . linking heart and mind. . . . It is the process and not the content that is most important."[40]

Maver is a founder of the Seven Ray Institute, and an adjunct faculty member of Kean College in New Jersey. She is Co-Director for the Institute for Visionary Leadership and is serving on the design team of the U.N.'s Global Education Program for Peace and Universal Responsibility, sponsored by Robert Muller's University for Peace.

1991. In his introduction to America 2000, Lamar Alexander wrote, "On April 18, 1991, President Bush announced America 2000: An Education Strategy. It is a bold, comprehensive, and long-range plan to move every community in America toward the National Education Goals adopted by the President and the Governors last year." President Bush, who often mentions "new world order," called for "new schools for a new world" in his announcement.[41]

1991. "We've got to revolutionize education. The old answers are not good enough anymore,"[42] President Bush told students in May at the Saturn School of Tomorrow in St. Paul, Minnesota, a national model for educational innovation which proved to be a disaster academically.

1991. At the request of President Bush on July 8, American business leaders formed the New American Schools Development Corporation (NASDC), a private, nonprofit, nonpartisan organization. Its Board of Directors included seven Council on Foreign Relations members and five members of the Committee for Economic Development.[43]

"The private sector is charging ahead, helping clear the way for reform,"[44] said Education Secretary Lamar Alexander three years later. (One of the ways privatization can "clear the way" is by avoiding the accountability due elected officials.) As Dr. Hamburg, chief negotiator for the Soviet exchange admitted, "privately endowed foundations can operate in areas government may prefer to avoid."[45]

1991. Referring to Oregon's controversial School-to-Work legislation, Lamar Alexander said on a visit to the model state in August, "Oregon has taken a pioneering step, and America will be watching and learning."[46]

What would America be learning? The Oregon Education Act for the 21st Century (HB 3565) decreed that all tenth-grade students must pass an outcome-based test to earn their Certificate of Initial Mastery (CIM).[47] Those who fail will move on to special Learning Centers.[48] Since people can neither attend college[49] nor be employed[50] without the CIM, the bill implies that homeschoolers and students in Christian schools whose responses fail to reflect new global values would also have to be remediated and tested until they conform to state and national standards.

1991. The U.S. Coalition for Education for All (USCEFA) held a conference from October 30 to November 1 on "Learning for All: Bridging Domestic and International Education," with First Lady Barbara Bush as the "honorary chair." The coalition is part of a 156-nation network working to reform education worldwide. One of the conference programs was "Education for a New World Order," with keynote speaker Elena Lenskaya, deputy to the Minister of Education of Russia.[51]

1991. UNICEF, UNESCO, UNDP, and The World Bank convened the International Consultative Forum on Education for All in Paris on December 4.

1992. (November 11). In an exuberant eighteen-page letter to Hillary Clinton, Marc Tucker, NCEE president, shared his "vision" of a new "human resources development system" that would include a private, tax-funded standard-setting board with little or no accountability to parents. Fresh from a meeting with David and John Rockefeller, John Sculley [Apple Computer], David Hornbeck and other key change agents, he explains the plan to the newly elected presidential couple:

> What is essential is that we create a seamless web of opportunities to develop one's skills that literally extends from cradle to grave.... regulated on the basis of outcomes.... in which curriculum, pedagogy, examinations, and teacher education and licensure systems are all linked to the national standards... a system that rewards students who meet the national standards with further education and good jobs....
>
> Institutions receiving grants and loan funds under this system are required to provide information . . . [that includes] characteristics and career outcomes for those students. . . .
>
> Create National Board for Professional and Technical Standards. Board is private, not-for-profit, chartered by Congress . . . Neither Congress nor the executive branch can dictate the standards set by the board.[52]

1993. Howard Gardner, author of the influential, much quoted book, *Frames of Mind: The Theory of Multiple Intelligences,* gives a glimpse of the restrictions on human freedom that would accompany the managed economy envisioned by global change agents:

> Ultimately, the educational plans that are pursued need to be orchestrated across various interest groups of the society so that they can, taken together, help the society to achieve its larger goals. Individual profiles must be considered in the light of goals pursued by the wider society; and sometimes, in fact, individuals with gifts in certain directions must nonetheless be guided along other, less favored paths, simply because the needs of the culture are particularly urgent in that realm at that time.[53]

1993. (January). The 240 international affiliates of the NEA and the AFT (American Federation of Teachers) joined in Stockholm in January to form Education International (EI).

1993. The third annual conference of the National Association for Multicultural Education (NAME) during February 11-14 brought together multicultural educators from all 50 states. Keynote speaker Lily Wong Fillmore, a professor of language at the University of California at Berkeley, asserted that the radical curriculum reform they propose will provoke "definite clashes with the practices, beliefs and attitudes that are taught in many homes...."[54]

1993. At the annual NEA convention in San Francisco during July 2-5, delegates approved resolutions supporting multicultural/ global education, abortion rights, school-based clinics, legal protection for teachers *against censorship,* and "early childhood education programs in the public schools for children from birth through age eight." President Clinton addressed the delegates and assured them that his goals paralleled theirs: ". . . we have had the *partnership* I promised in the campaign of 1992, and we will continue to have it. . . . *You and I are joined in a common cause,* and I believe we will succeed."[55]

1994. The Carnegie Foundation for the Advancement of Teaching (CFAT), along with the National Association of Secondary School Principals (NASSP), announced that they will appoint a 13-member group to study school reforms to develop a "holistic" plan for U.S. high schools.[56]

1994. The State of South Dakota passed House Bill No. 1262, "an act to require that home school teachers be certified by the year 2000." Neither Christian school teachers nor parents will be able to teach without going through the psychological training required to teach children the new beliefs and attitudes. Home-schooled children will take "the same tests designated to be used in the public school district. . . ."[57]

1994. The Second Annual Model Schools Conference in Atlanta, June 2-6, sponsored by the International Center for Leadership in Education (ICLE), featured a Chinese boarding school. Su Lin, the founder of the China International Intellectual Resources Development Center for Children, explained why she recommends her boarding school:

- Most parents are too busy working to pay enough attention to the education of their own children.

- Children from broken homes find comfort. Some prefer not to go home on weekends.

- Uneducated parents know nothing about how to bring up children.

- Children without siblings need to learn a sense of equality, solidarity, and independence.

"We have established a school for the parents," said Su Lin, "where people can learn how to educate their own children."[58]

1994. Educators from around the world gathered in Baltimore during December 11-14 for a USCEFA (United States Coalition for Education for All) conference titled "Revolution in World Education: 'Toward Systemic Change.'" The theme highlighted the move toward global as well as community partnerships: "The traditional African belief that 'it takes an entire village to raise a child' is proving increasingly true. As we enter the next century, it may well take an entire nation—or world—to educate our children."

The brochure announcing the conference stated: "Nearly five years ago the world came together at the World Conference on Education for All in Jomtien, Thailand, to ensure the right to education for all people. Since then, education systems around the world have embarked on significantly different programs of systemic reforms. . . ."[59]

• • •

"So where are we?" asks Charlotte Iserbyt. "All is in place except for 'universal' education. That means that home schoolers, independent, private, religious schools must somehow be coerced into the international system. How to accomplish that? Heat up the debate over OBE, publish outrageous outcomes, get the controlled media to beat the drums about how bad public education is.

"In other words, create the problem, people scream, impose the solution. . . .

"An inclusive international education system is being implemented at this very moment. Conservatives can negotiate and compromise all they want about bad outcomes and the need for choice, but what they will get if they accept one penny of tax money is the carefully planned OBE/Mastery-Learning choice schools of the global workforce training system. Once that is in place, they can forget about changing the outcomes. It will be too late.

"The soil has been tilled and the seeds have been planted. We now await the blossoming of what John Dewey and his followers have worked for since the early 1900s: universal socialist/internationalist education for the world government's planned economy."

• • •

Without the peace and hope which God offers every person who trusts Him, we might be tempted to give up. But we must not. We are on the winning team, for our God reigns! He has already won the war. To put this disturbing information into a biblical perspective, remember Psalm 2:

Why do the nations rage and the people plot a vain thing? The kings of the earth set themselves, and the rulers take counsel together, against the Lord, and against His Anointed, saying, "Let us break their bonds in pieces and and cast away their cords from us."

He who sits in the heavens shall laugh; the Lord shall hold them in derision. Then He shall speak to them in His wrath. . . .

"I have set My King on My holy hill. . . . Blessed are all those who put their trust in Him" (Psalm 2:1-6,12 NKJV).

• • •

You can order Dr. Cuddy's entire *Chronology of Education with Quotable Quotes* from the Pro Family Forum, Inc., P.O. Box 1059, Highland City, FL 33846. His booklet, *The Grab for Power: A Chronology of the NEA*, can be ordered from the Plymouth Rock Foundation, P.O. Box 577, Marlborough, NH 03455. 1-800-210-1620.

You can order Charlotte T. Iserbyt's *Back to Basics Reform Or . . . OBE Skinnerian International Curriculum?* and "Soviets in the Classroom: America's Latest Educational Fad" from her office at 1062 Washington Street, Bath, ME 04530.

SECTION D

Symbols and Their Meanings

Occult symbols are fast replacing Christian symbols in our culture. Many are used by people who trust occult powers rather than God. Therefore it is important for Christians to recognize them and have nothing to do with them. This list will help you. Use it to warn others, especially Christian children who like them because they are popular. But keep in mind that some of these symbols have double meanings. For example, the pentagram has been used to transmit occult power in all kinds of rituals for centuries, but to Christians the same shape may simply represent a star—a special part of God's creation.

ALL-SEEING EYE: A universal symbol representing spiritual sight, inner vision, higher knowledge, insight into occult mysteries.

AMULET: A magic charm worn to bring good luck and protection against illness, accidents, and evil forces.

ANCHOR: A reminder to Christians of our security in Christ, but it may represent sea gods and goddesses to pagans.

ANKH: An Egyptian cross symbolizing eternal life, rebirth, and the life-giving power of the sun.

ASHES: A universal symbol of death and mourning, guilt and remorse, or purification and resurrection.

BAT: A symbol of good fortune in the East, it represented demons and spirits in medieval Europe.

CELTIC CROSS: A standard cross with a ring around the point where the two lines cross. The section inside the (sacred) circle is identical to the Wiccan quartered circle or the Native American medicine wheel.

CHRISTIAN CROSS: While anyone—even pagans—now use the cross as decoration or as an occult symbol, Christians must continue to treasure the cross of Calvary. But be careful what kind of cross you wear and what message you communicate to others.

CIRCLE (hoop, ring): A universal symbol of unity, perfection, wholeness, time, and infinity. To many pagans it means Earth as well as heaven, the cosmos as well as a small sacred place.

COMPASS (MASONIC): As with the ancient Chinese, the Masonic symbol of the compass and the T-square represents movement toward perfection and the balance between spirit and matter. Gifts to schools from Masons often carry this occult symbol.

COW: It symbolized the sky goddess Hathor to Egyptians, enlightenment to Buddhists, and one of the highest and holiest stages of transmigration (reincarnation) to Hindus.

CRESCENT MOON: A symbol of the aging goddess (crone) to contemporary witches and victory over death to many Muslims. In Islamic lands, a crescent can be seen enclosing a lone pentagram.

DRAGON: A mythical monster made up of many animals: serpent, lizard, bird, lion. It may have many heads and breathe fire. To Medieval Europe it was dangerous and evil, but people in Eastern Asia believe it has power to help them against more hostile spiritual forces. In the Bible it represents Satan, the devil.

ELEMENTS: The four basic elements to many pagans are **earth, water, air** (or wind), and **fire.** In pagan rituals, they correspond to the spirits of the four directions: north, east, south and west.

EYE OF HORUS: A favorite crafts project in schools, it represents the eye of Egyptian sun god Horus, who lost an eye battling Set, the god of evil. Pagans use it as a charm to ward off evil.

EYE IN PYRAMID: Masonic symbol for the all-seeing eye of God—a mystical distortion of the biblical God. You can find this symbol on the U.S. dollar bill.

HEXAGRAM or SIX-POINTED STAR: An occult sign of the "Divine Mind" (a counterfeit of God's wisdom) to numerous occult groups through the centuries. Many still use it in occult rituals. But Jewish people and many others see it as good and call it the Star of David.

INVERTED CROSS: Represents Satanism and its mockery of Christ.

MASK: Used by pagans around the world to represent animal powers, nature spirits, or ancestral spirits. In pagan rituals the wearer may chant, dance, and enter a trance in order to contact the spirit world and be possessed by the spirit represented by the mask.

MEDICINE SHIELD: A round shield decorated with personal symbols and pictures of the animal spirit(s) contacted on a spirit quest or through a classroom visualization simulating an American Indian ceremony.

PEACE SYMBOL or NERO'S CROSS: A broken, upside-down cross. To Roman emperor Nero, who hated and persecuted the early Christians, it meant the destruction of Christianity. Revived in the sixties by hippies and others who protested nuclear weapons, Western culture, and Christian values, it now symbolizes a utopian hope for a new age of global peace and earth-centered unity. But many heavy metal rock fans would agree with Nero and use it to mock Christ and His followers.

PENTAGRAM or FIVE-POINTED STAR: A standard symbol for witches, Freemasons, and many other pagan or occult groups. To witches it represents the four basic elements (wind, water, earth, and fire) and a pantheistic spiritual being such as Gaia or Mother Earth.

PENTAGRAM, INVERTED: The horned god to many contemporary witches, it represents Satanism when inside a circle.

SERPENT or SNAKE: Most earth-centered or pagan cultures worshiped the serpent. It usually represents rebirth (because of its molting), but might also symbolize protection against evil, either male or female sexuality, rain and fertility, or a mediator between the physical and spiritual world. The list is almost endless, but in the Bible it represents sin, temptation, destruction, and Satan. (See **Dragon.**)

SPIRAL: Ancient symbol of the goddess and fertility.

STAR: See **Pentagram** or **Hexagram**.

SWASTIKA: Ancient occult symbol of the sun and the four directions. Revived by Hitler, it represents racism and the "white supremacy" of neo-Nazis.

TOTEM: Carved, painted representation of power animals or animal-human ancestors. To American Indians in the Northwest, who believe that all of nature has spiritual life, the animals in their totem poles represent the spiritual powers of animal protectors or ancestors.

UNICORN: To many New Agers it means power, purification, healing, renewal, and eternal life.

WHEEL: A universal symbol of cosmic unity, astrology, "the circle of life," and evolution. See **Medicine Wheel** and **Circle**.

YIN YANG: A Chinese Tao picture of universal harmony and the unity between all opposites: light/dark, male/female, etc. Yin is the dark, passive, negative female principle. Yang is the light, active, positive male principle.

SECTION E
Glossary of Educational Terms

These definitions were compiled with help from researchers Elizabeth Stoner (Mississippi), Betty Lewis (Michigan), Marla Quenzer (Iowa), and Cynthia Weatherly (Georgia).

ACHIEVEMENT-BASED EDUCATION: See **Outcome-Based Education**. Remember, the labels change as often as needed to keep ahead of critics.

AFFECTIVE DOMAIN: The area of learning that deals with feelings, beliefs, values, attitudes, and motives—all those inner factors that determine behavior and responses to stimuli. By changing or modifying the affective domain, educators can control behavior, or so they believe. (See **Mastery Learning**.)

ARTS EDUCATION: "Art is humanity's most essential, most universal language," contends the Goals 2000's "Arts and Education Reform" report. An effective tool for transforming beliefs and values, it "celebrates diversity while building unity."[1]

ASSESSMENT: A means of measuring student progress toward national and state goals. (See **Authentic Assessment**.)

AT RISK: Any "student who is at risk of not meeting the goals of the educational program . . . or not becoming a productive worker"[2] (Iowa State Standards). Programs such as Parents As Teachers (PAT), 21st Century Schools, Healthy People 2000, and others define at-risk in categories. (See **Parents As Teachers**.)

AUTHENTIC ASSESSMENT: Alternative tests which assess student ability to solve problems and perform task under simulated "real-life" situations. It measures student responses which demonstrate what students *think, do,* and have *become.* These outcomes are recorded during normal classroom involvement. Teachers may use hand-held computer scanners that scan the students' bar-coded name and responses, then transfer the information into a computer later.

BENCHMARKS or MILESTONES: Tangible, incremental steps toward meeting specific goals and national standards.

BRIDGING: A teacher helping students make connections between what they are studying and real-life, out-of-school experiences.

CERTIFICATE OF ADVANCED MASTERY (CAM): An advanced achievement credential that follows the CIM and supposedly proves mastery of "higher-level educational outcomes."

CERTIFICATE OF INITIAL MASTERY (CIM): Replacing the high school diploma, the CIM is the "new job ticket"—the reward for demonstrating "mastery" in the various attitudes and citizenship skills deemed necessary for employment and citizenship.

CHANGE AGENT: A term utilized by many people, including President Clinton and leading educators, to identify educators who change our schools, our children, our nation, and the world.

CHARACTER EDUCATION: An attempt to teach students global or core values. The process will involve the entire community, establish a new layer of governance, and promote the acceptance of core values by all parts of the community. These new values will be determined by the community, not parents, and will be the basis for making decisions and resolving controversial issues. Traditional morality will no longer fit nor be tolerated.

CHARTER SCHOOL: A public school created by a partnership between the private sector and government for the purpose of providing additional academic choices for parents. It must comply with federal and state laws to receive funding.

CHOICE: Allowing parents to enroll their children in any public schools within the district or inter-district, or—depending on the scope of the choice program—providing tax credits that can be applied toward tuition in private schools. All schools receiving federal funding must adopt "voluntary" national standards which force students to conform to core beliefs, values, and attitudes. "Such choices should include all schools that serve the public and are accountable to public authority" (America 2000).

CITIZEN: The new type of person needed for the next century workforce and community. (See **Global Education**.)

CLIMATE CONTROL: Creating the proper mood or feeling, not temperature, in the school. A "positive school climate" means a "psychologically facilitative climate."

COGNITIVE DISSONANCE: Mental confusion and emotional tension caused by incompatible values. Created through classroom stimuli such as hypothetical stories or pagan rituals that conflict with home-taught values, it forces most children to rethink and modify their values to resolve the conflict.

COLLABORATIVE LEARNING: Group learning. Views all knowledge as "the common property of a group."[3]

COLLECTIVE: The opposite of individualism and free enterprise, it emphasizes Utopian ideals such as Marxist equality and "serving the greater whole." Examples: a commune or a Communist farm "owned" and operated by all the people.

COMMON GROUND: A place of compromise; a nice-sounding strategy developed by change agents for silencing opposing voices and winning community support. Relies heavily on misleading euphemism and friendly responses that promise cooperation, but in the end it usually ignores conflicting suggestions. (See **Consensus Building**.)

COMMUNITY EDUCATION: Integrating physical and human resources in a concerted effort to develop the "whole person" through community **service programs** and **Lifelong Learning**.[4]

COMPREHENSIVE HEALTH EDUCATION: A sequential pre-K through 12 curriculum to address the physical, mental, emotional, and social (including holistic) dimensions of health.

COMPREHENSIVE SCHOOL HEALTH PROGRAM: The school as the hub of the community offers health education and services, integrated school and community health promotion, nutrition/food service, guidance-counseling, etc.

CONFLICT RESOLUTION: A psychological technique for dealing with (often hypothetical) conflicts. It manipulates a child's value system, trading old absolutes and convictions for compromise positions. In a legal context, it is used to avoid litigation. (See **Consensus Building** and **Common Ground**.)

CONSCIOUSNESS: Individual or **collective** (cultural) awareness or the moral and spiritual consciousness of a nation which defines its worldview or **paradigm**.

CONSENSUS BUILDING: The process by which students, schools, communities, or groups of people learn to compromise individual beliefs and ideas in order to work for "common goals." These may be dictated from the top down (national to local), yet be promoted as grassroots idealogies. It changes beliefs through pressure to conform to group thinking. (See **Synthesis**.)

CONTENT STANDARDS: Descriptions of what students should know and demonstrate in each subject area.

CONTEXT: The setting of circumstances that surround a particular event, statement, or story. Since most events or stories are understood or interpreted according to their context, a teacher can change meanings by altering the context. The biblical word "truth" acquires a totally different meaning when used in an Indian myth.

COOPERATIVE LEARNING: Groups of two to five students with varied abilities who learn to share responsibility for achieving group goals. High-achieving students carry the weight of a group assignment for which all receive the same group grade. It is supposed to eliminate competitiveness and individualism while teaching cooperation, problem-solving, and responsibility for achieving group success instead of personal success. Promoting collectivism, it lowers academic standards by forcing high achievers to bear the burden of success for others.

CREATIVE THINKING: Generating new ideas, changing or reshaping goals, imagining new possibilities, using imagination freely, and making connections between seemingly unrelated ideas.

CRITICAL THINKING: Challenging students' traditional beliefs, values, and authorities through **Values Clarification** strategies and **Mastery Learning**.

DELPHI TECHNIQUE: Communication technique used to get a diverse group to arrive at consensus position through circulating information for comment in several rounds synthesizing the responses until all agree. If a participant's view cannot be synthesized with the groups after repeated rounds, then the premise must be declared invalid and abandoned.

DISSONANCE: See **Cognitive Dissonance**.

EARTH-CENTERED SPIRITUALITY: A pantheistic, monastic blend of the world's pagan religions. It views all life as being interconnected and trades God for a spiritualized Mother Earth, nature spirits, or other supernaturals. (See **Gaia**.)

EDUCATIONAL ESTABLISHMENT: The national and international bipartisan leadership that plans and promotes today's transformation. Diverse and often divided, it is bonded by a common vision of the transformative role of education and of its own role as a change agent.

ELECTRONIC PORTFOLIO: The computer-based permanent record for each learner, which contains and discloses personal information.

EQUALITY: All schools conforming to an "equal" standard determined by the needs of the slowest learner. It limits a student's ability to excel and explains why OBE is often referred to as "dumbing down."

FABIAN SOCIALIST: A member of the Fabian Society, which sought the gradual worldwide spread of socialism by peaceful means.

FACILITATOR: 1) A nondirective, nonjudgmental teacher/ leader who creates an environment for learning, records student progress, and motivates students to exercise self-direction in determining and achieving educational goals. 2) A change agent who chairs handpicked committees or groups to direct discussion toward the "right" predetermined conclusions or consensus. This process is called "managed change." See **Consensus Building** and **Common Ground.**

GAIA: 1) The name of the ancient Greek earth-goddess. 2) A "scientific" hypothesis by James Lovelock, who views the earth as a living, self-directing organism. 3) A feminine, pantheistic life-force that embodies, nurtures, and guides the evolution of all life.

GENDER NORMING: Grading students not on merit alone but on subjective expectations by staff based on student's gender coupled with class performance. An attempt to "level the playing field."

GLOBAL EDUCATION: Prepares students to be global, interdependent citizens by developing a global **consciousness** which embraces "universal" values and pantheistic, **earth-centered** beliefs that supposedly will save the planet and unify its people. Teaching global idealism and training students in political activism, it builds a malleable young army ready to support the United Nations and other organizations calling for a world government.

GLOBAL SPIRITUALITY: A blend of the world's New Age and earth-centered religions. Since all are pantheistic, monistic, and polytheistic, they fit together but exclude monotheism, especially biblical Christianity.

GUIDED IMAGERY: A **visualization** exercise directed by a teacher/facilitator to produce a relaxed or altered state of consciousness.

HIGHER ORDER THINKING SKILLS (HOTS): Psychological manipulation using "application, analysis, synthesis, and evaluation" (the higher level of Bloom's Taxonomy) without the factual knowledge needed for rational and objective thinking. The student draws conclusions based on biased, politically correct information and disinformation.

HOLISTIC EDUCATION: Education involving the whole person—body, soul, and spirit. It integrates all subjects and infuses everything with a pantheistic, monistic spirituality. (See **Systemic Change**.)

HUMAN CAPITAL or RESOURCE: The new label for all children, who are being shaped to match the supposed needs of the global economy. The trained work force product of global/national schooling.

INCLUSION: Assigning *all* students to regular classrooms, including those with severe disabilities, thus turning each class into a special education class.

INDIVIDUAL EDUCATION PLAN (IEP): The individualized behavior modification plan for changing a student's beliefs and behavior through stimuli, response, assessment, and remediation. The control mechanism of **Mastery Learning**, it adapts to each student's rate of change and degree of resistance and indicates corrective measures. Masquerades as an academic plan.

INFUSION: A strategy that hides or blends politically correct social philosophies and matching activities into the basic content of the curriculum.

INTEGRATIVE EDUCATION or CURRICULUM: Organizing learning around broad themes, thus making it easy to infuse global, new-paradigm suggestions and activities into standard lessons.

INTRINSIC MOTIVATION: A system of rewards based on the inner feelings of the child.

JOURNAL: A daily record in which students express and deal with their feelings and emotions. When included in the student's assessment portfolio, it violates the students' right to privacy.

LIFE SKILLS, LIFE ROLE COMPETENCIES: Preparation for all life roles. The total development of the child—body, mind, and spirit as a learner, worker, consumer, family member and citizen. What the student will believe, think, and do to meet the exit outcomes.

LIFELONG LEARNING: A continuous program of training the masses to meet societal needs throughout their lifespan. All adults must meet the social, psychological, and work skills standards required for work and citizenship. (See **Citizen**.)

LITERACY, CULTURAL: Viewing life, people, and nature from a politically correct or new-paradigm perspective.

LITERACY, FUNCTIONAL: Basic literacy skills (such as reading a map or following instructions) needed to live and participate in society. Does not necessarily mean ability to read in the traditional sense.

LITERACY, WORKPLACE: Literacy focused on specific job skills; learning the factual, communication, reading, and math skills needed to perform required functions.

LITERATURE BASE: Teaching language arts, civic responsibility, and character through literature. It enables teachers to manipulate a child's belief system by choosing new-paradigm literature and/or interpreting literature according to the new paradigm.

LOCAL CONTROL: A euphemism to pacify critics, since all control rests with those who determine the national standards and assessments. Local educators are free only to find ways to meet those national standards.

LOWER-ORDER THINKING SKILLS: Includes knowledge, comprehension, and memorization, the cornerstones of traditional schools. (See **Mastery Learning**.)

MAGNET SCHOOLS: A public school focused on a specialized area of learning, which may have formed a partnership with a private organization.

MASTERY LEARNING: A psychological process based on the premise that all children can learn if given enough time and help. It uses behavior-modification techniques (stimulus, response, assessment, remediation) to change the students' beliefs, attitudes, values, and behavior. The student must "master" each sequential step toward the required "outcome" (and demonstrate this mastery by modifying behavior patterns) before advancing to the next stage. (See **IEP, OBE, Global Education**.)

MEDICINE (AMERICAN INDIAN): Magic; spiritual power as used by tribal medicine men. (See medicine wheel in Symbols and Their Meanings.)

MIND MAPPING: A new way of diagramming complex conceptual relationships. With their imagination, students create a network of lines connecting words and brief phrases.

MONISM: The belief that all is one; everything is interconnected, bound together through a pantheistic force that infuses everything with spiritual life. (See **Global Spirituality**.)

MULTICULTURAL EDUCATION: Teaching tolerance, respect, and appreciation for the world's diverse cultures, belief systems, and lifestyles. It shows little tolerance for biblical Christianity, but embraces homosexual lifestyles.

MYTH: A culturally significant fiction or fantasy story which attempts to explain some aspect of reality (the origin of the coyote, why it rains, etc.) but has no basis in factual reality.

NATIONAL ASSESSMENT OF EDUCATION PROGRESS (NAEP): "The Nation's Report Card" which measures student progress by testing different subject areas in alternate years. Also gathers personal data on children and families to fill out longitudinal profiles that include beliefs, attitudes, behavior and values. (See Anita Hoge's report on p. 207.)

NATIONAL CENTER ON EDUCATION AND THE ECONOMY (NCEE): Founded by Marc Tucker, it conceived the **CIM** in a 1990 report called "America's Choice: High Skills or Low Wages." (See **New Standards Project**.)

NATIONAL SKILLS STANDARD BOARD (NSSB): Has authority to identify occupation clusters and define the student skill level required for certification to work within these clusters. Both schools and businesses would be expected to follow government guidelines and adopt these standards. In other words, students would have to meet the government standards in order to be certified for various kinds of jobs.

NEW STANDARDS PROJECT (NSP): A partnership formed by Marc Tucker (head of NCEE) and Lauren Resnick to establish a "world-class" system of standards and assessment that reflects international standards and culminates with the **CIM** and **CAM**.

NON-GRADED SCHOOLS: Teaching children of different ages and ability levels together, without dividing the curriculum into steps labeled by grade designation. Rather than passing or failing at the end of the year, students progress at their own individual rates. Letter grades are usually replaced by **Authentic Assessments**.

OUTCOME-BASED EDUCATION (also called OBE, Standards-Driven Education, Achievement-Based Education, Performance-Based Education): The national, multilevel delivery system for **Mastery Learning**. Driven by national standards which match international standards, it forces states and local schools to teach according to national guidelines, curriculum frameworks, work-skills competencies, etc. by tying much-needed federal funding to compliance. Almost every other definition in this glossary list describes a facet of OBE, so scan the entire list.

OUTCOMES: "What students must *know,* and be able to *do,* and be *like.*" Determined at the national and international level, they must be met locally. Called learning goals, performance objectives, standards, competencies, or capacities, they all require students to embrace "new thinking, new strategies, new behavior, and new beliefs."[5]

PAGAN: A person who embraces a polytheistic/pantheistic (earth-centered) religion. Many people call themselves pagans, which they consider a good, not a derogatory, name.

PAIDEIA PROPOSAL: An education plan based on an ancient holistic Greek concept explained by Marilyn Ferguson in *The Aquarian Conspiracy.* "The paideia referred to the educational matrix created by the whole of Athenian culture, in which the community and all its disciplines generated learning resources for the individual, whose ultimate goal was to reach the divine center in the self."[6] Its four-step process—pretest, teach/train, post-test, and remediation—matches **Mastery Learning**. It was adapted as a model for **Outcome-Based Education** by Mortimer Adler, a zealous advocate of a one-world government.

PANTHEISM: The belief that all is God; a universal spiritual force infuses all things with spiritual life. It can be called the Great Spirit, Gaia, Mother Earth, a cosmic force, the Source, ultimate wisdom, etc.

PARADIGM: A worldview; a mental framework for thinking, for organizing information, and for understanding and explaining reality.

PARENTS AS TEACHERS (PAT): Brings the state educator into homes to make sure each child starts school "ready to learn" and "able to learn." The child is given a personal computer code number, and a computer record is initiated that will enable the national data system to track each child for the rest of his life. Parents as well as children are evaluated. (See Chapter 7.)

PARTNERSHIP: A unified effort by two or more entities — private, public or a combination—to implement the national goals.

PEER TUTORING: Children teaching children. Assigning fast learners to tutor slow learners limits the progress of the former and may subject the latter to peer ridicule.

PERFORMANCE-BASED ASSESSMENT: An assessment system which leans heavily on open-ended answers and extensive writing, and uses multiple evaluators. According to government research, it often falls short in validity, content, disparate impact, objectivity, and scoring reliability. (See **Paideia Proposal**).

PHONICS: Learning to read by decoding words. Students break words down into component parts and relate letters and groups of letters to the sounds of spoken language. (Contrast with **Whole Language**.)

POLYTHEISM: Belief in many gods, spirits, counterfeit angels, or other supernaturals.

PORTFOLIO ASSESSMENT: Measuring student progress by evaluating his or her "portfolio": a collection of work which includes art projects, written assignments, journaling, and a variety of other work that demonstrate learning. (See **Performance-Based Assessment**.)

PRIVATIZATION: Transferring educational policy-making and implementation from the public domain into the private or business arena, where educational leaders become accountable to wealthy funders (such as the Carnegie, Ford, Danforth, Rockefeller, Spencer, and Annenberg foundations) and multinational corporations rather than concerned parents and their representatives.

QUEST: A generally ineffective antidrug program based on situation ethics and values clarification strategies. Undermining a child's sense of right and wrong, it opens the door for students to think and do the unthinkable.

REGIONAL EDUCATION LABORATORIES: Private, non-profit corporations funded with tax money, in whole or in part, under Title IV of the Elementary and Secondary Education Act (ESEA) of 1965. They develop programs that link their research to practices in the schools of their respective regions. Far West Regional Educational Laboratory (FWREL) and Mid-Continent Educational Laboratories (McREL) lead in the national/ international transformation.

RELEARNING: Dismantling the old ways and establishing new ways of thinking and choosing; it applies to adults as well as children. (See **Community Education.**)

REMEDIATION: A stage in the **OBE/Mastery Learning** loop which applies to students who resist change or fail to show expected progress. Remediation continues until the student learns the re-quired outcomes and demonstrates them on designated assessments.

RESTRUCTURING: A systemic or system-wide movement to change the entire education model in order to achieve the new national goals. This revolutionary, never-ending change process includes: **Mastery Learning, Outcome-Based Education,** and **partnerships** with business and community leaders, churches, and parents. Almost every word in this glossary describes a part of today's restructuring effort. (See **Systemic Change.**)

SCANS—THE SECRETARY'S COMMISSION ON ACHIEV-ING NECESSARY SKILLS: Commission created under Elizabeth Dole as Secretary of Labor. It links education to the Department of Labor in a joint effort to create a workforce that meets the future needs for a global workforce and produces students that are com-petent in prescribed work skills, including attitudes and group thinking. It can direct students into specific training, limit their options, and bring intrusive government influences into all aspects of life. (See **Certificates of Initial** and **Advanced Mastery.**)

SCANS COMPETENCIES: An official list of competencies from the U.S. Department of Labor describing work skills that "effective workers can productively use." (See Pam Hoffecker's Report on p. 215.)

SCHOOL-BASED DECISION-MAKING: A form of school governance that replaces elected school boards or school system administrators with a council consisting of principals, teachers, and selected parents who support the new system. Designed to implement the changes with minimal hindrance, it is not accountable to elected officials or dissenting parents.

SCHOOL-TO-WORK or -CAREER: Legislative initiative which changes focus on education to workforce training instead of information-based learning. The link or partnership between the schools and businesses established through the SCANS competencies, which provide a criterion both for testing and training the global workforce. (See **SCANS.**)

SCHOOL/COMMUNITY-BASED CLINICS: Comprehensive health services offered near or at the school. Individual health plans (for treatment, prevention, birth control, abortion counseling, and psychological tests) are developed for each student and eventually for all family members. Family planning services are provided to minors without parental consent. (See **Community Education.**)

SERVICE LEARNING: Combining community service with politically correct classroom instruction that encourages students to see social problems from a collective or new-**paradigm** perspective.

SITE-BASED CURRICULUM: Though written by local teachers, this curriculum must be designed to prepare students tomeet the national outcomes. Often compiled from various sources, it is not easily identified or understood by concerned parents.

SITE-BASED MANAGEMENT: A nonelected management (made up of the principal, selected staff, lead/master teachers, and a few supportive parents and students) which either replaces the elected school board or reduces its members to figureheads. Parents and taxpayers who oppose the transformation lose all representation.

SPECIAL EDUCATION (redefined): Planned for all children "**at risk**" of not meeting the national standards.

SPEEDE/EXPRESS: Transmission process for student's academic progress recorded in the **CIM** databank in an **IEP** format to be sent to higher educational institutions, agencies, or corporations when indicated. Part of the NCS's (National Computer System) microcomputer-based software for K-12 schools.[7]

STAFF DEVELOPMENT: A long-term process which facilitates the top-down, nationwide systemic change in education. Since teachers cannot manage the behavior modification strategies until they themselves have been properly trained, their "development" is essential to the change. Like their students, they must be pretested, trained, evaluated, retrained, and retested throughout their entire career.

STANDARDS: The national criteria for student performance. It provides benchmarks set to the "highest in the world" to assure "competitiveness" and "citizenship" in the coming global economy. (See **Mastery Learning**.)

STANDARDS-DRIVEN EDUCATION: See **Outcome-Based Education**.

STUDENTS: Includes teachers, parents, and other adults; all must be retrained. (See **Lifelong Learning**.)

SYNTHESIS: One of the **higher-order thinking** skills in Bloom's Taxonomy. Uses the principles of Hegelian Dialectics to join the beliefs or ideas (theses) of individual students into a new joint belief—the compromise solution or synthesis. (See **Consensus Building**, **Common Ground**, **Values Clarification** and **Delphi Technique**.)

SYSTEMIC CHANGE or SCHOOL REFORM: Total holistic transformation—top-down, system-wide, international as well as national and practical. "Systemic" means one mind directing one body with many parts. It includes preschools, public elementary and high schools, private schools, colleges, universities, health clinics, and every other kind of community partners. The change "must occur all at once,"[8] wrote Thomas Kuhn who coined the word paradigm. Iowa educators call it "meaningful change that cannot be accomplished piecemeal by disconnected projects or quick fixes."[9] The planned deadline is school year 2000-2001.

THEMATIC LEARNING: All subjects revolve around one central theme, such as American Indians or Aztec culture.

THRESHOLD: The point where a stimulus of increasing strength produces the desired response. In **Mastery Learning** it shows how much psychological stimuli—and what kinds of conditions—will cause a student to behave the desired way (the required outcome).

TOTAL QUALITY MANAGEMENT (TQM): A strategy for managing continual improvement through statistical tools and decision-making techniques. Administered through site-based management, it emphasizes the "customer" or "stakeholder," which includes everyone but the concerned parent.

TRANSFORMATION: The process of rethinking our present educational system and reshaping it to meet present and future needs of students and society.

TRANSFORMATIONAL OBE: The third stage of William Spady's program for OBE—Traditional, Transitional and Transformational. An anti-intellectual, highly politicized plan for eliminating traditional education and changing the beliefs of students through psychological formulas for behavior modification. (See **Mastery Learning.**)

UNGRADED PRIMARIES: Since students "progress at their own speed," they remain in the ungraded primary class for as many years as it takes to achieve the stated outcomes. (See **Mastery Learning.**)

UNIVERSAL VALUES: Honesty, integrity, tolerance, and other values believed to be common to all the world's culture (counter to the facts of history).

VALUES CLARIFICATION: A strategy for changing a student's vaues. It prods students to criticize traditional values, then choose "their own" values based on personal opinions and group consensus. (See **Synthesis**.)

VISUALIZATION: Mental images formed in response to specific suggestions, which can lead children into an altered state of consciousness ranging from simple relaxation to a deep hypnotic trance. Children may or may not encounter or communicate with spiritual entities such as "their animal spirit" or "a wise person" during the exercise.

VOUCHERS: Tuition credits used by parents to pay for their child's education in a private school of their choice. "A simple fact of political life is that public regulation follows money. . . . Private schools that operate with *public money* will be subject to public regulations. . . ."[10]

WHOLE CHILD: Pertaining to every aspect of the child, including health, nutrition, values, attitudes, beliefs, and resulting behaviors.

WHOLE LANGUAGE: A reading and learning method which trains students to focus on words, sentences, and paragraphs as a whole rather than on letters. Sometimes called the "look-say" method, it ignores the proven success of phonics and tells children to find meaning by guessing, by recognizing whole words they have memorized, by looking at pictures, and by creating a context based on surrounding words. It encourages students to construct their own meaning, not retrieve or comprehend the intended meaning of the author.

WORK-BASED LEARNING: Programs designed to teach older students (grades 7 and up) work skills on the job site, thereby assuring that the student can perform the task needed by local employers when he or she graduates from public school.

WORKLINK: A computer-based student record system that "enables students to assess their skills . . . make work-related decisions and transmit data to [potential] employers."[11] According to its own brochure, it "encourages cooperation among high schools, the business community, and students." Could replace individual choice with computerized and politicized placement of future workers.

WORKPLACE SKILLS STANDARD: The broadly defined "essential" skills for competency in various occupations.[12]

WORLDVIEW: A learned perception of reality, a mental framework for thinking, believing, and understanding reality. (See **Paradigm**.)

WORLD-CLASS EDUCATION: Noncompetitive system based on national standards and benchmarks that match international standards. Students must embrace a common set of universal beliefs and values in preparation for the next century. (See **Global Education**.)

WORLD-CLASS STANDARDS: Standards for citizens in the new global economy. Planned by international leaders, they include attitudes, values, and beliefs that reject or minimize national sovereignty and emphasize collectivism rather than individualism.

WORLD CONFERENCE ON EDUCATION FOR ALL (WCEFA): International organization working with the United Nations, many nongovernmental organizations (NGO), and individual nations to plan and promote **OBE** and **Mastery Learning** for all. (See **Systemic Change**.)

YOUTH SERVICE: Programs designed to help students meet the national goal of "responsible citizenship" by instilling an attitude of service to the community or collective.

Notes

Before You Begin . . .

1. 2 Corinthians 12:9,10; Philippians 3:13,19; Deuteronomy 31:6.

2. Chester Finn, Jr., "Reinventing Local Control," *Education Week* (January 23, 1991); p. 32.

3. Sponsored by the International Center for Leadership in Education. For more information, see June 26-29, 1994, in "Chronology of Events" in Part 2.

4. Cynthia Weatherly, "The Second Annual Model School Conference," *The Christian Conscience* (January 1995); p.36.

5. John R. Champlin, "News and Views from the Institute for Quality Learning," *Journal of Quality Learning,* April 1995, p. 7.

6. Deuteronomy 1:30 NKJV.

Chapter 1: New Beliefs for a Global Village

1. The term "global village" refers to the envisioned global society of the twenty-first century—a world of people no longer separated by oceans and national borders but brought together as one community through fast-spreading communication links.

2. Benjamin Bloom, *All Our Children Learning* (New York: McGraw Hill, 1981), p. 180.

3. Former President George Bush announcing America 2000 at the White House on April 18, 1991. *America 2000: An Education Strategy* (Washington, D.C.: U.S. Department of Education, 1991), pp. 50, 51, 55.

4. Marilyn Ferguson, *The Aquarian Conspiracy* (New York: J.P. Tarcher, Inc., 1980), p. 280.

5. Michael J. Caduto and Joseph Bruchac, *Keepers of the Earth* (Golden, CO: Fulcrum, Inc., 1988), p. 188.

6. Ibid., p. 7

7. Vincent Rogers, *Teaching Social Studies: Portraits from the Classroom* (National Council for the Social Studies Bulletin, No. 82), p. 20.

8. Information sent by concerned parent.

9. Cited from copy of original program from elementary school in Portland, Oregon.

10. Reported by a parent in Mountain View, California.

11. Reported in a telephone conversation with the Colorado mother.

12. A term coined by educators who call themselves "change agents." See explanation in "Before You Begin" at the beginning of this book.

13. The historical record through the centuries, as documented both by biblical scribes in ancient Israel and historians in other lands, shows the violence, torture, and occult fears that characterized earth-centered cultures. The false idea that polytheistic cultures demonstrated harmony and concern for nature came primarily from counterculture activists during the seventies and eighties.

14. These assignments were parts of North Carolina's basic K-12 competencies. Only the threat of a lawsuit forced Craig Phillips, the state Superintendent of Public Instruction, to provide concerned parents with this information. Charlotte Iserbyt, *Back to Basics Reform Or . . . OBE Skinnerian International Curriculum?* (Bath, ME, 1993), pp. 20-21.

15. William Carr, "On the Waging of Peace," in *NEA Journal,* October 1947, p. 496.

16. Ibid.

17. See Pam Hoffecker's report on p. 215.

18. At the time of this writing, that entrance pass is the Certificate of Initial Mastery (CIM), which will be required for entrance to work, college, or a university. This will be explained later in the book.

19. Lee Droegemeuller, "Assessment! Kansas Quality Performance Accreditation (QPA)," Kansas State Board of Education, Topeka, KS, January 1992. This will be explained in detail in Chapters 3, 4, and 5.

20. Alan A. Glatthorn and Jonathan Barron, "The Good Thinker," in *Developing Minds: A Resource Book for Teaching Thinking* (Alexandria, VA.: The Association for Supervision and Curriculum Development, 1985), p. 51. Included in *Caught in the Middle: Educational Reform for Young Adolescents in California Public Schools,* Report of the Superintendent's Middle Grade Task Force (Sacramento: California State Department of Education, 1987), p. 14.

21. Raymond English, "Research and Improvement in the Social Studies: Reflections of a Private Sector Practitioner," presented to the National Advisory Council on Educational Research and Improvement, April 2, 1987.

22. To protect this mother and her children, I have used a fictitious name.

23. Cornel Pewewardy and Mary Bushey, "The American Indian School," p. 58. This copy of the article was available to visitors to the school, but it did not indicate the name of the publisher.

24. From Mrs. Holm's written record of her dialogues with teachers and students at the school.

25. *101 Ways to Learn Vocabulary,* p. 72. This used portion of the curriculum was sent to me by a parent in Texas.

26. Robert Muller, *World Core Curriculum Journal,* Vol. 1 (Arlington, TX: The Robert Muller School, 1989), p. 19.

27. This concept will be clarified and illustrated in Chapter 4.

28. James Quina, "Aldous Huxley's Integrated Curriculum," in *Holistic Education Journal,* December 1993, p. 54.

29. This story was included in the first grade curriculum in New Pittsburgh, Pennsylvania. The story was also told—using the new paradigm context—at a parents' meeting explaining Character Education. Anita Hoge, Pennsylvania mother and researcher, reported the story to me.

Chapter 2: The International Agenda

1. Al Gore, *Earth in the Balance: Ecology and the Human Spirit* (New York: Houghton Mifflin Company, 1992), pp. 354-55.

2. Harold Drummon, "Leadership for Human Change," in *Educational Leadership*, December 1964, p. 147.

3. James Becker, ed., *Schooling for a Global Age* (New York: McGraw-Hill Book Company, 1979), pp. xxiii, xvii.

4. Deborah Sharp, "A culture clash divides Florida," in *USA Today*, May 18, 1994.

5. Christine Bennet, *Comprehensive Multicultural Education* (Boston: Allyn and Bacon, 1990), p. 12.

6. Humanist Manifesto II, Tenet 12.

7. Philip Vander Velde and Hyung-Chan Kim, eds., *Global Mandate: Pedagogy for Peace* (Bellingham, WA: Bellwether Press, 1985). Cited by Dennis Laurence Cuddy, Ph.D., *Chronology of Education* (Highland City, FL: Pro Family Forum, Inc., 1993), p. 76.

8. One of the primary vehicles for transmitting revisionist history into schools in every state is the attractive, easy-to-use Houghton-Mifflin Social Studies program authored by Gary Nash, who debated Lynne Cheney in the following debate. Nash's textbooks will be discussed in Chapter 5.

9. *The Columbus Controversy: Challenging How History Is Written*, Videogram, Current Affairs Series, American School Publishers (McMillan-McGraw Hill School Publishing Company, 1991).

10. Gary Nash's social studies texts published by Houghton-Mifflin will be discussed in Chapter 5.

11. Lynne Cheney, "The End of History," in *Wall Street Journal*, October 20, 1994.

12. The Hindu and Buddhist concept of Karma, the belief that a person's actions in one life determine the person's life-form, social position, and destiny in the next reincarnation.

13. "New Study Finds Convergence of School Curricula Worldwide," in *Chronicle of Higher Education*, March 6, 1991, p. A8. Summarized in *Magazine Article Summaries* at Los Altos Public Library, CA.

14. Susan Hooper, "Educator Proposes a Global 'Core Curriculum,'" in *Education Week*, November 27, 1985, p. 8.

15. Robert Muller, *New Genesis: Shaping a Global Spirituality* (Garden City: Image Books, 1984), p. 49.

16. Hooper, "Educator Proposes," p. 8.

17. Vaclav Havel, "Creating a New Vision," in *Earthlight,* Spring 1995, p. 9.

18. Norway's Prime Minister, Gro Brundtland, has been a leading spokesperson for global environmental strategies and population controls.

19. *World Core Curriculum Manual* (Arlington, TX: Robert Muller School, 1986), Preface.

20. Chairperson of the accreditation team for the Southern Association of Colleges and Schools, Eileen Lynch, Professor of Political Science, Brookhaven College, October 1984.

21. Muller, *New Genesis,* p. 127.

22. Presented by Cordell Svengalis in lecture titled "Global Education: Reaching for Common Visions," at educational conference, "Iowa to Iowan . . . Defining World Class Education," sponsored by BEL (Business and Educational Leadership Associates) and the Iowa Department of Education, Des Moines, IA, October 17-18, 1990.

23. A copy of the words were sent to me by a concerned teacher at the Sunnyvale school.

24. From an address to the Seeking the True Meaning of Peace Conference, June 1989, cosponsored by the UN Population Fund, the University of Peace, and the Government of Costa Rica.

25. *Encyclopedia Britannica,* Vol. 21 (Chicago; William Benton Publisher, 1968), p. 203.

26. Andy LePage, *Transforming Education* (Oakland, CA: Oakmore House, 1987), pp. 122, 128, 160.

27. From the text of the Declaration of Human Responsibilities for Peace and Sustainable Development, adopted at San Jose, Costa Rica, during "The Conference in Search of the true Meaning of Peace," held June 23-30, 1989.

28. The two goals added to the Bush Adminstration's America 2000 to form the Clinton Administration's Goals 2000 focus on professional development for teachers and increased parental training and invovement.

29. *Learning for All: Bridging Domestic and International Education,* Conference Report, United States Coalition for Education for All (Arlington, VA: October 30, 31, November 1, 1991), p. 1.

30. Ibid., p. vii.

31. *The Revolution in World Education: Toward Systemic Change,* U.S. Coalition for Education for All, December 1994, p. 5.

32. Ibid., p. 2.

33. Ibid., p. 3.

34. These exchanges were documented and explained by Charlotte Iserbyt. Additional information will be included in other parts of this book.

35. Thomas Sowell, "A Road to Hell Paved with Good Intentions," in *Forbes,* January 17, 1994, pp. 62, 63, 64.

36. Chapter 7 will explain in detail the myth of "local control. "

37. Thomas Sowell, "Indoctrinating the Children," in *Forbes,* February 1, 1993, p. 65.

38. 2 Corinthians 2:14 NKJV.

Chapter 3: A New Way of Thinking

1. Shirley McCune, Senior Director, Mid-continent Educational Laboratory, address at the 1989 Governors' Conference on Education. Transcribed from conference video.

2. Donald A. Cowan, at a 1988 forum address at the Dallas Institute of Humanities and Culture. This address formed the nucleus for Cowan's book *Unbinding Prometheus: Education for the Coming Age* (published by the Dallas Institute Press).

3. Aldous Huxley, *Brave New World* (New York: HarperCollins, 1932), p. 55.

4. This quote is written according to Ashley's recall.

5. Lee Droegemueller, Commissioner of Education, "Assessment! Kansas Quality Performance Accreditation (QPA)," Kansas State Board of Education, Topeka, KS, January 1992.

6. Marc Tucker, "How We Plan to Do It," in *Proposal to the New American School Development Corporation: National Center for Education and the Economy,* July 9, 1992.

7. Chester Finn, Jr., "The Biggest Reform of All," in *Phi Delta Kappa,* April 1990, p. 589.

8. Ibid., p. 592.

9. Marilyn Ferguson, *The Aquarian Conspiracy* (Los Angeles: J.P. Tarcher, Inc., 1980), pp. 289-90.

10. Robert Muller, *The Birth of a Global Civilization* (Anacortes, WA: World Happiness and Cooperation, 1991), p. 12.

11. Charlotte Iserbyt, *Back to Basics Reform Or . . . OBE Skinnerian International Curriculum?* (Bath, ME: 1993), p. 24.

12. John Goodlad, "Report of Task Force C: Strategies for Change," in *Schooling for the Future,* a report to the President's Commission on Schools Finance, Issue #9, 1971.

13. B. F. Skinner, *Science and Human Behavior* (New York: Macmillan & Co., 1953). Cited by Iserbyt.

14. Richard Evans, *B. F. Skinner: The Man and His Ideas* (New York: E. P. Dutton & Co., 1968). Cited by Iserbyt.

15. Howard Witt, "New Age teaching spells trouble in California," in *Chicago Tribune,* May 14, 1995.

16. Ibid.

17. See "SCANS: Outcome-Based Education's School-to-Work Manual," by Pamela Hobbs Hoffecker on page 215.

18. Thomas Sticht and Willis Harman, "Experts Say Too Much Is Read Into Illiteracy Crisis," in *The Washington Post,* August 17, 1987. Iserbyt, "OBE Choice: the Final Solution," p. 4.

19. Dustin H. Heuston, "Discussion—Developing the Potential of an Amazing Tool," in *Schooling and Technology,* Vol. 3, *Planning for the Future: A Collaborative Model*, published by Southeastern Regional Council for Educational Improvement, P. O. Box 12746, 200 Park, Suite 111, Research Triangle Park, NC 27709. Grant from National Institute of Education, p. 8. Cited by Charlotte Iserbyt, *Back to Basics Reform Or . . . OBE Skinnerian International Curriculum?* (Bath, ME: 1993), p. 27.

20. Jeannie Georges, "Outcome Based Education" (*Media Bypass Magazine,* P. O. Box 5326, Evansville, Indiana 47716), p. 12.

21. "Developing Leaders for Restructuring Schools: New Habits of Mind and Heart," report of the National LEADership Network

Study Group on Restructuring Schools, August 1990. Foreword written by Bruno Manno, Assistant Secretary of the Office of Educational Research and Improvement, U.S. Department of Education. Cited by Dennis Cuddy, *Chronology of Education,* p. 93.

22. Jeannie Georges, p. 3.

23. Marc Tucker, "How We Plan to Do It," proposal to the New American School Development Corporation: National Center for Education and the Economy, July 9, 1992.

24. The Regional Educational Laboratories are private, nonprofit corporations which are funded, in whole or in part, under Title IV of the Elementary and Secondary Education Act of 1965. Each lab operates under a contract with the Division of Educational Laboratories, Bureau of Research, U.S. Office of Education.

25. Transcribed from a video recording of the Governors' Conference on Education in Wichita, Kansas, November 1989.

26. Benjamin Bloom, *All Our Children Learning* (New York: McCraw Hill, 1981), p. 180.

27. David Krathwohl, Benjamin Bloom, and Bertram Massia, *Taxonomy of Educational Objectives, The Classification of Educational Goals, Handbook II: Affective Domain* (McKay Publishers, 1956), p. 55.

28. From paper distributed to students at Homestead High School, Cupertino, CA.

29. Anita Hoge, from audiocassette portion of *Talking Papers: A "Hands on" Tool for Parents to Understand Outcome Based Education* (West Alexander, PA: self-published, 1994). "The National Assessment of Educational Progress (NAEP) developed nine general citizenship objectives. . . . These national objectives were used to provide the frame of reference for what was to be measured."

30. Ibid., p. 18 of written portion of the *Talking Papers.*

31. Ibid.

32. Ibid., pp. 11, 14.

33. Gustave Le Bon, *The Crowd* (Burlington, VT: Fraser Publishing Co., 1982), pp. xvi, xx, 9.

34. Alan Bloom, *The Closing of the American Mind* (New York: Simon & Schuster, 1987), p. 246.

35. Donald A. Cowan. See note #2 in this chapter.

36. Jeffrey Kane, "Reflections on the Holistic Paradigm," in *Holistic Education Review,* Winter 1993, p. 3.

37. Ibid.

38. "Teaching of Values," Title III Grant, Northwood Public Schools, Grand Rapids, Michigan, 1968. According to Anita Hoge, this is the federal grant that funded Sidney Simon's development of values clarification techniques.

39. Andy LePage, *Transforming Education* (Oakland, CA: Oakmore House Press, 1987), p. xii.

40. *To Nurture Humaneness: Commitment for the '70's* (Washington D. C.: Association for Supervision and Curriculum Development, NEA, 1970); Cuddy, pp. 46-47.

Chapter 4: Establishing a Global Spirituality

1. From promotional brochure for summer course for educators titled *Teaching, Learning and Communicating in a Global Society: A Leadership Training for Transforming Education* sponsored by The Institute for Educational Studies (TIES). Phil Gang is the Founding Director of TIES and Executive Director of Global Alliance for Transforming Education (GATE).

2. Kevin McCullen, "Expert on spiritual beliefs of Indians capitalizes on a prophecy," in *Rocky Mountain News,* August 23, 1992.

3. Aldous Huxley, *Brave New World* (New York: HarperCollins, 1932), p. 52.

4. Article 13, WCEFA World Declaration, p. 3. Cited by Patrick James in "America 2000/Goals 2000, Citizens for Academic Excellence" (P.O. Box 1164, Moline, IL 61265), p. 151.

5. USCEFA-I: Designing Education for the 21st Century: Access and Reform, pp. 5-6. Cited by Patrick James, "America 2000/-Goals 2000," p. 151.

6. Patrick James, p. 25.

7. John R. Champlin, "Leadership: A Change Agent's View," in *Quality Outcomes-Driven Education, Journal of the National Center for Outcome Based Education,* February 1994, pp. 15-16.

8. Ibid.

9. Lee Droegemueller, Commissioner of Education, "Assessment! Kansas Quality Performance Accreditation (QPA)," Kansas State Board of Education, January 1992.

10. *Spaceship Earth: Our Global Environment,* a project of the American Forum for Global Education (New York). Contributors include Ted Turner's Better World Society, Gaia Corporation, and the National Wildlife Federation.

11. *World Goodwill Newsletter,* 1993, No. 1.

12. C. William Smith, "God's Plan in America. " Quoted from a copy of the original article written in New Orleans, for an unknown publication.

13. Robert Muller, *New Genesis: Shaping a Global Spirituality* (Garden City, NY: Image Books, 1984), p. 37.

14. Most of the following illustrations were reported to me by parents whose children participated in the classroom activities or assignments. Some parents asked to remain anonymous.

15. After the guided journey, the taped instructions continued: " . . . write down your journey while it is still fresh in your mind. Let your first line begin where you were poised at the edge of the opening waiting to jump in. Move through the whole adventure again as your write. . . . Enjoy the telling as much as the adventure itself. For writing too is journey. " From "A Journey Beneath Your Feet," in *READ* (Delran, NJ: Weekly Reader Corporation).

16. Dan Dekock, *Honor—A Simulation of Coming of Age* (Lakeside, CA: Interaction Publishers, Inc., 1988), p. 46.

17. "Fun with Chinese Horoscopes," in *Teacher Created Materials,* Inc., 1992. A used portion of the assignment was sent to me by a parent.

18. Vincent Rogers, ed., *Teaching Social Studies: Portraits from the Classroom* (National Council for the Social Studies Bulletin, No. 82), p. 20.

19. These occult practices were taught to seniors in preparation for a Mountain View High School graduation celebration. For several

years, more occult practices have been added. These practices are also taught through a growing assortment of multicultural textbooks and programs used in classrooms across the country, such as *Native American Crafts Workshop,* by Bonnie Bernstein and Leigh Blair, *Ethnic Celebrations Around the World,* by Nancy Everix, and *Anti-Bias Curriculum*, by Louise Derman-Sparks.

20. "Look Into My Crystal Ball," in *101 Ways to Learn Vocabulary.* This portion of the curriculum was sent by a parent in Texas.

21. Reported by a teacher in a public elementary school in San Jose, CA.

22. A detailed written report was sent by a participating student's mother.

23. Starhawk, *The Spiral Dance* (San Francisco: Harper & Row, 1979), pp. 62, 123-24.

24. From a copy of the original program.

25. Louise Derman-Sparks, *Anti-Bias Curriculum* (Washington D. C.: National Association for the Education of Young Children, 1989), p. 92.

26. God withdraws His protection: Numbers 14:9; Micah 1:11; Deuteronomy 8:6-20; 31:17; Ezra 8:22; 1 Corinthians 10:1-11.

27. Sun Bear, *The Path of Power* (Spokane, WA: Bear Tribe Publishing, 1983), pp. 244-45.

28. Starhawk, p. 23.

29. *Sexuality and Man*, a collection of articles written and compiled by Lester Kirkendall and other SIECUS board members.

30. Huxley, p. 28.

31. Richard W. Paul, "Moral Education in the Life of the School," in *Educational Leadership*, May 1988, p. 11.

32. Ibid., p. 18.

33. *From Sea to Shining Sea*, Teacher's Edition (New York: Houghton-Mifflin, 1991), p. 79.

34. Ibid.

35. *America Will Be* (New York: Houghton-Mifflin, 1991), pp. 185-86.

36. *The Original Land,* Unit One of McDougal Literature (McDougal, Littel & Co., 1989), p. 24.

37. Ibid.

38. Read 1 Corinthians 1:18–2:14.

39. Jeffrey Kane, "On a New Vision of Science and Science Education," in *Holistic Education Review,* Fall 1992, p. 2.

40. Lamar Alexander, *Steps Along the Way: A Governor's Scrapbook* (Nashville: Thomas Nelson Publishers, 1986), p. 85.

41. René Dubos, *A God Within: A Positive Approach to Man's Future as Part of the Natural World* (New York: Charles Scribner's Sons, 1972), pp. 42-43.

42. Bess Clayton, *The Truth About the Moon* (Boston: Houghton-Mifflin, 1983).

43. Rhoda Blumberg, *The Truth About Dragons* (D. C. Heaths & Co., 1989).

44. *America Will Be*, p. 98.

45. Clark Wissler, *Indians of the United States* (New York: Anchor Books, Doubleday, 1966), pp. 131-32.

46. See John 10:10; 3:16; Romans 3:23,24; 5:8; 6:23; John 1:12; 3:1-8; Ephesians 2:8,9.

47. Ann McGovern, *If You Lived with the Sioux Indians* (New York: Scholastic Inc., 1974), p. 44.

48. See 2 Corinthians 4:4.

49. Leah Mowery, "Mystical Misconceptions Haunt Students," in *The Talon*, June 7, 1991.

50. See also Romans 13:14; John 14:20.

Chapter 5: Saving the Earth

1. Pledge and curriculum prepared by Global Education Associates (GEA), 552 Park Avenue, East Orange, NJ 07017.

2. Education 2000, Global Alliance for Transforming Education (GATE), "The Vision Statement," p. 9.

3. Alexander King & Bertrand Schneider, *The First Global Revolution* (New York: Pantheon Books, 1991), p. 115.

4. Kathryn Sheehan and Mary Waidner, *Earth Child* (Tulsa: Council Oak Books), p. 71.

5. Gary Nash, *From Sea to Shining Sea* (New York: Houghton-Mifflin, 1991), p. 86.

6. Ibid., p. 87.

7. Ibid., p. 88.

8. Ibid.

9. Ibid., p. 89.

10. Beverly J. Armento and Gary B. Nash, *America Will Be,* Teacher's Edition (New York: Houghton Mifflin, 1991), p. T30.

11. Ibid., p. 101.

12. Ibid.

13. Dixy Lee Ray, *Environmental Overkill* (Washington: Regnery Gateway, 1993), p. 114.

14. Jim Petersen, "Think Globally, Act Locally," in *Evergreen,* Summer 1993, p. 7, citing information from the U.S. Forest Service.

15. "Environmentalists' Can't See the Forest for the Trees," Posthaste Facts on the Environment #8, in *Forests Today & Forever,* Vol. 8, Issue 2, May 6, 1994.

16. Steven Chapman, *Chicago Tribune,* October 8, 1992.

17. Prepared remarks, typescript distributed at the United Nations Earth Summit in Rio de Janeiro, June 1992.

18. Dixy Lee Ray, p. 101.

19. Ibid.

20. Al Gore, *Earth in the Balance* (Boston: Houghton Mifflin Company, 1992), pp. 259-61.

21. Ibid., pp. 237, 259.

22. Ibid., p. 1.

23. Ibid., p. 355.

24. Bob Garfield, "Little Chop of Horrors," in *Washington Post,* May 1, 1994.

25. *Rescue Mission Planet Earth,* The Children of the World, in association with the United Nations (New York: Kingfisher Books, 1994), p. 65.

26. Ibid., p. 10.

27. Dr. Gordon Dobson wrote a review of his ozone discovery in the March 1968 issue of *Applied Optics. Cited in *Fact Sheet: A Hole in the Ozone,* by Edward Krug, Ph.D.

28. *New York Times,* October 12, 1990.

29. For more information and specific data, contact either CFACT (see next footnote) or Dr. Krug. The address for his newsletter is given later in this chapter.

30. Edward C. Krug, *Fact Sheet: A Hole in the Ozone,* Committee for a Constructive Tomorrow, Box 65722, Washington D.C. 20035.

31. Frederick Seitz, *Global Warming and Ozone Hole Controversies: A Challenge to Scientific Judgment* (Washington D.C.: George C. Marshall Institute, 1994), pp. 25, 27, 33.

32. *Rescue Mission Planet Earth,* p. 13.

33. Warren T. Brooks, "The Global Warming Panic," in *Forbes,* December 25, 1989, p. 97.

34. Ibid., p. 98.

35. Sherwood B. Idso, "The Greenhouse Effect: Just a Lot of Hot Air," in CFACT, Washington D.C.

36. "Stay Cool," in *The Economist*, April 1, 1995, p. 11.

37. "Facts and Fiction of Global Warming," in *The San Francisco Chronicle,* February 4, 1991.

38. Jonathan Schell, "Our Fragile Earth," in *Discover*, October 1989, p. 44.

39. Linda MacRae-Campbell and Micki McKisson, *Our Troubled Skies* (Tuscon: Zephyr Press, 1990), p. 6.

40. *Rescue Mission Planet Earth,* p. 45.

41. "Climate History Invalidates Global Warming Models: Part II," in *Environment Betrayed*, January 1994, p. 8.

42. George Will's syndicated column on January 8, 1992. Cited by Edward C. Krug, "A Hole in the Ozone," *Fact Sheet,* CFACT, Washington D.C.

43. Jonathan Porritt, *Captain Eco and the Fate of the Earth* (New York: Dorling Kindersley, Inc., 1988), p. 5.

44. Ibid., pp. 46-47.

45. The Associated Press, in "Earth Day Celebrations Include Kids," in *The Oakland Press*, April 23, 1992.

46. Matt Holland, "Planetary Networking for Kids," in *In Context*, No. 34, p. 43.

47. Iowa Department of Education, *Iowa's Clean Sweep* (Des Moines: Department of Education, 1992), pp. 4-5.

48. Robert Lilienfeld and Wiliam L. Rathje, "Six Enviro-Myths," in *The New York Times,* January 21, 1995.

49. Sources of facts about the political quest for planetary management which fuels the environmental movement.

50. "Censored Science," in *The Observer* [London], April 24, 1994.

51. Sir Frederick Hoyle, "Hoyle on Evolution," in *Nature,* November 12, 1981, p. 105.

52. Stephen Jay Gould, "Evolution's Erratic Pace," in *Natural History,* April 1977, p. 14.

53. Roger Lewin, "A downward slope to greater diversity," in *Science,* September 1974, p. 1239.

54. Francis Crick, "In the beginning . . . " in *Scientific American,* February 1991, p. 125.

55. Dr. David Raup, "Conflicts Between Darwin and Paleontology," in *Field Museum of Natural History Bulletin,* January 1979, p. 25.

56. H. S. Lipson, "A Physicist Looks at Evolution," in *Physics Bulletin,* May 1980, p. 138.

57. Quoted by Henry M. Morris and Gary E. Parker, *What Is Creation Science?* (El Cajon, CA: Master Books, 1982), p. 21.

58. Al Gore, *Earth in the Balance* (Boston: Houghton-Mifflin, 1992), p. 263.

59. Lamar Alexander, *Steps Along the Way: A Governor's Scrapbook* (Nashville: Thomas Nelson Publishers, 1986), p. 85.

60. René Dubos, *A God Within: A Positive Approach to Man's Future as Part of the Natural World* (New York: Charles Scribner's Sons, 1972), pp. 38, 41.

61. Thomas Sowell, "Revelations for the Anointed," in *Forbes,* January 18, 1993, p. 65.

62. Genesis 2:15.

63. Genesis 1:26.

Chapter 6: Serving a Greater Whole

1. Harold G. Shane, "America's Next Twenty-five Years: Some Implications for Education," in *Phi Delta Kappan,* September 1976. Cited by Charlotte Iserbyt, *Back to Basic Reform Or . . . OBE Skinnerian International Curriculum?* (Bath, ME: 1985), p. 13.

2. Aldous Huxley, *Brave New World* (New York: HarperCollins, 1932), p. xvii.

3. Lois Lowry, *The Giver* (New York: Bantam, 1993).

4. Ibid., 149-151.

5. Oregon, a national model for implementing the Certificate of Initial Mastery (CIM), established the CIM by law in 1991. When fully implemented, the Oregon code will require students to earn their CIM before they can enter college, university, or the workplace. Those who fail to pass the affective qualifications for the CIM, including homeschoolers, will be indoctrinated with global beliefs and attitudes at special learning centers before they can take their place in the new society.

6. Chester Finn, Jr., *We Must Take Charge* (New York: The Free Press, 1991), p. 257.

7. The Tennessee Education Association, "Kill It," in *TEA News,* January 1995.

8. Ibid. The first half of this statement was also included in Lamar Alexander's address at the 1989 Governors' Conference on Education.

9. Huxley, p. xvii.

10. Lori Aratani, "Out of the Classroom, into the Community," in *San Jose Mercury News,* March 3, 1994.

11. Ibid.

12. The Thirteenth Amendment to the U.S. Constitution states that "neither slavery nor involuntary servitude, except as punishment for crime, whereof the party shall have been duly convicted, shall exist within the United States. . . . "

13. Aratani. "Out of the Classroom."

14. Lori Aratani, "Service becomes requirement," in *San Jose Mercury News,* September 25, 1995.

15. Glenn F. Bunting, "'Points of Light' Group May have Misspent Millions," in *San Francisco Chronicle,* January 9, 1995.

16. Bob Herbert, "A Season of Service," in *The New York Times,* September 31, 1994.

17. William Carlsen, "Gore Rallies Idealists at 'Boot Camp,'" in *San Francisco Chronicle,* June 22, 1993.

18. Aratani. "Service becomes requirement."

19. Charlotte Iserbyt, *Back to Basic Reform Or . . . OBE Skinnerian International Curriculum?* (Bath, ME, 1993), p. 14.

20. Ernest L. Boyer, *High School* (New York: Harper & Row Publishers, Inc., 1983). Quoted by David Hornbeck in testimony before the Maryland State Board of Education in support of mandated community service, January 25, 1984. Cited by Charlotte Iserbyt, p. 14.

21. According to *The Blumenfeld Educational Letter,* February 1994, p. 6, "Prominent educators were among the earliest trustees of the various foundations. For example, Nicholas Murray Butler, who was president of Columbia University from 1901 to 1945, was an original trustee of the Carnegie Foundation for the Advancement of Teaching, a trustee of the Carnegie Corporation of New York, and president of the Carnegie Endowment for International Peace. He was also president of the National Education Association in 1895. "

22. Beverly Eakman, *Educating for the "New World Order"* (Portland, OR: Halcyon House, 1991), pp. 218-19.

23. Charlotte T. Iserbyt, *Soviets in the Classroom: America's Latest Educational Fad* (America's Future Inc., 514 Main St., New Rochelle, NY 10801). Order brochure from 1062 Washington St., Bath, ME 04530.

24. Ibid.

25. "Transforming the Education of Young Adolescents," reprinted from *Turning Points: Preparing American Youth for the 21st Century* (Washington D.C.: Carnegie Council on Adolescent Development, 1989), pp. 51-52.

26. Pierrette Hondagneu-Sotelo and Sally Raskoff, "Community Service-Learning: Promises and Problems," in *Teaching Sociology*, July 1994, p. 248.

27. Ibid.

28. Ibid., p. 250.

29. Dinesh D'Souza, *Illiberal Education* (New York: Vintage Books, 1992), p. 16.

30. Ibid., pp. 9-10.

31. Hondagneu-Sotelo, pp. 252-53.

32. Ibid., p. 253.

33. Huxley, p. xvii.

34. Ibid., pp. xiv-xv.

35. Maxine Shideler, "Mandatory National Service Is a Tool to Indoctrinate Youth into Socialism," in *Colorado Christian News*, October 1994, p. 15.

36. J. Noakes and G. Pridham, eds., *Nazism: A History in Documents and Eyewitness Accounts*, 1919-1945, Department of History and Archaeology, University of Exeter (New York: Schocken Books Inc., 1983), pp. 440-41.

37. 1 Corinthians 10:1-12; Deuteronomy 8:10-20, 28:1-50; Numbers 14:9.

38. Alice Bailey, *Education in the New Age* (New York: Lucis Publishing Company, 1954), p. 20.

39. 2 Thessalonians 2:9,10; 2 Timothy 4:3,4.

40. "The New Group of World Servers," a pamphlet distributed by World Goodwill, an activity of Lucis Trust, pp. 6-7. Quoted in *Global Tyranny* by William F. Jasper (Appleton, Wisconsin: Western Islands, 1992), p. 216.

41. From personal telephone interview with Roy Hanson, Jr.

42. Matthew 4:10.

Chapter 7: Silencing the Opposition

1. Ronald G. Havelock, *The Change Agent's Guide to Innovation in Education* (Englewood Cliffs, NJ: Educational Technology Publications, 1973), p. 122.

2. Aldous Huxley, *Brave New World* (New York: HarperCollins, 1932), p. xvii.

3. *B-Step, Teacher Training Manual* (National Training Institute for Applied Behavioral Science, 1240 North Pitt, Suite 100, Alexandria, VA 22314, 800-777-5227). (Was in Bethel, ME.) Cited by Cherrilyn Gulbrandson, *Edu-gate America—The Deconstruction of a Culture* (Provo, Utah; World Class Education Research Institute, Inc., 1994), p. 183.

4. From keynote address to the Association for Childhood Education International (Denver, April 1972) by Chester M. Pierce, Professor of Education and Psychiatry in the Faculty of Medicine at Harvard University.

5. Kathy Collins, "Children Are Not Chattel," in *Free Inquiry,* a publication of CODESH (Council for Democratic and Secular Humanism), Fall 1987, p. 11.

6. A term coined by Lamar Alexander in his address at the 1989 Governors' Conference in Kansas.

7. Fred M. Newmann, "Schoolwide Professional Community," in *Issues in Restructuring Schools*, Center on Organization and Restructuring of Schools, Spring 1994, p. 1.

8. "Goals 2000—Details You Can Use," in *Self-Evident,* March 1995, p. 3.

9. *The Iowa Initiative for World-Class Schools, Final Report,* prepared by the Iowa Business and Education Roundtable, December 1990, pp. 11-12.

10. Massell Smith, *Social Change*, Vol. 7, no. 2, 1977. Cited by D. L. Cuddy in *Chronology of Education*, p. 61.

11. Chester Finn, Jr., "Reinventing Local Control," in *Education Week,* January 23, 1991.

12. Chester Finn, Jr., *We Must Take Charge: Our Schools and Our Future* (New York: The Free Press, 1991), p. 233.

13. Ibid., p. 246.

14. Finn, "Reinventing Local Control. "

15. Gen Yvette Sutton's comments in a private telephone conversation.

16. Dennis Laurence Cuddy, *Chronology of Education* (1994, Pro Family Forum, Box 1059, Highland City, FL 33846), p. 39. Dr. Cuddy's full explanation is worth reading.

17. Kurt Waldheim, Secretary-General of the U.N., addressing the Executive Board of UNICEF, April 1972. Cited by D.L. Cuddy, p. 51.

18. Laura Rogers, "In Loco Parentis I," in *Chronicles Magazine,* a publication of the Rockford Institute, February 19, 1991, p. 42.

19. Ibid., pp. 42-43.

20. Ibid., p. 43.

21. Dana Mack, "Child-abuse bureaucracy a new parent trap," in *The Sacramento Bee,* February 20, 1994.

22. Missouri Department of Elementary and Secondary Education, Parents As Teachers National Center, Missouri.

23. Laura Rogers, p. 43.

24. Ibid.

25. Laura Rogers, "In Loco Parentis II," in *Chronicles Magazine,* a publication of the Rockford Institute, September 1992, p. 47.

26. Ibid.

27. Rogers, "In Loco Parentis I," p. 44.

28. "Guide to Getting Out Your Message," in *National Education Goals Panel Community Action Toolkit: A Do-It-Yourself Kit for Education Renewal,* September 1994, p. 6.

29. *The New Lexicon Webster's Dictionary of the English Language* (New York: Lexicon Publications, Inc., 1989), p. 801.

30. Adolf Hitler, *Mein Kampf* (Cambridge: Houghton-Mifflin Company, 1943), p. 582.

31. Ibid., pp. 581-82.

32. Sponsored by the International Center for Leadership in Education. For more information see June 26-29, 1994, in "Chronology of Events."

33. Cynthia Weatherly, "The 2nd Annual Model School Conference," in *The Christian Conscience*, January 1995, p. 36.

34. "Organizing Your Community to Reach the National Education Goals," in *Goals 2000: Educate America,* May 18, 1993, p. 2.

35. Ibid.

36. Ibid., p. 14.

37. "Community Organizing Guide," in *National Education Goals Panel Community Action Toolkit,* September 1994, p. 36.

38. Richard Riley, "Statement of Common Purpose of Religious Leaders," (U.S. Department of Education, December 16, 1994).

39. Ibid.

40. Richard P. Manatt, *When Right Is Wrong* (Lancaster, PA: Technomic Publishing Co., Inc.), p. 2.

41. Joy Perry, "Workshop: 'Responding Democratically to Opposition Groups,'" in *Wisconsin Report*, December 16, 1993, p. 1.

42. CTA Human Rights Department and CTA Division of Governmental Relations, "Primer on the Extremist Attacks on Public Education," June 1994, p. 13.

43. Ibid., p. 19.

44. Discussed in telephone conversation with Kim Shaw.

45. Starhawk, *The Spiral Dance* (San Francisco: Harper & Row Publishers, 1979), p. 23.

46. Corinne and Gordon Davidson, *Spiritual Politics* (New York: Ballantine Books, 1994), p. 147.

47. *World Goodwill Newsletter*, 1993, No. 4, p. 2.

48. Cover story of *Parade*, December 25, 1994.

Chapter 8: What You Can Do

1. Proverbs 22:6. Laura Rogers, "Societal Structures vs. Restructuring," sent directly to me by author.

2. Dietrich Bonhoeffer, *The Cost of Discipleship* (New York: The Macmillan Company, 1963), p. 22.

3. Richard Wurmbrand, "Preparing for the Underground Church," in *The Voice of the Martyrs*, p. 13.

4. Moms in Touch International (P.O. Box 1120, Poway, CA 92074-1120).

5. Laura Rogers, "Societal Structures vs. Restructuring."

6. Romans 1:18-32; Deuteronomy 8,11,28.

7. Ephesians 6:12.

8. Romans 13:12,14.

9. From a personal letter from Catherine Elizabeth Warncke.

10. 1 Corinthians 1:9.

Section A: Making a Difference

1. The EQA Inventory measured attitudes and opinions and collected frequency data. Non-cognitive areas collected information on students' attitudes, opinions, or feelings or their opportunities for participation in activities. EQA Commentary, Division of Educational Testing and Evaluation, Pennsylvania Department of Education, 1985.

2. "World of Work," EQA test questionnaire, Educational Quality Assessment, Pennsylvania Department of Education, 1975.

3. "Citizenship," EQA test questionnaire, Educational Quality Assessment, Pennsylvania Department of Education, 1975.

4. "Understanding Others," EQA test questionnaire, Educational Quality Assessment, Pennsylvania Department of Education, 1975.

5. National Assessment of Educational Progress (NAEP), Part C, Sec. 3401; P. L. 100-297.

6. Beyond Text or "Extended Questions: Answers to questions not available in the written text of a story or writing prompt, answers that require the student to respond to and think beyond the text" (like EQA questions), Pennsylvania Education, vol. 20, no. 6, March 14, 1989.

7. Citizenship refers to a behavior-referenced model incorporating elements related to the "psychological notion of threshold." The reference to threshold refers to that set of conditions necessary to bring about the desired responses by varying situations of reward and punishment. "Getting Inside the EQA Inventory," Pennsylvania Department of Education, 1975.

8. Whole Child Theory: A Plan for Evaluating the Quality of Educational Programs in Pennsylvania, Educational Testing Service, 1974, p. 9.

9. Nolan Russell, ed., "Minimum Positive Attitude Definition: Getting Inside the EQA Inventory," 1975, pp. 109-99.

10. Ibid.

11. "Resources for Improvement, Citizenship," Pennsylvania Department of Education, 1981.

12. Max Rafferty, Superintendent of Public Instruction, "A Planning, Programming, Budgeting System for the State of California School Districts," An Educational Planning and Evaluation System, 1970.

    Donald R. Miller, San Mateo County Superintendent, "Toward the Management of Society": Operation PEP, 1970.

    California PACE Narrative Report, Projects to Advance Creativity in Education, Dept. of Education, 1969.

    Emery Stoops, "California State Plan: Report of the Study Title III," ESEA, Bureau of Program Planning, California State Department of Education.

13. Basic Education Circular 8-90, issued by the Pennsylvania Department of Education to all 501 school districts, April, 1990, to resolve Hoge Complaint by the U.S. Department of Education.

14. "ED Unveils New Data Collection Program," *Education Daily,* March 31, 1986, "Bennett Names Study Group to Evaluate Student Assessment," *Education Daily,* May 15, 1986.

15. SPEED/ExPRESS: An interstate student records transfer system called the Exchange of Permanent Records Electronically for Students and Schools, administered by the Chief State School Officers, March 31, 1992.

16. PENNDATA: Pennsylvania Department of Education computer network to input data for a management information on special education students, August, 1994.

17. "Electronic verification system" is the transfer of personal data from one government agency to another via electronic transmission done through the SSN. Incorporated in waiver granted to Pennsylvania for Family Care Network, Department of Health & Human Services; Sally Richardson, Medicaid Bureau, October 14, 1993.

18. Governor Bob Casey, "Children's Cabinet," Executive Report of Community Delivery Services, 1994.

19. Instructional Support Team, Initiative of the Pennsylvania Special Education Department to screen ALL children in the regular classroom to find "developmental delays" in meeting OBE outcomes, 1990.

20. Medical Assistance Bulletins, Pennsylvania Department of Public Welfare, January 1994, January 1995.

21. Waiver through Health Care Financing Administration. See note 17.

22. A non-binding Resolution 293 sponsored by Ron "Huck" Gamble won 150 to 47 to slow OBE process down in Pennsylvania (April, 1992). Representative Gamble began his infamous "Gamble Grams" newsletter to inform parents and the legislature about OBE research.

23. Resolution 37 passed the House of Representatives in Pennsylvania, 175 to 25, to investigate the Department of Education and the links to Medicaid.

24. Secretary's Commission on Achieving the Necessary Skills (SCANS), Department of Labor, 1992.

25. Superintendent Cercone, Freedom School District "Goals, 2000," grant to a local district in Freedom, Pennsylvania, that connects all the federal pieces to the strategic plan and testing on the local level.

Section B: SCANS

1. Bill Graves, "Rites of Passage," *The Oregonian,* June 17, 1994. A1.

2. Renee Cook press statement, Cottage Grove, Oregon, June 10, 1994.

3. Graves, "Rites of Passage," A23.

4. Lonnie Harp, "Ore. Bill Would End Traditional Schooling After the 10th Grade," *Education Week* (May 15, 1991), pp. 1, 20.

5. During the 1990's states began either legislating or piloting the CIM. However, to give an appearance of uniqueness, its name is often changed.

6. Phone interview by author with Janice Kincaid, July 8, 1994.

7. *Learning a Living: A Blueprint for High Performance: a SCANS Report for America 2000* (U.S. Department of Labor, April 1992), p. 62. To order a *SCANS* manual call the U.S. Government Bookstore (Washington, D.C.), 1-202-512-1800.

8. *SCANS*, xvi.

9. Ibid., xix.

10. Ibid., xiii.

11. Ibid., xv.

12. Ibid., xvii.

13. Edward L. Lederman, "High Tech Hustle," *National Review* (September 20, 1993), p. 56.

14. "Center for the New West Learning Community Proposal," Figure 1, Grant proposal, nod., E3.

15. Joseph A. Braun, Jr. and Kurt A. Slobodzian, "Can Computers Teach Values?" *Educational Leadership* (April 1982), p. 509.

16. *Education Week*, August 31, 1983, credits Skinner with developing Mastery Learning (OBE's previous name).

17. B. F. Skinner, *Beyond Freedom and Dignity* (New York: Vintage Books, 1972), p. 3.

18. Ibid., first inside page.

19. *Teaching the SCANS Competencies* (U.S. Department of Labor, 1993, p. 102.

20. *SCANS*, p. 71.

21. As quoted in *U.S. Congressional Record*, House of Representatives, October 23, 1989, pp. 3517-3519.

22. *SCANS*, p. 60.

23. Associated Press, "Rand Study Points to Problems in Vermont's Portfolio Assessment Program," *The Executive Educator* (February 1993), p. 6.

24. *SCANS,* p. 72.

25. Barbara Kantrowitz and Pat Wingert, "Putting Value in Diplomas," *Newsweek* (July 15, 1991), p. 62.

26. *SCANS,* p. 62.

27. Ibid., p. 64.

28. Ibid., p. 66.

29. Hillary Rodham Clinton and Ira Magaziner, "Will America Choose High Skills or Low Wages?" *Educational Leadership* (March 1992), p. 12.

30. *SCANS,* p. 61.

31. Nicholas D. Kristof, "Where Each Worker Is Yoked to a Personal File," *New York Times International,* March 16, 1992, p. A4.

32. "WORKLINK System Helps East Transition from High School to Work," *ETS Developments* (Spring 1994), pp. 4, 5.

33. Joseph Stinson, "Beyond Shop Talk," *Electronic Learning* (February 1994), p. 21.

34. *The Alliance* (The National Center on Education and the Economy, February/March 1995), 2. The NCEE was established in 1988 to continue the policy development work begun by the Carnegie Forum on Education and the Economy.

35. *The Challenges of Change: Standards to Make Education Work for All Our Children* (National Alliance of Business, January 1995), p. 7.

36. "How Americans Grade the School System, *Business Week* (September 14, 1992), p. 85.

37. Phone interview by author with Virginia K. Miller, May 9, 1995. Miller cited Marcus W. Brauchil, "Wary of Education But Needing Brains, China Faces a Dilemma: State Fears Loss of Control," *Wall Street Journal,* November 15, 1994, p. A1.

38. "Eye on America," CBS-TV (Summer 1995).

Section C: Chronology of Events

1. You can order the entire chronology from the Pro Family Forum, Inc., P. O. Box 1059, Highland City, FL, 33846.

2. Cuddy, p. 18.

3. The *Humanist Manifesto I* (1933) was the first public declaration of the views and objectives of modern humanism. It rejected God and His values but affirmed humanist faith in the power and evolution of man. The Humanist Manifesto II (1973) reaffirmed and amplified this man-centered, relativistic, Utopian belief system.

4. Willard Givens presented a report titled "Education for the New America" at the 72nd Annual Meeting of the NEA, held in Washington D.C. in July 1934. Cuddy, p. 20.

5. "Report of the Commission on the Social Studies," *The American Historical Association,* 1934, pp. 16-17. Cited by Charlotte Iserbyt.

6. Joy Elmer Morgan, "The United Peoples of the World," in *The NEA Journal,* December 1942, p. 261.

7. J. Elmer Morgan, "The Teacher and World Government," *The NEA Journal,* January 1946, p. 1.

8. G. B. Chisholm, "The Re-establishment of Peacetime Society," in *Psychiatry,* February 1946, pp. 7, 9-10, 16, 18.

9. Dennis Cuddy, *The Grab for Power: A Chronology of the NEA* (Marlborough, NH: Plymouth Rock Foundation, P.O. Box 577, 1993), p. 8.

10. *Chicago Sun-Times,* October 1962. Cuddy, pp. 34-35.

11. John I. Goodlad, *Citizens for the 21st Century* (Sacramento: State Committeee on Public Education, 1969), pp. 461-462.

12. John I. Goodlad & Associates, *Curriculum Inquiry—the Study of Curriculum Practice* (New York: McGraw Hill, 1979), p. 261. Iserbyt, p. 25.

13. *To Nurture Humaneness: Commitment for the '70's* (Washington D.C.: Association for Supervision and Curriculum Development, NEA, 1970), pp. 50-51.

14. Ibid., pp. 106-07.

15. Ibid., p. 79.

16. Ibid., p. 181.

17. Promotional pamphlet titled "An Invitation to Collaboration with Global Education Associates in Building a More Humane World Order," 552 Park Ave., East Orange, NJ 07017. Undated.

18. "Man, Education and Society in the Year 2000," a report issued by the Institute for Chief State School Officers, 1974. Summary written by Dr. Grant Venn, CSSO Institute Director. Cuddy, pp. 55-56.

19. Harold Shane, "America's Next 25 Years: Some Implications for Education," *Phi Delta Kappan* (September 1976). Cuddy p. 59.

20. Vladimir Turchenko, *The Scientific and Technological Revolution and the Revolution in Education* (1976). Cuddy, p. 60.

21. *Project Global 2000: Planning for a New Century* (New York: Global Education Associates, 1991), p. 2.

22. *Human Intelligence International Newsletter,* P. O. Box 1163, Birmingham, MI 48012 (March/April 1981), p. 1. Iserbyt, p. 16.

23. Benjamin Bloom, *All Our Children Learning* (New York: McGraw-Hill Paperbacks, 1981), pp. 33, 35. Iserbyt, p. 25.

24. Board members include Lester Brown, President of Worldwatch Institute, and representatives from the World Bank and The Council for a Parliament of the World's Religions.

25. Chairperson of the accreditation team for the Southern Association of Colleges and Schools, Dr. Eileen Lynch, Professor of Political Science, Brookhaven College, October 1984. Quoted from a copy of the accreditation report which is included in the appendix of the *Robert Muller World Core Curriculum Manual.*

26. Charlotte T. Iserbyt, *"Soviets in the Classroom: America's Latest Educational Fad"* (1062 Washington St., Bath, ME 04530).

27. Susan Hooper, "Educator Proposes a Global Core Curriculum," *Education Week* (November 27, 1985), p. 8.

28. From ASCD's brochure announcing the conference.

29. Thomas Sticht and Willis Harman, "Experts Say Too Much Is Read into Illiteracy Crisis," *The Washington Post,* August 17, 1987.

30. "The United States Prepares for Its Future: Global Perspectives in Education, Report of the Study Commission on Global Educa-

tion," 1987. The report is financed by the Rockefeller, Ford and Exxon Foundations. Cuddy, p. 80.

31. Cuddy, p. 80.

32. From a brochure publicizing the conference.

33. Muller's speech transcribed by Virginia Meves, ed., *Wisconsin Report*, Box 45, Brookfield, WI 53008.

34. Transcribed from videotape of conference.

35. Malachi Martin, *The Keys of This Blood: The Struggle for World Dominion* (New York: Simon and Schuster, 1990). Cuddy, p. 85.

36. Learning for All: Bridging Domestic and International Education, Conference Report (United States Coalition for Education for All, 1991), p. 1.

37. "The Goodwill Vision," *World Goodwill Newsletter,* No. 3, 1993, p. 2.

38. From telephone interview with Dr. Dennis Cuddy, April 5, 1994.

39. *Education 2000: A Holistic Perspective* (Brandon, VT: Global Alliance for Transforming Education, 1991). Cuddy, p. 87.

40. From the tape of Dorothy Maver's 1990 message, which has been widely distributed.

41. *America 2000: An Educational Strategy* (U.S. Department of Education), p. 51.

42. Richard Chin, "Bush Pushes Education Plan," *St. Paul Pioneer Press*, May 23 1991.

43. Cuddy, p. 92.

44. Lamar Alexander, "Breaking the Mold," *Business Week* (October 17, 1994), p. 122.

45. Charlotte Iserbyt, "The Soviet-American Exchange," *America's Future*, Box 1625, Milford PA 18337.

46. Stuart Wasserman, "Nation Will Be Watching Oregon's 'Pioneering Step,'" *The Los Angeles Times*, October 17, 1991.

47. Oregon bill, HB 3565, Sec. 20:1-3.

48. Ibid., Sec. 20:5.

49. Ibid., Sec. 20:4.

50. Section 25:1 in the original bill states, "By July 1, 1996, it shall be unlawful for an employer to employ any person under 18 years of age who has not obtained a Certificate of Initial Mastery." Other portions of the bill cover adult certification. The final bill deleted the most objectionable statements, but left the framework which would achieve the same result. Oregon's law matches the goals of the National Center on Education and the Economy (Hillary Clinton on Board of Trustees) which recommends (1) that "all students achieve a Certificate of Initial Mastery," (2) Youth Centers for continued pursuit of the Certificate, and (3) "occupational certification programs" only for those who have their Certificates of Initial Mastery, (4) "The assessment standard would be the same for both adults and students." The latter explains the need for Lifetime Learning. *America's Choice: High Skills or Low Wages!* NCEE (June 1990), pp. 71-72.

51. Ibid., 94.

52. From a copy, in my possession, of the letter written by Marc Tucker, MNCEE President, on November 11, 1992.

53. Howard Gardner, *Frames of Mind: The Theory of Multiple Intelligences* (New York: Basic Books, 1993), p. 392.

54. Lily Wong Fillmore, keynote speaker at the third annual conference of the National Association for Multicultural Education, Los Angeles, February 11-14, 1993. Cuddy, p. 102.

55. Cuddy, p. 107.

56. Cuddy, p. 110.

57. From a copy of the bill sent to me.

58. Cynthia Weatherly, "The 2nd Annual Model Schools Conference," *The Christian Conscience* (January 1995), p. 37.

59. From the flier announcing the December 11-14 USCEFA conference in Baltimore.

Section E: Glossary of Educational Terms

1. The Arts and Education Reform: Ideas for Schools and Communities, background paper for the Goals 2000 Satelite Town Meeting, January 18, 1994 (The U.S. Department of Education), pp. 5, 1.

2. National Goals 253.37 matches Iowa code.

3. Kenneth A. Bruffe, "Social Construction, Language and the Authority of Knowledge: A Bibliographical Essay," in *College English*, December 1986, pp. 773-90.

4. Ruth Feld, "An Exposé: Community Education," unpublished report.

5. Lee Droegemueller, Commissioner of Education, "Assessment! Kansas Quality Performance Accreditation (QPA)," Kansas State Board of Education, Topeka, KS, January 1992.

6. Marilyn Ferguson, *The Aquarian Conspiracy* (Los Angeles: J.P. Tarcher, Inc., 1980), p. 307.

7. "News from the Vendors," *Speede/Express Newsletter*, September 1994, p. 4.

8. Thomas Kuhn, *The Structure of Scientific Revolutions*, 1962. Cited by Marilyn Ferguson, *The Aquarian Conspiracy* (Los Angeles: J.P. Tarcher, Inc., 1980), pp. 26, 27.

9. "Definitions of Terms," K-12 Education Reform Committee Addendum, Iowa, Revised 8-12-1992.

10. Thomas A. Shannon, Executive Director of the National School Boards Association (1981).

    In March 1984 the U.S. Supreme Court ruled that private schools are subject to government regulations even if they receive no direct federal funds. A private school may be held accountable for federal rules because it enrolls students who receive tuition money from the government. Even though the checks are payable to individual students, not the school, the Court said any scholarships, loans, or grants to students "constitute federal financial assistance to that entity."

    "On March 22, 1988, pp. L 100-259 became the law of the land. The legislation would make it clear that the entire institution must not discriminate if any component receives federal aid." (*Congressional Quarterly Weekly,* p. 774). Cited by Virginia Birt Baker, "Educational 'Choice,'" *Free World Research Report*, March 1993.

11. A brochure promoting Worklink.

12. A Goals 2000 Glossary, *Basic Education* (June 1994), p. 10.

Index